Interactional Competences in Institutional Settings

Simona Pekarek Doehler • Adrian Bangerter •
Geneviève de Weck • Laurent Filliettaz •
Esther González-Martínez • Cécile Petitjean
Editors

Interactional Competences in Institutional Settings

From School to the Workplace

palgrave
macmillan

Editors
Simona Pekarek Doehler
Centre for Applied Linguistics
University of Neuchâtel
Neuchâtel, Switzerland

Geneviève de Weck
Center of Logopedics
University of Neuchâtel
Neuchâtel, Switzerland

Esther González-Martínez
Department of Social Sciences
University of Fribourg
Fribourg, Switzerland

Adrian Bangerter
Institute of Work and Organizational Psychology
University of Neuchâtel
Neuchâtel, Switzerland

Laurent Filliettaz
Faculty of Psychology & Educational Sciences
University of Geneva
Geneva, Switzerland

Cécile Petitjean
Center for Applied Linguistics
University of Neuchâtel
Neuchâtel, Switzerland

ISBN 978-3-319-46866-2 ISBN 978-3-319-46867-9 (eBook)
DOI 10.1007/978-3-319-46867-9

Library of Congress Control Number: 2016962317

Printed on acid-free paper

This Palgrave Macmillan imprint is published by Springer Nature
The registered company is Springer International Publishing AG
The registered company address is: Gewerbestrasse 11, 6330 Cham, Switzerland

Acknowledgments

This book has originated in a collaboration among the editors in a large-scale research project funded by the Swiss National Science Foundation (SNSF): The inter-university Sinergia project *Interactional Competences in Institutional Practices: Young People between School and the Workplace* (*IC-You*) (2012–2015, SNSF, grant no. CRSII1_136291). We are grateful to all the people who participated in data collection. Without their contributions, the studies presented in this volume would have not been possible. We address our thanks to all those colleagues who commented on the issues and data discussed here in various workshops, conferences and data sessions: Their input helped us to sharpen our arguments and analysis. We also thank the Secteur Recherche et Innovation of the University of Neuchâtel for its support with regard to the proofreading of the book.

Contents

Notes on the Contributors

Adrian Bangerter is Professor of Work Psychology at the University of Neuchâtel (Switzerland). He does research on coordination processes in conversation, especially coordinating parallel activities and interruptions and the relationship between pointing gestures and language. He also does research on interactions between recruiters and applicants in personnel selection. A third focus of his research is cultural transmission of knowledge and popular beliefs, especially the case of public understanding of science and scientific topics.

Stephen Billett is Professor of Adult and Vocational Education in the School of Education and Professional Studies at Griffith University (Brisbane, Australia). He has worked as a vocational educator, educational administrator, teacher educator, professional development practitioner and policy developer within the Australian vocational education system and as a teacher and researcher at Griffith University. Since 1992, he has researched learning through and for work and has published widely in the fields of vocational learning, workplace learning and conceptual accounts of learning for vocational purposes.

Virginie Degoumois is a doctoral student at the Center for Applied Linguistics, University of Neuchâtel (Switzerland). Using conversation analysis, she works on French as a first-language classroom interaction, focusing on how students manage epistemic stances in opinion formulation.

Geneviève de Weck is Professor of Logopedics in the Department of Language Sciences and Communication at the University of Neuchâtel (Switzerland). She is a specialist of language impairment in childhood and adolescence, which she studies from an interactionist point of view. Her studies focus on the pragmatic-discursive dimension of social interactions and the scaffolding strategies (of mothers and adults such as speech and language therapists) therein. She also studies interventions in speech and language therapy.

Laurent Filliettaz is Professor of Adult and Vocational Education at the University of Geneva (Switzerland). He received his PhD in linguistics in 2000 and has developed an expertise in discourse analysis and multimodal approaches to interaction. He has conducted much research over the years on topics like language use in professional contexts and social interaction in vocational education and training.

Gwendoline Fox is a postdoctoral researcher in the Department of Language Sciences and Communication at the University of Neuchâtel (Switzerland). She adopts a usage-based approach in her research and focuses on the role of experience, in particular the contribution of input, in the construction of linguistic knowledge. She currently examines how the dynamics of dialogue in speech therapy sessions, in addition to pre-designed exercises, provide a support for the treatment of adolescents with language impairments.

Esther González-Martínez is Associate Professor of Sociology in the Department of Social Sciences at the University of Fribourg (Switzerland). Her area of specialization is the analysis of social interactions in institutional settings, including several projects on nurses at work. Her research adopts an ethnomethodological perspective as well as conversation and multimodal analysis, supplemented by ethnographic fieldwork.

Paloma Gosteli-Corvalan is a doctoral researcher at the University of Neuchâtel (Switzerland). She works on young people's interactional competences in conversation, especially narrative competence, investigating how applicants and recruiters use storytelling in the institutional setting of job interviews. Her research also includes aspects of self-presentation and impression management, exploring the way these are implemented in interaction.

Janet Holmes is Emeritus Professor of Linguistics at Victoria University of Wellington in New Zealand and a Fellow of the Royal Society of New Zealand. She is Associate Director of the Wellington "Language in the Workplace" project, an ongoing study of communication in the workplace. The team is currently researching the hospitality industry.

Keely Kidner recently completed her PhD in Applied Linguistics at Victoria University of Wellington in New Zealand. Her thesis dealt with environmental discourses, critical discourse analysis and multimodality. She also works with the Wellington "Language in the Workplace" project.

Vassiliki Markaki is a postdoctoral researcher in linguistics at the Ecole Normale Supérieure of Lyon (France). Her current research deals with the multimodal practices and resources participants mobilize within professional training and learning interactions. More particularly, she focuses on the ways professionals organize and assess learning activities within complex settings, such as multiparty interactions or human-machine interactions.

Meredith Marra is Director of the Wellington 'Language in the Workplace' Project and has been involved in collecting and analyzing naturally occurring data in New Zealand organizations since 1998. Her primary research interest is the language of business meetings, and she has published in the areas of humor, gender and ethnicity in workplace interactions.

Helen Melander is Assistant Professor in Education at the Department of Education, Uppsala University (Sweden). Building on a conversation analytic framework, her main research interests concern knowledge and learning in interaction, covering various areas such as learning in interaction within peer groups and instructional work in encounters between students and teachers.

Hanh Thi Nguyen is Associate Professor of Applied Linguistics at Hawaii Pacific University (United States). She is the author of *Developing Interactional Competence: A Conversation-Analytic Study of Patient Consultations in Pharmacy* (Palgrave-Macmillan, 2012) and several papers using conversation analysis longitudinally to investigate the development of interactional competence in workplace communication and second-language learning.

Christy Noble is a Medical Education Officer at the Gold Coast Hospital and Health Service (Queensland, Australia). Originally trained as a pharmacist, through her doctoral studies, she has developed an interest and expertise in the development of clinical skills in practice settings.

Simona Pekarek Doehler is Professor of Applied Linguistics in the Department of Language Sciences and Communication at the University of Neuchâtel (Switzerland). Her research is dedicated to exploring the development of interactional competence, based on longitudinal conversation analysis, as well as the role of grammatical resources in the organization of social interaction. She has been the principal investigator of the large-scale research project *Interactional Competence in Institutional Practices: Young People between School and the Workplace (IC-You)*, which many of the contributions to this volume stem from.

Cécile Petitjean is a postdoctoral researcher at the Center for Applied Linguistics, University of Neuchâtel (Switzerland). She has carried out research on interactional competence, primarily in classroom settings and, in collaboration with other colleagues, also in workplace settings and in speech therapy sessions. Her research focuses on the ways participants mobilize humor and laughter in talk-in-interaction. Her work has been published, among others, in *Classroom Discourse*, *Langage et Société* and *Journal of Pragmatics*.

Anca-Cristina Sterie has just accomplished her PhD in Sociology in the Department of Social Sciences at the University of Fribourg (Switzerland). In her dissertation, she examines nurse–doctor telephone calls at the hospital in which the nurse produces a report on medical problems as a vehicle for requesting the doctor's intervention.

Audrey Sublon is a doctoral student at the Center of Logopedics at the University of Neuchâtel (Switzerland). She works, from an interactionist perspective, on storytellings during speech therapy sessions involving adolescents, investigating both the nature and the functions of such tellings. She also explores the dynamics of dialogue by studying mechanisms of coproduction such as reiterations or questions.

List of Figures

List of Tables

1

Introduction: Interactional Competences in Institutional Settings – Young People Between School and Work

Simona Pekarek Doehler and Cécile Petitjean

Interactional Competences in an Ever-changing World[1]

Increasing mobility of students and workers, the emergence of a knowledge- and service-based economy and the growing diversification of our economic and cultural landscapes highlight the importance of people's adaptive capacities and mastery of communicative tools. Interactional competences, in particular, are central components of the wider social abilities by which people gain access to multiple institutional worlds, enabling them to pursue educational and professional goals in ever-changing environments. These competences are key to learning, academic or professional selection, identity construction, workplace socialization, professional integration and much more. Both education

S. Pekarek Doehler (✉) • C. Petitjean
Center for Applied Linguistics, University of Neuchâtel,
Neuchâtel, Switzerland

S. Pekarek Doehler et al. (eds.), *Interactional Competences in Institutional Settings*, DOI 10.1007/978-3-319-46867-9_1

and industry have recognized this issue but often consider young people's interactional competences to be suboptimal—and this at a time when the social integration of young people through school and the professions has come into unprecedented critical scrutiny. This raises two important questions. The first concerns the extent to which institutional expectations regarding people's interactional competences are explicitly formulated, or how far hidden curricula or otherwise implicit criteria for evaluating these competences are at work. The second question concerns the extent to which these expectations vary across institutions and across people's individual trajectories.

Studies of work (e.g., Garfinkel 1986), workplace studies (Luff et al. 2000) as well as the institutional talk program (Drew and Heritage 1992) have uncovered how people interact in different institutional (typically work-related) settings, and how such interactions vary depending on the details of these settings. Investigations into educational interactions have shed light on the way people engage into classroom interactions of various types and at different levels of schooling or education (for classical studies, see Mehan 1979; Macbeth 1990; Seedhouse 2004). Analyses of vocational and professional training have stressed the interdependencies between individual and contextual factors in learning processes as they occur within social practices (Billett 2001, 2010). More specifically, they have highlighted how people develop expertise and knowledge through their social interactions with others (e.g., de Saint-Georges and Filliettaz 2008; Filliettaz 2010) and how they recontextualize such expertise and knowledge across situations (see the papers collected in Tuomi-Gröhn and Engeström 2003a). In much earlier work, Jacoby (1998) and Jacoby and McNamara (1999) have drawn our attention to the fact that an important part of such expertise is the object of what they refer to as "indigenous assessment," that is, assessment practices used by specialists in assessing the communicative performance of novices as part of any professional culture, many of which are built into everyday interactions and hence become observable for researchers through the analysis of such interactions. More recently, there has been an increased interest in how newcomers negotiate their membership in workplace communities (see the papers collected in Angouri et al. 2016). In the field of workplace discourse analysis, factors such as the role of workplace preparation and apprenticeship have been explored (e.g., Filliettaz et al. 2010) as well as the mechanisms that shape transitions into the work market (e.g., Bradley and Devadason 2008; see also section "Young People's Interactional Practices Within Institutional Settings"). In all these studies, people's ability to interact has been shown to be core to learning, identity construction, sociability, socialization and professional integration. As Zemel and Koschmann (2014) have prominently shown, talk-at-work involves both participants' systematic procedures for accomplishing situated actions and the deployment of instructed actions.

At the current state of research, we understand that talk-at-work is a site of both the use and the development of interactional (and other) competences as well as of their assessment. Yet, little is known about the precise demands various institutional settings put on the interactional competences of the people who interact within them. Also, a detailed understanding of the nature of interactional competence is still missing. In particular, current research needs to show how interactional competences are deployed and solicited in very diverse contexts, and what challenges ensue for people interacting in these contexts.

This volume brings together scholars from a variety of disciplines (linguistics, sociology, education, psychology of work and speech therapy) who share an interest in uncovering what it takes to interact within institutional settings that are key to young people's socialization between school and the workplace. We ask:

- What aspects of interactional competence are relevant for participation in practical activities within emblematic settings on the pathway between school and the workplace?
- What are the interactional procedures through which interactional competence is recognized, legitimized and possibly assessed in the course of practical activities?
- How do these procedures both shape and reflect social institutions and people's understanding of them?

While indebted to various research traditions, the contributions to this volume share an understanding of social interaction as the core site where the institutional order is brought into being (Blumer 1969; Garfinkel 1967; Goffmann 1983; Sacks 1992). As Giddens (1979, 69) put it, "the structural properties of social systems are both the medium and the outcome of the practices that constitute those systems." This position implies an analytic focus on the local organization of practical activities within the institution—which may be quite different from the declared institutional order as made explicit, for instance, through guidelines or rules provided in written or oral form. The contributions also converge on an understanding of interactional competence as profoundly implicated in action (see section "Interactional Competence"): Interactional competence materializes in the course of practical activities as a set of systematic procedures through which participants coordinate their actions and deal with the local contingencies of the courses of action they are engaged in (Garfinkel 2002; Psathas 1990).

The present collection represents the first consolidated effort to discuss, in a comprehensive and integrated way, young people's interactional competences across a variety of institutional settings and to reflect on the related institutional order by scrutinizing how such competences are interactionally treated within everyday practices. The volume as a whole is designed to further an interdisciplinary understanding of concepts that are fundamental to research in the humanities and social sciences: interactional competence, norm, institution and context. Most centrally, the volume provides original qualitative contributions to understanding much neglected aspects of how young people engage with institutions on the transition from school to work—an issue that has been analyzed traditionally by means of longitudinal quantitative methods (Booth et al. 1999; Corijn and Klijzing 2001; Settersten et al. 2005; Bergman et al. 2011). The cumulative evidence emanating from the studies collected in this volume stresses the need to better understand how young people cope with the institutional demands put on their interactional competences on their pathway from school to workplace integration.

In this introduction, we briefly outline the purpose of the volume against the background of current research on young people's interactional practices in institutional settings (section "Young People's Interactional Practices Within Institutional Settings") and offer a critical discussion of the notion of interactional competence and its relevance for understanding social interactional practices, larger social institutional environments and how people navigate them (section "Interactional Competence").

We then present findings of a large-scale research project that motivated the present collection, and which many of the contributions in this volume stem from, addressing the role of interactional competences in different institutional settings on the trajectory between school and work (section "The 'IC-You' Project: (Dis)continuities in Institutional Exigencies Regarding Interactional Competences Between School and the Workplace"). We close by presenting the contributions to this volume (section "Contributions to the Volume").

Young People's Interactional Practices Within Institutional Settings

Recent research on work, education and organizations underlines the prevalence of verbal interaction in a variety of work and educational settings. The discursive construction of identities and competences of young people, through the use of language, has been addressed within such diverse approaches as discourse analysis, sociolinguistics and sociocultural theory (see e.g., the papers collected in Androutsopoulos and Georgakopoulou 2003; Tuomi-Gröhn and Engeström 2003a; Perret-Clermont et al. 2004; Angouri et al. 2016). One prominent line of research on young people's practices within institutional settings has been concerned with boundary crossing, that is, the crossing between organizations and communities of practice (Beach 1999; Tuomi-Gröhn and Engeström 2003a; Angouri et al. 2016) and the related transfer of knowledge. Going back to Lave's (1988) and Lave and Wenger's (1991) classical documentations of how mathematical problem-solving is accomplished differently in mundane situations than in formal institutional settings, situated approaches to cognition and learning (see Tuomi-Gröhn and Engeström 2003b, for a discussion) have identified the challenges of the transfer of knowledge and competences from school to the workplace. This line of research emphasizes the central import of the affordances that learning situations—as they materialize in practical activities—offer for participants.

Yet, to date, only a few studies explore the competences of young people via analysis of the micro-level organization of the verbal interactions in which they participate (but see the growing literature on children's interactional competences; e.g., Wootton 1997; Filipi 2009; and the papers collected in Hutchby and Moran-Ellis 1998; Gardner and Forrester 2010; see also Jacoby and McNamara's 1999 early critical discussion on the context-dependency of the assessment of spoken interaction). The existing studies draw on ethnomethodology and conversation analysis (CA), including studies of work (Garfinkel 1986), the institutional talk program (Drew and Heritage 1992) and workplace studies (Luff et al. 2000), or on discourse analysis, including, for instance, workplace discourse (see the papers in Angouri et al. 2016). Most of the studies on young people's competences focus on formal learning environments such as classrooms (Mehan 1979; Macbeth 1990), second language learning environments (see the papers collected in Hall et al. 2011; Palotti and Wagner 2011), tutorial meetings (e.g., Glenn and Koschmann 2005) or workshops (e.g., de Saint-Georges and Filliettaz 2008; Filliettaz et al. 2010). These studies demonstrate how features of organizational settings, such as social identities and competences, are shaped by social interaction via ordinary practices.

In the quoted research, the detailed qualitative analysis of naturally occurring interactional practices informs us about the interactional resource participants put to work and about how the institutional order is embodied in these very same practices. Only few microanalytic studies have been carried out comparing work-related or educational practices within different organizational or educational settings so as to analyze convergences between these practices and between the related institutional orders (e.g., Lindström and Lindholm 2009; Koskela and Palukka 2011). Accordingly, research faces the challenge of showing how interactional competences are deployed and solicited in very diverse contexts (on the challenges of comparative and longitudinal CA see the papers collected in Sidnell 2009 and Pekarek Doehler et al. forthcoming, respectively; see also Nguyen, this volume).

Interactional Competence

When participating in social interaction, people coordinate their actions, make these recognizable to each other and continuously adapt them according to the needs of the moment. Chatting around a cup of coffee, interacting in a professional meeting and engaging in a verbal exchange at a sales counter all require highly organized socially coordinated procedures for action. The ability to interact develops from early childhood on, all along our lives.

Whereas technical skills or specific types of knowledge are relevant for some settings and irrelevant for others, the ability to interact represents a general instrument for problem-solving, participation, recognition and success across a large variety of settings that is both context-independent (it is needed everywhere) and context-sensitive (it is needed differently in different settings and may be flexibly adapted to the exigencies of the moment). Interactional competence is currently attracting much attention in the fields of applied linguistics (Young 2003; Hall et al. 2011; Nguyen 2012; Pekarek Doehler and Pochon-Berger 2015), education sciences (Filliettaz and de Saint-Georges 2006), sociology of work (Schwartz 2000) or human resource management (Johnsson et al. 2012), and existing studies draw on a range of different understandings of what interactional competence consists of.

One of the most prominent lines of research that informs us about the workings of interactional competence is CA. As Heritage put it: CA is "concerned with the analysis of *competence* which underlies ordinary social activities" (Heritage 1984, 241, original emphasis). Classic work in CA focuses on the generic organization of actions and the systematic procedures participants employ to accomplish that organization locally. While it provides a strong basis for understanding how members put to use these systematic procedures as part of their interactional competence in the course of practical activities, classic CA does not in general explicitly address interactional competence, and even less so its development. Yet, it unveils the fine-grained procedures participants deploy to engage in social interaction—participants that are most typically treated as full members, that is, competent participants (but see Wootton 1997, for pioneering work on a child's development).

The most important body of empirical research explicitly focusing on interactional competence and its development over time has been carried out within CA research on second language acquisition—often referred to as applied CA. Based on an understanding of interactional competence in terms of members' "methods" (i.e., systematic procedures, see

Garfinkel 1967) for organizing social interaction, relating to such issues as turn-taking, repairing, opening or closing a conversation (Mondada and Pekarek Doehler 2004; Hellermann 2008; Pekarek Doehler 2010), studies in this field define interactional competence as being both thoroughly rooted in practical activities and context-sensitive (i.e., contingent upon the very interactional environments in which they are deployed). A recent discussion of longitudinal research on second language interactions (Pekarek Doehler and Pochon-Berger 2015) suggests that the existing findings identify increased efficiency in recipient-designing actions and increased "fittedness" of one's conduct to the local circumstances of the interaction as key components of the development of interactional competence over time.

In line with such findings, a recent transdisciplinary line of research drawing on ethnomethodology and CA has developed a notion of "competence-in-action" according to which competences are not discrete context-independent characteristics of the individual but are products of the interaction within which they are attributed (or not) to an individual through largely implicit or informal operations of assessment and legitimization (Mondada and Pekarek Doehler 2004; Pekarek Doehler 2006, 2010; see also Firth and Wagner 2007). Participants in interaction mobilize representations to which they give the status of shared interpretive markers used for assessments of their own and others' competences. Competences thus are understood as transcending any specific interaction: Not only do they survive it, but they are also interpreted according to collectively shared and valid principles (Mondada 2009; Petitjean 2013).

Although not all of the studies presented in this volume are based on CA, they all analyze interactional competence in exactly these terms, that is, as the situated deployment of context-sensitive conduct designed to be understood, attended to and accepted by co-participants. They investigate interactional competence as consisting of practical procedures (of turn-taking, requesting, telling stories, etc.) through which participants in an interaction coordinate their actions, guide each other, accomplish roles and relationships and give their encounter features of typicity, objectivity and normality which make it transcend the here and now (Psathas 1990; Garfinkel 2002; Young 2003). Accordingly, they study interactional competences as materializing in the local organization of practical activities within the different institutions under scrutiny.

The "IC-You" Project: (Dis)continuities in Institutional Exigencies Regarding Interactional Competences Between School and the Workplace

The present volume originates in a large-scale interdisciplinary research project investigating the dynamic relationship between young people's interactional competences and the larger social institutions within which they operate: *Interactional Competences in Institutional Practices: Young People between School and the Workplace (IC-You)*. Generously funded by the Swiss National Science Foundation (interuniversity Sinergia project, grant CRSII1_136291, 2012–2015)[2], the project's empirical focus was on a set of key moments in the social trajectories of young people (see the studies presented in Part I of this volume): obligatory and post-obligatory schooling (Degoumois et al. this volume), speech therapy sessions (de Weck et al. this volume), professional training (Markaki and Filliettaz this volume), job interviews (Bangerter and Gosteli-Corvalan this volume) and the first steps into working life (Sterie and González-Martínez this volume). The empirical data consist of audio- and video-recorded naturally occurring everyday interactions involving young people aged between 13 and 25 as well as others (teachers, trainers, recruiters, co-workers, etc.) within different institutions in French-speaking Switzerland. The interactions were transcribed and subjected to interaction analysis drawing to various degrees on CA. The precise data under scrutiny as well as some of the results for the institutional settings investigated are presented in the chapters in Part I of this volume; here we summarize the overall picture that emerges from the studies as to the continuities and discontinues between the demands that different institutional settings put on young people's interactional competences.

Overall, findings confirm the key role of people's interactional competences in order for them to "do their job" and be recognized as doing a good job—be it as a student in school or a trainee in vocational training, a candidate for a job or a professional on the job. Interactional competences are identified as central vectors for people's gaining recognition for what they are doing, for how they comply with the normative orders of the social institutions and groups they are involved in and ultimately for how others perceive them as members of the communities of practice at hand. This is also further corroborated by the chapters presented in Part II of this volume.

Yet, as young people move from school to the workplace, they are faced with ever-changing institutional demands as to their abilities for interaction. While interactional competences are a pervasive resource to deal with these demands because they are central instruments for participation, task accomplishment, self-presentation as well as membership, they are differentially called upon at various key moments on the pathway into professional life.

Continuities

Many of the demands young people encounter in work-related interactions outside of school build on interactional competences that were called upon and valued in the classroom—especially at the upper secondary level: This relates, for instance, to active initiative-taking for participation, offering personal points of view, prudent dealing with delicate matters and taking of epistemic (and affirmative) stance toward one's claims or views, all of which are implicitly and explicitly encouraged in school (see Petitjean 2013; Petitjean and González-Martínez 2015; Degoumois 2014; Degoumois et al. this volume). The reasons for these issues being at stake may differ between school and other institutional settings (e.g., dealing with delicate matters can be related to such diverse issues as disclosing personal opinions or requesting actions from superiors); yet, the basic resources used to manage them (e.g., displaying epistemic stance, laughter, humor) are already at work in classroom interaction—increasingly so as students move from compulsory to post-compulsory schooling. Significant in this regard is the strong continuity between lower and upper secondary school (Petitjean 2013, 2015; Degoumois et al. this volume): Processes of implicit legitimization at work at the lower secondary regarding issues like interactional autonomy, assertiveness, local adaptation of one's conduct to ongoing activities tend to become appropriated by students as normative patterns of reference guiding conduct at upper secondary levels. And it is exactly these patterns that are called for in work-related situations, such as job interviews (Bangerter and Gosteli-Corvalan this volume) or actual workplaces (González-Martínez and Petitjean 2016; Sterie and González-Martínez this volume). Also, adolescents undergoing speech therapy displays competences that are equally at work in classroom and professional settings: For example, they mobilize laughter to manage interactional troubles (Petitjean and Cangemi 2016) in a way similar to what has been observed in the classroom (Petitjean and González-Martínez 2015) and the workplace (González-Martínez and Petitjean 2016). Hence, with regard to the above-mentioned issues, there is a remarkable continuity on the pathway that leads young people from lower to upper secondary school, and how that pathway prepares for some future challenges.

Recalibrations

Young people also face new interactional demands when moving beyond school into the world of work. The complexity of participation is drastically increased. Multitasking (Markaki and Filliettaz this volume), adjusting to multiple types of interlocutors (Sterie and González-Martínez this volume) and dealing with flexible and changing participation frameworks (Markaki and Filliettaz this volume; Filliettaz 2015; Rémery and Markaki 2016) are among the pervasive new demands young people encounter on their pathway toward the workplace. Also, increased responsibility and agency are called upon in work-related social interactions, as materializing in the need for inviting or instructing others to act or for actively structuring social interaction through personal initiative (Markaki and Filliettaz this volume; Filliettaz et al. 2014, 2015; Filliettaz and Rémery 2015; Sterie and González-Martínez this volume). Finally, such issues as expectations of self-presentation (e.g., in job interviews, Bangerter and Gosteli-Corvalan this volume) or time pressure (e.g., in work-related telephone interactions; Sterie and González-Martínez this volume; Sterie 2016), as well as decreased permissibility of disruptive actions during work-related interactions (Sterie and González-Martínez this volume; Sterie 2016) are among further challenges. The findings suggest that in the face of these challenges, young people are not unprepared; yet, the new situations require them to adapt and further elaborate the resources available to them to deal with the novel exigencies at hand. While we do not have empirical evidence for the process of such adaptation (longitudinal studies would be needed for this), the quoted studies document the products of such recalibrations in how young people deal with social interactions during for instance vocational training, in job interviews or on a new job, and how their actions are accepted, scaffolded or ignored by others.

Discontinuities

Strong discontinuities were identified at one key moment in the transition between school and work: when young people leave school directly after the lower secondary level, that is, after compulsory schooling. Although the project touched upon this issue only to a limited extent, namely through the study of job interviews (Bangerter and Gosteli-Corvalan this volume), the study clearly shows that adolescents applying for a job directly after compulsory school tend to encounter considerable difficulties in dealing with the demands of job interview interactions. The lack of initiative-taking displayed by many candidates echoes the question-answering scripts that operate in school settings at the lower secondary level (Petitjean 2013), where pupils are typically not involved in extended turns at talk and are not expected to use questions, for instance, as opportunities for extended self-presentation (see also Degoumois 2014). Interestingly, for the many young people who suffer from language and communicative impairments, the interactional dynamics during speech therapy provides a complement to school practices: de Weck et al., this volume, show that speech therapy favors adolescents' use of storytelling as an institutionally legitimate resource for conveying a positive self-image, just as this is called for in job interviews (Bangerter and Gosteli-Corvalan this volume).

In sum, then, the empirical studies conducted within the framework of the *IC-You* project show that there is continuity, recalibration, and at times discontinuity, between school and further steps into working life regarding young people's interactional competences and how these are recognized and assessed within everyday interactions in the related institutions. The cooperative participatory culture based on the student's initiative, the diversification of turn-taking practices and the negotiation of knowledge observed at the upper end of the school trajectory in particular reverberates with the increased demands for interactional flexibility encountered in diverse work-related situations. In order to face these demands, young people are required to revise earlier experiences, adapt existing competences and elaborate new ones.

The institutional requirements regarding young people's interactional competences on the trajectory between school and the workplace call for an *increased diversification of resources and practices, allowing for increasingly context-sensitive conduct* (and this resonates with findings on the development of interactional competence over time; see section "Young People's Interactional Practices Within Institutional Settings"). This is indicated by increased demands in terms of *patterns of participation* and *interactional multitasking* (diversification of participation structures and navigation between these; managing various parallel lines of action) as well as by an augmented need for fine-tuned *recipient design* (diversification of interlocutors; time pressure) and increased demands on *self-positioning* and *self-presentation.*

One further finding is worth mentioning. The mechanisms through which young people's interactional competencies are recognized and treated as more or less legitimate evolve from being explicit (lower secondary school) to highly implicit (on the job: González-Martínez et al. 2016; González-Martínez and Petitjean 2016; Petitjean et al. 2016), passing through intermediate stages based on a differential implementation of overt and tacit norms of conduct (e.g., vocational training: Filliettaz 2015; Filliettaz and Rémery 2015; upper secondary schooling: Petitjean 2013, 2015; speech therapy: de Weck 2003, 2004; Rezzonico et al. 2013). This suggests an *increased role of hidden curricula* regarding the interactional competences required on the transition between school and the workplace. It also reveals the importance of everyday institutional interactional practices as sites where the institution-specific normative order is both enacted and transmitted, that is, where facets of young people's interactional competence are treated as more or less legitimate. This further stresses the existence of powerful normative orders that both underlie institutional interactions and are perpetuated by them (Melander this volume). Even in situations where no official documents pertain to these orders, they remain *adaptable through practice*—and in particular through mutual orientations between "novices" and "experts," and the related negotiations of stance, epistemic entitlement, mutual positionings, as well as task accomplishment in the course of social interactions.

Of course, the overall picture that emerges from the above-mentioned results is based on a selective set of snapshots of emblematic institutional settings and social interactions therein that young people are involved in when they move from school into the workplace. Yet, this picture is further detailed by the studies presented in Part II, which identify the need for local adaptation as well as the mostly implicit (embedded in interactional practices) nature of the normative order at hand in such diverse settings as pharmacists' or doctors' training sessions in Sweden, the USA and Australia, or workplace interaction among builders in New Zealand. Gaps remain to be filled by means of further qualitative research (other types of schools, professional training or workplaces, as well as other transitions from one type of institution to another, e.g., from compulsory school directly to vocational training). Yet, taken together, the findings of the *IC-You* project boil down to this: The pathway between school and the workplace requires young people to exhibit a *growing degree of interactional flexibility*, the *capability of continually revising and adapting their own conduct* as a basis for refining their abilities for interaction and an *increased ability to "read between the lines" of the explicit institutional order*, that is, to monitor social interactional practices for how others react to their own conduct as indicators of the institutional legitimacy of that very conduct and, in the end, of the institutional value of their competences for social interaction. The contributions to this volume empirically substantiate these issues, while addressing their broader social and scientific relevance.

Contributions to the Volume

The volume is organized into two parts. Part I presents five studies emanating from the *IC-You* project designed to identify the institutional demands put on interactional competences of young people in emblematic settings between school and the workplace: the classroom, speech therapy sessions, professional training, job interviews and work. The empirical data for all these studies were collected in the French-speaking part of Switzerland. Part II comprises four contributions which address issues of young people's transition into work across four continents: training sessions involving nursing students in Sweden, pharmacists training during role-play and at actual pharmacies in the USA, workplace interactions among builders in New Zealand and junior doctors co-working with pharmacists in an Australian teaching hospital.

Part I opens with Degoumois, Petitjean and Pekarek Doehler's study on how young people deal with the challenges of expressing personal opinions within a primary site of their socialization—the classroom—as part of their interactional competence. Based on a CA analysis of French (L1) classroom interactions at the lower secondary level, the study documents how students (aged between 13 and 14) succeed in expressing opinions in a way that is attended to and accepted by others, by subtly navigating between the use of humor and epistemic disclaimers. By means of epistemic disclaimers, students downgrade their commitment and hence offer the opportunity for co-participants to disaffiliate from the opinion being proffered; by means of humor, they maximize their assertiveness while playing on degrees of non-seriousness. Thereby, they ultimately augment the public acceptance of their conduct by peers in a way that also conforms to the institutional order at hand, as displayed by teachers' reactions. When moving from lower to upper secondary schooling, students progressively comply with the normative orders of the classroom as enacted through the teacher's implicit interactional sanctioning or accepting of students' conduct, and they display increased assertiveness in publicly committing to their own opinions.

De Weck, Sublon and Fox analyze the role of storytelling in speech and language therapy, an institutional setting involving young people suffering from language impairments that is designed to help their social, educational and professional integration. In their socio-interactionist study, based on qualitative and quantitative analyses, the authors show that adolescents use storytelling efficiently to report their learning experiences and are encouraged to do so by therapists. These personal storytellings, the authors argue, allow adolescent and therapist to establish a common ground of understanding that might be useful for the therapy itself. Yet, the authors also show that reports of past events are accepted by therapists only if they do not disrupt the ongoing course of action during the sessions; otherwise, such tellings are met with silence or are overtly sanctioned (i.e., treated as illegitimate). Interactional competence is evident in the fact that most often, the storytellings are finely tuned to the ongoing interaction, and the adolescent tellers manage to take the therapist aboard as a story recipient.

In their study on vocational training of students learning to become early childhood educators, Markaki and Filliettaz focus on schisming, that is, the simultaneous emergence of two interactional spaces within the same group of participants. They document how early childhood educator students navigate through such complex participation frameworks, simultaneously maintaining focus on specific participants and monitoring the parallel interaction going on. For instance, they keep their engagement constant toward the children while monitoring the co-present mentor's disciplining a specific child. The mentor in turn provides the students with examples of "good" conduct by asking questions in specific ways to the children or by eliciting specific actions from them. When students follow such examples when interacting with children, they display their understanding of what is locally appropriate conduct as a caregiver, while at the same time treating the children's conduct as more or less legitimate. The authors conclude: "It is precisely the experience of becoming a source of legitimation in interaction that may constitute a key ingredient of vocational training practices, and that could be seen as an important milestone in the journey from school to work" (Markaki and Filliettaz this volume, 112).

Bangerter and Gosteli-Corvalan scrutinize how young people take initiatives in job interviews by means of extended responses to questions (including storytelling), as part of their impression management. Based on analyses of interviews involving adolescents applying for an internship or a first job, the authors document the role recruiters play in creating opportunities for candidates to take initiatives, for instance by asking open questions, by prompting via follow-up questions or by using assessments to display alignment with candidates. Yet, young candidates often deploy only minimal initiative-taking and exhibit little responsiveness. Frequently, they respond hesitantly and limit themselves strictly to the scope of the question, using few resources for displaying the relevance of their responses to the ongoing interaction. While some candidates do show extended initiative-taking, which is rendered legitimate by recruiter's display of alignment and appreciation, the authors suggest that the often minimal taking of initiatives indicates the young candidates' difficulty of "emancipating themselves" from the routine interactional patterns they have experienced as students in the classroom.

Novice nurses' telephone calls to porters and doctors in a hospital setting are the object of Sterie and González-Martínez's study. In these calls, novice nurses often make requests for future action. They format their requests according to the specific other they are addressing and the routine character of the request: Inquiries about ability of the recipient (e.g., "can you?") are routinely used for requests addressed to porters; when addressing doctors, this format is used only when a routine medical task is at issue. By contrast, nurses most typically use reports of a problematic situation to request an action on the part of doctors, most often inviting him or her to say what should be done in the problematic situation at hand. By these two distinct ways of doing requests, nurses display their relative entitlement to make the request, their orientation to the recipient's ability to grant the request, as well as their orientation to who the participants are relative to one another. Recipients, in turn, by routinely granting these requests, treat each format as legitimate for the situation and purpose at hand, thereby accepting the nurses' entitlements and orientations. Through request formats and responses to these, participants' orientation to the normative institutional order is shaped into being.

Part II "Young People's Interactional Practices Within Institutional Settings" opens with Melander's study on training sessions in which nursing students at a Swedish hospital learn how to insert peripheral venous catheters. Drawing on ethnomethodology and CA, Melander documents how students deal differently with problems encountered in a mock setting (working on a model) than in situations similar to the workplace (performing the insertion on a fellow student). Yet, in both situations, they deploy conversational resources to embody what they consider as the social norms and moral expectations of their future profession. For instance, in the mock situation, problems with the stiff plastic arm occasion the telling of an atrocity story about an incompetent nurse's practices from which the students, implicitly, distance themselves. With the live-body situation, the fellow student feeling pain is treated as an occasion to discuss how to use this experience in future encounters with patients. Training sessions are thus analyzed as offering a glimpse on how nursing students orient to the transition from education to medical contexts: They explore norms of proper nursing conduct, talking into being what the author calls "the moral order of the institutional context."

In her contribution, Nguyen traces the roots of the notion "competence" in ethnomethodology and CA and outlines a set of methodological procedures for longitudinal analysis of competence development. She then illustrates these procedures based on an empirical analysis of a pharmacy student learning to counsel patients in classroom role-plays and at actual pharmacies in the USA. Focusing on the consultations' beginning, the analysis shows that during the role-played patient consultations, over time, the target pharmacy student shifted from stating to inquiring about the drug therapy's purpose. By contrast, in subsequent workplace patient consultations, the same student only occasionally inquired about the therapy purpose, and when he did, this was done for different purposes compared to the role-plays (e.g., during pre-closing to build a relation with the patient). These findings suggest that practices developed in training may be repurposed in locally contingent ways at the workplace, providing a case in point for the local, adaptive nature of interactional competence (see section "Interactional Competence").

Marra, Holmes and Kidner investigate the challenges participation may involve for workplace newcomers when joining a new team. The study, undertaken within the framework of workplace discourse, focuses on social interactions in a New Zealand building team. It documents how different values and norms become relevant within interactions in the workplace context. For instance, societal "macro-level" values such as egalitarianism and gender order manifest themselves in workplace interaction through the implementation of non-technical topics such as sports. Moreover, meso-level appropriations of relevant professional values and micro-level uses of legitimate conduct are related to "unwritten rules of the building industry" (see section "The 'IC-You' Project: (Dis)continuities in Institutional Exigencies Regarding Interactional Competences Between School and the Workplace" on the importance of "hidden curricula"). The study concludes: "Developing interactional competence in a new work environment entails developing awareness of relevant societal values and the related constraints (macro level), navigating the unfamiliar norms of a specific workplace team or community of practice (meso level) and learning how to move smoothly between activities and between different frames within workplace activities (micro level)" (Marra et al. this volume, 245).

The object of Noble and Billett's chapter is how junior doctors learn to develop their prescribing capacities through co-working with pharmacists in an Australian teaching hospital. The study departs from the rest of this volume by using interview data as a basis for analysis. Interviews conducted with pharmacists, consultant clinical supervisors and junior doctors show that, for the latter, the transition from medical school to actual prescribing practice is challenging. While junior doctors refrain from asking questions or seeking clarification to avoid being seen as incompetent, they accept guidance, feedback on errors or provision of explanations by co-working pharmacists, which is seen as favoring their learning. As junior doctors gain experience, they become less reliant on pharmacists. According to the authors, this indicates a developmental trajectory of doctors' increasing competence in prescribing medicine and diminished reliance on direct guidance by others. In the conclusion, practical implications are drawn from the study as to how co-working can be effectively supported as junior doctors transition to clinical work.

All studies, from both Parts I and II, discuss implications for one or several of the key notions addressed in this volume: interactional competence, normative institutional order, integration into the workplace, and the affordances and constraints related to integration and transition. Together, the studies highlight the immense variety of interactional situations that young people face when moving from school to work, and identify the major challenges that they encounter, like the need for simultaneously dealing with multiple tasks, participants or participation structures, the need to adapt one's conduct to various types of institutional interlocutors and their roles, duties and entitlements, and the need to deal with delicate matters such as self-presentation through reports of past experiences or the expression of personal opinions. The studies thereby unveil the multilayered set of norms and values that pertain to people's integrating new interactional situations within new communities of practice—norms and values that, most often, are enacted (and appropriated) through engagement in social interaction and the local processes of legitimization or delegitimization accomplished therein, rather than being made explicit in some way or another. Last but not least, the studies also empirically corroborate an understanding of interactional competence (see section "Interactional Competence") as profoundly dynamic, adaptive and situated, involving the locally contingent and recipient designed use of resources for social interaction.

Notes

1. This introductory discussion is deeply indebted to the many stimulating debates we have had with our colleagues Adrian Bangerter, Geneviève de Weck, Laurent Filliettaz, Esther González-Martínez and their research teams as part of a large-scale research project in which this volume originated (the project is presented in section "The 'IC-You' Project: (Dis)continuities in Institutional Exigencies Regarding Interactional Competences Between School and the Workplace"). Those debates have influenced how we authors think about the issues addressed in this introduction to the volume. Our warmest thanks go to the above-mentioned colleagues and their teams for the intellectually stimulating and socially rewarding time spent together. Without them, this introduction would not be as it is, and--more importantly--it would not have a volume to introduce.
2. For more details, see: https://www2.unine.ch/ic-you/lang/en/accueil

References

Androutsopoulos, J. K., & Georgakopoulou, A. (Eds.). (2003). *Discourse constructions of youth identities*. Amsterdam: John Benjamins.

Angouri, J., Marra, M., & Holmes, J. (Eds.). (2016). *Negotiating boundaries at work*. Edinburgh: Edinburgh University Press.

Beach, K. (1999). Consequential transitions: A sociocultural expedition beyond transfer in education. *Review of Research in Education, 28*, 46–69.

Bergman, M., Hupka-Brunner, S., Keller, A., Meyer, T., & Stalder, B. E. (2011). *Transitions juvéniles en Suisse: résultats de l'étude longitudinale TREE*. Zurich: Seismo.

Billett, S. (2001). *Learning in the workplace: Strategies for effective practice*. Crows Nest: Allen & Unwin.

Billett, S. (Ed.). (2010). *Learning through practice*. Dordrecht: Springer.

Blumer, H. (1969). *Symbolic interactionism: Perspective and method*. Englewood Cliffs, NJ: Prentice Hall.

Booth, A., et al. (Eds.). (1999). *Transitions to adulthood in a changing economy. No work, no family, no future?* Westport: Praeger.

Bradley, H., & Devadason, R. (2008). Fractured transitions: Young adults' pathways into contemporary labour markets. *Sociology, 42*(1), 119–136.

Corijn, M., & Klijzing, E. (Eds.). (2001). *Transitions to adulthood in Europe*. Dordrecht: Kluwer.

Degoumois, V. (2014). The expression of personal opinions in the classroom: Insights into teachers' implicit legitimization of students' competences. In *4th international conference of Applied Linguistics and Professional Practice (ALAAP)*, University of Geneva, Geneva, Switzerland, 10–13 September 2014.

de Saint-Georges, I., & Filliettaz, L. (2008). Situated trajectories of learning in vocational training interactions. *European Journal of Psychology of Education, 23*(2), 213–233.

de Weck, G. (2003). Pratiques langagières, contextes d'interaction et genres de discours en logopédie/orthophonie. *Travaux Neuchâtelois de Linguistique, 38–39*, 25–47.

de Weck, G. (2004). Erreurs, normes et tâches dans l'acquisition de L1 et en pathologie du langage. In L. Gajo, M. Matthey, D. Moore, & C. Serra (Eds.), *Un parcours au contact des langues. Sociolinguistique du plurilinguisme et de l'acquisition: Textes de Bernard Py commentés* (pp. 73–76). Paris: Didier, Collection LAL.

Drew, P., & Heritage, J. (Eds.). (1992). *Talk at work. Interaction in institutional settings*. Cambridge: Cambridge University Press.

Filipi, A. (2009). *Toddler and parent interaction. The organization of gaze, pointing, and vocalisation*. Amsterdam: John Benjamins.

Filliettaz, L. (2010). Guidance as an interactional accomplishment: Practice-based learning within the Swiss VET system. In S. Billett (Ed.), *Learning through practice: Models, traditions, orientations and approaches* (pp. 156–179). London: Springer.

Filliettaz, L. (2015). Les ressources interactionnelles de la structuration des activités en contexte éducatif. *Bulletin Suisse de Linguistique Appliquée (VALS-ASLA), 101*, 11–26.

Filliettaz, L., & de Saint-Georges, I. (2006). La mise en discours du temps en situation de formation professionnelle initiale: le cas du trempage de l'acier. *Bulletin suisse de linguistique appliquée, 84*, 121–141.

Filliettaz, L., de Saint-Georges, I., & Duc, B. (2010). Skiing, cheese fondue and Swiss watches: Analogical discourse in vocational training interactions. *Vocations & Learning, 3*(2), 117–140.

Filliettaz, L., Durand, I., & Trébert, D. (2015). Learning through interactional participatory configurations. In L. Filliettaz & S. Billett (Eds.), *Francophone perspectives of learning through work: Conceptions, traditions and practices* (pp. 279–301). Dordrecht: Springer.

Filliettaz, L., & Rémery, V. (2015). Transmettre le travail par les mises en forme langagières de l'activité. In R. Wittorski (Ed.), *Comprendre la transmission du travail* (pp. 47–81). Editions Champ Social: Nîmes.

Filliettaz, L., Rémery, V., & Trébert, D. (2014). Relation tutorale et configurations de participation à l'interaction: analyse de l'accompagnement des stagiaires dans le champ de la petite enfance. *Activités, 11*(1), 22–46.

Firth, A., & Wagner, J. (2007). Second/Foreign language learning as a social accomplishment. Elaborations on a reconceptualized SLA. *The Modern Language Journal, 91*, 798–817.

Gardner, H., & Forrester, M. (Eds.). (2010). *Analysing interactions in childhood. Insights from conversation analysis*. Oxford: Wiley/Blackwell.

Garfinkel, H. (1967). *Studies in ethnomethodology*. Englewood Cliffs, NJ: Prentice Hall.

Garfinkel, H. (Ed.). (1986). *Ethnomethodological studies of work*. London: Routledge & Kegan.

Garfinkel, H. (2002). *Ethnomethodology's program. Working out Durkheim's aphorism*. Lanham: Rowman and Littlefield.

Giddens, A. (1979). *Central problems in social theory*. London and Basingstoke: The Macmillan Press.

Glenn, P., & Koschmann, T. (2005). Learning to diagnose. Production of diagnostic hypotheses in problem-based learning tutorials. In M. Maxwell, D. Kovarsky, & J. Duchan (Eds.), *Diagnosis as cultural practice. An account of the power of language in diagnosis* (pp. 154–178). The Hague: Mouton.

Goffmann, E. (1983). The interaction order. *American Sociological Review, 48*, 1–17.

González-Martínez, E., Markaki, V., & Bovey, F. (2016). 'Demandes régime dernière minute' lors de conversations téléphoniques infirmière-diététicienne. In K. Stroumza & H. Messmer (Eds.), *Langage et savoir-faire. Des pratiques professionnelles du travail social et de la santé passées à la loupe* (pp. 85–110). Geneva: Editions IES.

González-Martínez, E., & Petitjean, C. (2016). Le rire cordial dans les demandes téléphoniques par de jeunes infirmières à l'hôpital. *Activités, 13*(1), 2–19.

Hall, J. K., Hellemann, J., & Pekarek Doehler, S. (Eds.). (2011). *L2 interactional competence and development*. Clevedon: Multilingual Matters.

Hellermann, J. (2008). *Social actions for classroom language learning*. Clevedon: Multilingual Matters.

Heritage, J. (1984). *Garfinkel and ethnomethodology*. Cambridge, MA: Polity Press.

Hutchby, I., & Moran-Ellis, J. (1998). Situating children's social competence. In I. Hutchby & J. Moran-Ellis (Eds.), *Children and social competence: Arenas of action*. London: Falmer Press.

Jacoby, S. (1998). *Science as performance: Socializing scientific discourse through conference talk rehearsals*. Unpublished PhD, University of California, Los Angeles.

Jacoby, S., & McNamara, T. (1999). Locating competence. *English for Specific Purposes, 18*(3), 213–241.

Johnsson, M. C., Boud, D. J., & Solomon, N. (2012). Learning in-between, across and beyond workplace boundaries. *International Journal of Human Resources Development and Management, 12*(1–2), 61–76.

Koskela, I., & Palukka, H. (2011). Trainer interventions as instructional strategies in air traffic control training. *Journal of Workplace Learning, 23*(5), 293–314.

Lave, J. (1988). *Cognition in practice: Mind, mathematics and culture in everyday life*. Cambridge: Cambridge University Press.

Lave, J., & Wenger, E. (1991). *Situated learning: Legitimate peripheral participation*. Cambridge: Cambridge University Press.

Lindström, J., & Lindholm, C. (2009). 'May I ask' Question frames in institutional interaction. In M. Haakana et al. (Eds.), *Talk in interaction: Comparative dimensions* (pp. 180–205). Helsinki: Finnish Literature Society.

Luff, P. K., et al. (Eds.). (2000). *Workplace studies. Recovering work practice and informing systems design*. Cambridge: Cambridge University Press.

Macbeth, D. H. (1990). Classroom order as practical action. The making and un-making of a quiet reproach. *British Journal of Sociology of Education, 11*(2), 189–214.

Mehan, H. (1979). *Learning lessons: Social organization in the classroom*. Cambridge, MA: Harvard University Press.

Mondada, L. (2009). The embodied and negotiated production of assessments in instructed actions. *Research in Language and Social Interaction, 42*(4), 329–361.

Mondada, L., & Pekarek Doehler, S. (2004). Second language acquisition as situated practice. *The Modern Language Journal, 88*(4), 501–518.

Nguyen, H. T. (2012). *Developing interactional competence. A conversation-analytic study of patient consultations in pharmacy*. New York: Palgrave Macmillan.

Palotti, G., & Wagner, J. (Eds.). (2011). *L2 learning as social practice: Conversation-analytic perspectives*. Honolulu: The national foreign language resource center, University of Hawaii.

Pekarek Doehler, S. (2006). Compétence et langage en action. *Bulletin VALS-ASLA, 84*, 9–45.

Pekarek Doehler, S. (2010). Conceptual changes and methodological challenges: On language and learning from a conversation analytic perspective on SLA. In P. Seedhouse, S. Walsh, & C. Jenks (Eds.), *Conceptualising learning in applied linguistics* (pp. 105–127). Basingstoke: Palgrave Macmillan.

Pekarek Doehler, S., & Pochon-Berger, E. (2015). The development of L2 interactional competence: Evidence from turn-taking organization, sequence organization, repair organization and preference organization. In T. Cadierno & S. Eskildsen (Eds.), *Usage-based perspectives on second language learning* (pp. 233–267). Berlin: Mouton De Gruyter.

Pekarek Doehler, S., Wagner, J., & González-Martínez, E. (Eds.). (forthcoming). *Longitudinal studies in conversation analysis*. Basinkstoke: Palgrave Macmillan.

Perret-Clermont, A.-N., et al. (Eds.). (2004). *Joining society. Social interaction and learning in adolescence and youth*. Cambridge: Cambridge University Press.

Petitjean, C. (2013). Social representations of turn-taking in classrooms: From compulsory to post-compulsory schooling in French-speaking Switzerland. *Classroom Discourse, 5*(2), 138–157.

Petitjean, C. (2015). Les pratiques humoristiques dans des interactions en classe de français. Transition de l'école obligatoire à l'école post-obligatoire en Suisse romande. *Langage et Société, 154*, 101–126.

Petitjean, C., & Cangemi, F. (2016). Laughter in correction sequences in speech therapy sessions. *Journal of Pragmatics, 99*, 17–38.

Petitjean, C., & González-Martínez, E. (2015). Laughing and smiling to manage trouble in French-language classroom interaction. *Classroom Discourse, 6*(2), 89–106.

Petitjean, C., Sterie, A., Vaucher, C., & González-Martínez, E. (2016). "Je me permets de te déranger pour te demander un petit conseil": la gestion de l'expertise lors d'un appel téléphonique infirmier au service des Soins intensifs. *Cahiers de l'Institut de linguistique et des sciences du langage, 42*, 33–56.

Psathas, G. (Ed.). (1990). *Interaction competence.* Washington, DC: University Press of America.

Rémery, V., & Markaki, V. (2016). Travailler et former: l'activité hybride des tuteurs. *Education Permanente, 206*, 47–59.

Rezzonico, S., de Weck, G., Salazar Orvig, A., da Silva-Genest, C., & Rahmati, S. (2013). Maternal recasts and activity variations: A comparison of mother-child dyads involving children with and without SLI. *Clinical Linguistics and Phonetics, 28*(4), 223–240.

Sacks, H. (1992). *Lectures on conversation. Vol. I & II* (G. Jefferson, Ed.). Malden, Oxford, Victoria: Blackwell Publishing.

Schwartz, Y. (2000). *Le paradigme ergologique ou un métier de Philosophe (Texte 23: De la qualification à la compétence. La qualification à la recherche de ses conditions aux limites, pp. 467–477).* Toulouse: Octarès.

Seedhouse, P. (2004). *The interactional architecture of the language classroom: A conversation analysis perspective.* Malden, MA: Blackwell.

Settersten, R. A., et al. (Eds.). (2005). *On the frontier of adulthood. Theory, research and public policy.* Chicago: The University of Chicago Press.

Sidnell, J. (Ed.). (2009). *Conversation analysis. Comparative perspectives.* Cambridge: Cambridge University Press.

Sterie, A. (2016). *Nurses reporting problems in hospital telephone interaction. A practice for requesting doctor's intervention.* Unpublished PhD, University of Fribourg, Switzerland.

Tuomi-Gröhn, T., & Engeström, Y. (Eds.). (2003a). *Between school and work. New perspectives on transfer and boundary-crossing.* Howard House: Emerald Group Publishing.

Tuomi-Gröhn, T., & Engeström, Y. (2003b). Conceptualizing transfer: From standard notions to developmental perspectives. In T. Tuomi-Gröhn & Y. Engeström (Eds.), *Between school and work. New perspectives on transfer and boundary-crossing* (pp. 19–38). Howard House: Emerald Group Publishing.

Wootton, A. J. (1997). *Interaction and the development of mind.* Cambridge: Cambridge University Press.

Young, R. F. (2003). Learning to talk the talk and walk the walk: Interactional competence in academic spoken English. *North Eastern Illinois University Working Papers in Linguistics, 2*, 26–44.

Zemel, A., & Koschmann, T. (2014). "Put your finger right in here": Learnability and instructed experience. *Discourse Studies, 16*(2), 163–183.

Part I

Institutional Practices Between School and the Workplace

2

Expressing Personal Opinions in Classroom Interactions: The Role of Humor and Displays of Uncertainty

Virginie Degoumois, Cécile Petitjean, and Simona Pekarek Doehler

Introduction

The expression of personal opinions is ubiquitous to both ordinary conversation and institutional talk. When engaging in social interaction, we recurrently formulate our points of view on a myriad of issues related to the world and to our daily lives. The expression of personal opinions is a central part of the management of intersubjectivity in human communication, be it in the family, among friends, in the workplace, or elsewhere. It is instrumental to our establishing personal relationships, to our negotiating solutions to a given problem, and ultimately, to our sharing of a view of the world with others. Yet it also represents a delicate interactional endeavor that may generate disaffiliation on the part of co-participants.

V. Degoumois (✉) • C. Petitjean • S. Pekarek Doehler
Center for Applied Linguistics, University of Neuchâtel, Neuchâtel, Switzerland

S. Pekarek Doehler et al. (eds.), *Interactional Competences in Institutional Settings*, DOI 10.1007/978-3-319-46867-9_2

Although public opinion has become a major topic in numerous fields of research, including social, political, and media studies (see Bourdieu 1971, *inter alia*), few studies have focused on personal opinion (but see Myers 1998; Quéré 1995), particularly on how it is expressed verbally (see Mullan 2010). While there is a body of conversation analytic work on argument sequences (e.g., Coulter 1990; Hutchby 1996) in which participants present their views, little is known to date as to how the eliciting and offering of personal opinion is interactionally organized.

This chapter investigates how young people deal with the challenges of expressing personal opinions within a primary site of their socialization—the classroom—as part of their interactional competence. It focuses on the interactional resources students use for displaying the "fittedness" of their opinions to the local circumstances of the interaction and how, thereby, they promote opportunities for affiliation (or disaffiliation) on the part of co-participants. Expressing personal opinions is particularly challenging in classroom interaction—and specifically so at the lower secondary level of schooling. Students at that level go through a period in their life (puberty) during which they tend to be concerned with forging their personalities in response to the other. Gaining respect and recognition from others—especially peers—for how they act and think is a critical part of this process (Brinthaupt and Lipka 2012; Harter 1999). This is also the time when social group conformity or defiance, as well as dynamics of inclusion and exclusion, is prominently at play (Harter 1999). In the classroom, students' opinions are likely to be assessed by both teachers and classmates, and students therefore may be particularly concerned with managing opinion formulation so as to satisfy the teacher's expectations while minimizing risks of disaffiliation on the part of peers.

Based on a corpus of video-recorded French L1 lessons in a lower secondary school in Switzerland, the present study concentrates on cases where, in response to the teacher's prompts to offer personal opinions, students subtly navigate between displaying uncertainty and showing assertiveness as a means of dealing with the potentially delicate nature of opinion expression. The study particularly focuses on two interactional resources that students frequently use in this process: humor and claims of lack of epistemic access. Drawing on Conversation Analysis, the study identifies two recurrent trajectories of students' opinion formulation, each of which entails different interactional consequentialities. When the teacher selects a specific student as the next speaker, that student typically first designs his/her turn as uncertain and then shifts to humorous talk through which he or she offers a personal opinion. In this case, the display of uncertainty occurs first in the turn, and it projects the delicate nature of the incipient action, while the delivery of personal opinion occurs next and is proffered through humorous talk. This turn trajectory allows students to satisfy the sequential expectations ensuing from the teachers' questions so as to minimize the opportunity for participants to disaffiliate from the opinion being proffered, exactly because that opinion is designed as non-serious. By contrast, when the teacher elicits an opinion without selecting a specific next speaker, the self-selected student tends to first respond to the teacher's question by delivering his or her opinion in a humorous way and then shifts to uncertainty as a way of closing the humorous episode while downgrading his or her commitment to the previously proffered opinion. We argue that these two turn trajectories show how students minutely organize opinion formulations so as to augment their acceptability both for the teacher and classmates. The findings contribute to a better understanding of students' interactional competence by documenting the accountable ways in which, when expressing personal opinions, they subtly balance between assertiveness and uncertainty in response to the local circumstantial details of the ongoing interaction. The findings also shed light on what facets of students' conduct are treated as institutionally legitimate in the classroom. Finally, the findings provide insights into a ubiquitous yet little studied interactional endeavor: the expression of personal opinions.

The Art of Expressing Personal Opinions

The Expression of Personal Opinions as an Interactional Accomplishment

The notion of "opinion" is commonly defined as a personal way of thinking about a topic, and therefore the expression of personal opinions differs from stating facts. An opinion is a personal judgment that cannot be evaluated as right or wrong but rather pertains to a continuum ranging from acceptable to not acceptable in terms of morality and hence socially shared values. As Sacks points out:

> The notion of 'opinion' as contrasted to knowledge (and Plato made a great deal of the difference between them) and the sheer introduction of a notion of 'opinion' provides in part for professionals' talk to laymen. Because one of the characteristics of 'opinion' is that it's something which lay persons are entitled to have when they're not entitled to have knowledge—in the sense that they can offer it without ever proposing to have to then defend it. (Sacks 1992, 33)

Important here is the fact that the expression of personal opinions pertains to a moral rather than an epistemic order. Everyone may be entitled to have an opinion on a given issue; yet not everyone is equally entitled to offer his or her opinion in a given situation, and not all opinions will be equally assessed as 'morally' (i.e., normatively) acceptable (see Melander this volume, for related considerations on the moral order of social interaction). While much effort has been invested in defining what personal opinion is, only a few studies investigate such opinion in talk-in-interaction (but see Myers 1998, on displays of opinion in focus groups; see also Mullan 2010, on the use of discourse markers). Within conversation analytic research, personal opinion is mostly mentioned in studies on survey and interview settings (e.g., Antaki et al. 2000) and on argument structure (Coulter 1990; Hutchby 1996), without however representing an analytic focus *per se*. The expression of personal opinion is implicitly addressed in the extensive conversation analytic work on assessments (Pomerantz 1984; Goodwin and Goodwin 1987; Mondada 2009; Sidnell 2012; *inter alia*), in which assessment is commonly understood as the expression of one's 'positively or negatively valenced stance toward some person or object talked about' (Sidnell 2012, 304). In this sense, assessment can be considered as one type of personal opinion. Yet, while assessment and personal opinion both imply self-positioning (Du Bois 2007), they differ in terms of sequential organization: While assessments are typically organized 'within the turn at talk' (Goodwin and Goodwin 1987, 49), the expression of personal opinion is most often not confined to a single turn, rather it is dynamically co-produced by participants through extended sequences (see below). Therefore, we consider the action of assessing as one of many potential components involved in the activity of expressing personal opinion. And we document the expression of opinions in talk-in-interaction as a local accomplishment that is continuously adapted online to the local circumstantial details of the ongoing interaction, including co-participants' conduct. In this study, we set out to uncover how the expression of personal opinion is accomplished in the precise context where one participant has explicitly prompted the offering of a personal opinion by co-participants.

On the Delicate Nature of Opinion Formulation in the Classroom

In the classroom, the expression of personal opinion is an explicit object of instruction. According to the official curriculum for the lower secondary schools in French-speaking Switzerland,[1] students have to be trained in formulating an opinion, contributing to a debate and elaborating an argument. Yet, the expression of personal opinions is a challenging endeavor for students: They often have difficulties satisfying the sequential expectations ensuing from the teacher's opinion requests. In the following excerpt, the teacher (Tea) invites a student to offer her point of view regarding the opportunity for her to enroll in another school next year.

Ex. (1)[2]

```
1  Tea:   lisa qu'est-ce tu en penses toi.
          lisa what do   you think of it
2         (0.6)
3  Dom:   (xx)
4  Tea:   t'as l'air comme ça un peu:: triste dans ton coin,
          you seem like that a little sad in your corner
5         qu'est-ce tu en penses.
          what do you think of it
6         (0.3)
7         vas-y.
          come on
8  Lis:   °(ben) chais pas?°
           well  dunno
```

```
9          (0.9)
10         °°mais non mais si (x) chais pas°°
            but  no  but if/yes    dunno
11         (1.3)
```

Since the student does not respond (l. 2), the teacher recasts his question (l. 5). Lisa remains silent (l. 6), and the teacher again encourages her to take the floor (l. 7). Lisa's response (l. 8–10) starts off with a display of uncertainty (lower volume, claim of limited epistemic access, and final rising intonation) and is delivered hesitantly (repeats, very low volume, and pause, l. 9–10), displaying Lisa's orientation to the delicate nature of the called-for delivery of a personal opinion (see Lerner 2013, on speakers' hesitant turn delivery when dealing with delicate matters). Additionally, her turn-final *chais pas* "dunno" (l. 10) may be a way of opting out of the turn (Pekarek Doehler 2016; Degoumois 2013) and thereby displaying resistance to comply with the sequential implicature of the teacher's prompt. So, just as participants may show a special concern for such interpersonally sensitive matters as the voicing of a potentially offensive term (e.g., vulgar expletives), aspects of apparently delicate topics (e.g., sex or death, and derogatory reference to persons') (Lerner 2013, 95), they may also show a special concern for interpersonally sensitive matters like the expression of a personal opinion.

Although an opinion cannot be evaluated as right or wrong, it can be assessed as more or less acceptable by the other participants. In the following excerpt, a student—Maya—is expressing her view of her future life as a mother who will not abandon her profession.

Ex. (2)

```
1  May:    =ben à cinquante pour cent ouais p't'être,
           well at fifty percent      yeah maybe
2          mais pas euh:: (0.2) toute ma vie
           but  not             my whole life
3          rester à la maison [avec (mon m↑ari),      ]
           staying at home     with my husband
4  Car:                       [(mais pour la↓vi:e) ]
                                but for a lifetime
5          (0.7)
6  Tea:    CH::UT.
           hush
7          ((0.4, hubbub))
```

```
8  Dom:    MAIS C'QU'ELLE EST [NU::LLE.]
           but  what a dummy she is
9  Tea:                       [CH::UT. ]
                               hush
10         non non.
           no no
11         (0.2)
12         vous vous taisez,
           you keep quiet
13         c'est difficile de (0.4) dire ses idées,
           it is difficult to   express one's ideas
14         j'aimerais que vous écoutiez s'il vous plait.
           I want     you      to listen        please
```

Maya's view is met with a strong negative assessment by Dominique (l. 8). Dominique's taking a turn is immediately sanctioned by the teacher (l. 9), who subsequently explicitly addresses the difficulty of expressing opinions in the classroom (l. 13). This excerpt thus highlights the fact that offering personal opinions in the classroom is both susceptible to meeting with open criticism by others and is oriented to as delicate, or even difficult, by participants.

The above excerpts illustrate pervasive features of the interactional management of opinion expression in the classroom. On the one hand, expressing personal opinions is called for by the institutional agenda as implemented in the local unfolding of social interaction (in particular: teacher's prompts). On the other hand, it is treated as a delicate matter in the classroom, invoking a moral order that may be more or less shared among classmates (and the teacher), and therefore personal opinions may be subject to disapproval or even dismissal by others. Accordingly, in the classroom data scrutinized in this study, students mobilize systematic procedures for dealing with the delicate nature of opinion expressions—procedures by means of which they foster affiliation on the part of co-participants and ultimately augment the public acceptance of their opinions by others. Among these are namely humor and displays of uncertainty.

Data and Procedure

This study is based on a corpus of French-as-a-first-language classroom interactions at the lower secondary level in French-speaking Switzerland (CODI Corpus), with students aged between 13 and 14, representing a total of 7.5 hours of audio-video recordings. The data comprise debates and discussions from two different classes with two different teachers. Using conversation analysis, we analyze the interactional resources that students employ to manage opinion formulation in the classroom. While in ordinary conversation an opinion may be volunteered, occurring in that case as a first pair part (see the work on assessments quoted above), in our data, the expression of opinions is typically prompted by a teacher's questions ("what do you think of X?" and "what is your point of view?") and hence occurs as a second pair part. Accordingly, students offer personal opinions as responsive actions and more precisely as responses to questions. We compiled 20 excerpts in which students offer a personal opinion in response to the teacher's invitation to do so. These opinion-proffering sequences are often built in three parts including the teacher's prompts, the student's answer, and a teacher's reformulation as a sequence-closing third (see Schegloff 2007). By focusing on how students design their turns at talk in a way to ensure the recipient-designed production of their opinion, we document how students subtly navigate between cautiousness and assertiveness, adapting the trajectory of their opinion formulation according to how the teacher invites them to take the floor and according to the classmates' concurrent conduct.

How Students Manage the Expression of Personal Opinions in Classroom Interaction

In this section, we document two trajectories of students' opinion formulation in response to teacher's prompts: (i) When the teacher selects a specific student as the next speaker, the selected student first displays uncertainty before shifting to more assertiveness by producing humorous talk. By contrast, (ii) when the teacher produces a choral question addressed to the whole class without precisely selecting a student, the self-selected student assertively formulates his/her opinion in a humorous way before shifting to uncertainty as a way to close down the humorous episode and to soften the potentially 'subversive' nature of his/her humor. Through both trajectories, students manage the delicate nature of the expression of personal opinions by minimizing the opportunity for other participants to disaffiliate; by choosing one or the other trajectory in precise sequential environments, students calibrate their engagement in opinion formulation depending on whether they are (or not) personally invited to express their views.

From Displays of Uncertainty to Humor

In the following excerpt, that we quote in two parts, the teacher is asking the students what they think about their previous classes. Just before the start of the excerpt, the teacher has been discussing with Noémie about why she chose to join this specific class. The teacher prompts Noémie to formulate a personal opinion by asking her whether she thought that this class had a good reputation when she was in another class the year before (l. 1–3):

Ex. (3)

```
1  Tea:   mais: t'avais::,
          but   you had
2         tu pensais que cette classe avait bonne réputation,
          you thought that this class had a good  reputation
3         je veux dire [ça se sait] en dehors [des: des classes ou bien.      ]
          I mean        this is known outside      the classrooms or not
4  (?):                [°hhhi°    ]
5  Bra:                                       [£(xxx pas b'soin d'ça) £hihi hi]
                                                   no need of that
6  Teo:   £--------------------------------((until the end of line 7))--£
7  Tea:   dis-nous voir franchement noémie ça intéresse les autres.
          tell us       honestly    noémie this interests the others
8         (1.2)
```

Clearly, the teacher's question is oriented to by some students as potentially delicate, as indicated by co-occurring laughter (l. 4–5) and smiles (l. 6) (Jacknick 2013). The teacher does not react but further prompts Noémie to provide her personal opinion openly. By arguing that the whole class is interested by Noémie's opinion, the teacher preempts the students' unsolicited turns while encouraging Noémie to express her views. Noémie then provides a response:

Ex. (3')

```
8            (1.2)
9  Noe:      >°s'ils ont une bonne (t-) réputation°<,
             if they  have a good       reputation
10           ben j'sais pas des fois euh::,
             well I don't know sometimes
11           (1.4)
12  (?):     [°hhhu°]=
13  (?):     [hihih ]=
14  (?):               =[°huhh° hhhh                                    ]
15  All:               =[((°°laughs°°))                                 ]
16  Noe:               =[>moi j'trouve qu'ils ont pas< qu'ils ont pas l'â(h)ge.]
                        me I think that they haven't that they haven't the age
17  Teo:     £-----------------------------((until the end of line 21))--£
18  (?):       HHHe[he]
19  (?):           [ha]haha
20  (?):     >he↓ha<
21           (1.7)
22  Bar:     £---£
23  Noe:     je les prends pour des gamins des fois.
             I take them    for    kids     sometimes
24  (?):     ° ·hhuu°
25  Noe:     enfin euh ça c'est l'âge des garçons hein.=
             well     that is      the boys'age
26  Bra:     =£faut le dire hein£.
             we have to say it
```

In this excerpt, Noémie faces a delicate matter: She has to respond to the teacher's question by formulating a personal opinion about the class' reputation, in front of the very class she is assessing—and as it turns out, this assessment is not exactly positive (see l. 23). Also, Noémie designs her response in a way to display that she is engaging in a delicate matter: After having delayed her answer (l. 8), she repeats part of the teacher's question with a lower volume (l. 9). She then starts to produce a response that is *well*-prefaced and followed by the epistemic disclaimer "I don't know." It can be argued that the *ben* "well" and the *je sais pas* "I don't know" operate a division of labor in projecting the potentially problematic nature of the upcoming response. As Schegloff and Lerner (2009) suggest, the *well*-prefacing of responses to wh-questions projects a non-straightforward response. In the present context, the subsequent *je sais pas* "I don't know" more specifically alerts the recipient to the possible delicate (and not only non-straightforward) nature of the upcoming response and by the same token prospectively downgrades the speaker's commitment to that response (see Weatherall 2011; Pekarek Doehler 2016). By delivering her turn in a non-straightforward way (see also the delayed start, the hesitation markers, the lower voice, and vowel lengthening, l. 8–10), Noémie further displays uncertainty. Also, at this moment, Noémie seems to encounter trouble that leads her to suspend her turn-in-progress (l. 10).

After a 1.4-second silence (l. 11)—and possibly in reaction to the sudden suspension of the preceding turn—several students begin to laugh (l. 12–13) and other classmates join in the students' laughter (l. 14–15). Petitjean and González-Martínez (2015) show that choral laughter after a student's problematic turn is an efficient resource for troubleshooting in the classroom. Interestingly, Noémie overlaps with the students' shared laughter and provides a critical assessment of the male students' behavior (l. 16), but this time in a more straightforward manner (see the turn-initial stance marker *moi je trouve* "me I think," the absence of hesitation markers and the conclusive intonation, but see also the repetition which introduces slight disfluency). By using a preferred action format to produce an action that is disaffiliating with the stance conveyed by the teacher (namely that the class had a good reputation), Noémie displays some non-seriousness of her very disaffiliation (see also the laugh particle in line 16).

Conversation analytic studies document how participants make their talk hearable as humorous by producing a sequential disjunction (Clift 1999), accomplishing a dispreferred action in a preferred action turn-shape (see also Waring 2013; Petitjean 2015). This breach between the expected action and the way the action is performed indexes the non-seriousness of that action, which routinely generates affiliation on the part of co-participants. This is exactly what happens in excerpt (3'). The sequential disjunction is recognized by Noémie's classmates: By smiling and jointly laughing (l. 17–22), they display understanding of the previous turn as not having the usual sequential implication it would have if it has been built as a serious action (Holt 2013). We observe the same configuration in line 23, when Noémie assertively produces another critical assessment of the male students: She delivers her turn without any kind of mitigation, within a single intonation unit ending on final falling intonation, emphasizing the item "kids." In terms of lexical choice, Noémie switches the periphrastic formulation "they haven't the age" (l. 16) to the more informal "kids" (l. 23). The non-seriousness of Noémie's turn is oriented to by a peer who laughs in the next turn (l. 24). By producing her opinion in a humorous yet assertive way (see Holmes 2000; Petitjean and Degoumois 2014 for the interrelation between humor and assertiveness), Noémie satisfies the teacher's question (i.e., formulating her personal opinion) and takes responsibility for her views ("me I think") while fostering the class' affiliation (displayed by the students' laughter and smiles). In short, her display of non-seriousness allows Noémie to accomplish a "subversive" action (criticizing co-students) without being sanctioned for it.

It is important to point out that humor is at times a risky business, particularly in the classroom (Korobkin 1988; Petitjean 2015). Possibly because the students' laughter decreases (see the brief laugh by a single student in line 24) after her second humorous critical assessment (l. 23), Noémie orients toward the closing of the humorous episode she had initiated (l. 25) by shifting to a more hesitant delivery (see the delayed turn-start, the discourse marker *enfin* "well" followed by a hesitation marker) and delivering an aphorism, that is, a sequence-closing implicative expression (see Drew and Holt 1998). By the same token, she appeals to shared knowledge, as boys are known to be less mature than girls, and receives Brandon's overt support for her position (l. 26).

In the following excerpt, another student organizes the expression of his opinion in a similar way. The class is discussing the question of how to reconcile family and work life. Students claim that they would give priority to family, except Yann. The teacher asks Yann to explain why he would prefer to work rather than to take care of his (future) children, thereby inviting Yann to offer his personal take on the issue at hand.

Ex. (4)

1 Tea: yann tu as dit plutôt le boulot toi.=
yann you have said you'd prefer working

2 Yan: =non mais en- en fait euh:=
no but in- in fact

3 Tea: =oui.=
yes

4 Yan: =c'est trop chou ces petits,
kids are so cute

5 mais euh: chais pas s'en occuper tout le temps tout le temps: euh:,
but I dunno taking care of them all the time all the time

```
6            au bout d'un moment euh:
               after a while
7            [°c'est peut-être un peu chiant°. ]
              it's    maybe      a bit shitty
8  All :     [((hubbub until line 21))          ]
9  Bar :     £-----------------------------((until the end of line 10))--£
10  (?):     °qu'est-ce que tu f'rais dans la vie (xxx)°.=
             what  would    you  do   for a living
11  Tea:     =°>mhm mhm<°.=
12  Yan:     =(xxx) (ouais:) comment ils sont,
                    yeah     how      they are
13           (0.7) s'ils sont comme moi [£ben:: n(h)on£ ].=
                   if they are like me      well no
14  (?):                                [ou(hh)ais hehe ]=
                                            yeah
15  Yan:     £-----------------------------((until the end of line 19))--£
16  Car:     =[HHE:]
17  Tea:     =[°hhh][huhuhu°]=
18  (?):            [(xxx)  ]=
19  Tea:     =CH::::T.
              hush
20           (0.6)
21  Tea:     ne parlez pas en même temps.
             don't talk at the same time
22           (0.4)
23  Tea:     ·h euh,
24           (0.2) yann il est: il est toujours plein d'humour,
                   yann he is  he is  always   full of humor
25           faut bien l'écouter:?
             we have to listen to him carefully
26           >il dit< s(h)i i(h)ls s(h)ont comme m(hh)oi,
             he says  if      they     are    like    me
27           (0.2) o(h)n préf(h)ère aller b(h)osser.
                   we     prefer     going  to  work
```

Since Yann's point of view differs from the class' consensus, he subsequently seeks to explain why he does not agree with his classmates. And he resorts to both humor and the display of uncertainty to accomplish the interactional work of formulating his divergent opinion while sustaining affiliation on the part of the other participants.

Yann begins to deliver his turn cautiously: He starts off (l. 2) by foreshadowing a dispreferred response and announcing further elaboration (see the turn-initial *non mais* "no but," the hesitation marker *euh*: with a final vowel lengthening and the continuative intonation). The teacher's *yes* token (l. 3) invites Yann to continue. Yann completes his response with a general positive assessment about kids (l. 4), which he then mitigates by displaying uncertainty: He delays his upcoming turn (l. 5) by means of *mais* "but" followed by a hesitation marker with final vowel lengthening and a *chais pas* "I dunno." Here the epistemic marker does not index a lack of knowledge but prefaces the upcoming talk as uncertain (Weatherall 2011). Yann concludes by providing a negative assessment (l. 7) with a lower voice and hedges ("maybe," "a bit"), which mitigate the item *chiant* "shitty"—quite an impolite term in French. Yann's explanation, however, does not seem to satisfy his classmates' expectations: While some students begin to chat (l. 8), one classmate challenges Yann by asking him what he would do for a living (l. 10), to which the teacher appears to affiliate (l. 11). So, Yann's diverging opinion appears to be treated as non-legitimate, both by being ignored by some students and by being overtly challenged.

Interestingly, although Yann seems to pass over his classmate's question, it is exactly at this moment that he shifts from serious to non-serious talk (l. 12–13): He straightforwardly produces a negative self-assessment, with laugh particles and smiley voice in turn-final position (l. 13), suggesting that he does not want to take care of children if they are as undisciplined as he is himself (see Glenn 1991/1992, on self-deprecation as a way of displaying non-seriousness). Yann's use of humor is aligned to by the other classmates (l. 14, 16), who join in with laughter, and by the teacher (l. 17), who comments on the humorous nature of Yann's talk (l. 23–27). By being humorous, Yann maintains his preceding affirmation and possibly even reinforces it by giving a reason for it, but at the same time he retrospectively downgrades the seriousness of this very affirmation and thereby fosters alignment and affiliation on the part of co-participants.

Intermediate Summary

Shifting from uncertainty to humorous assertiveness allows students to maintain a subtle balance between cautiousness and risk-taking in expressing personal opinions in the classroom. In the excerpts, a chosen student is directly prompted by the teacher to offer a personal point of view. In this sequential environment, the student is subjected to a high interactional "pressure" for providing a response. In the data, opinions delivered in response to prompts directly addressed to a chosen student typically follow a trajectory that includes, first, the display of uncertainty via a non-straightforward start of the responsive action (i.e., turn-initial delays, repetitions, "I don't know" tokens, and hesitation markers). In doing so, the speaker alerts recipients to the delicate nature of the upcoming action. Only in a second step does the speaker actually deliver his or her opinion, the seriousness of which he or she then often downgrades by shifting to humorous assertiveness after, for instance, encountering trouble in delivering his or her opinion (Ex. 3') or after recipients' displays of disalignment with or disapproval of the student's response (Ex. 4). By concluding the formulation of one's own opinion by means of some humorous comment, speakers maintain their earlier proffered position on some issue that is displayed as delicate, while at the same time retrospectively stepping down from the seriousness of that very position and thereby favoring alignment and affiliation by co-participants, which was exactly missing before. In short, then, by framing their personal opinions by means of uncertainty markers and humorous talk, students successfully adjust opinion formulation in the very course of their production to the local circumstances of the ongoing talk while responding to the institutional expectations related to the teacher's solicitation of a personal opinion. In this way, they take responsibility for their opinions while pre-empting potential disaffiliation on the part of co-participants.

From Humor to Displays of Uncertainty

In this section, we illustrate another trajectory of students' expression of personal opinions in the classroom. Here, the teacher elicits the students' opinion by producing an open question *without* addressing a particular student. In this case, a student *volunteers* his or her opinion rather than being other-selected by the teacher. This may explain why the student who responds tends to express his or her opinion more straightforwardly: The self-selected student first uses humor to express his/her views in an assertive way and only then resorts to uncertainty markers so as to minimize the risks of disaffiliation on the part of the co-participants. The student hence implements a trajectory of opinion formulation that is exactly opposite to what we have documented in the preceding section. This may be because humor itself is interactionally risky: It can lead to misinterpretation (Hay 2001; Priego-Valverde 2009) and can be perceived as aggressive (Priego-Valverde 2003). Moreover, students may perform humor in a way that does not fit in with the institutional expectations prevailing in the classroom (see Petitjean 2015).

In the following excerpt, the class is studying an article on discipline problems in a German school. The teacher asks the students why they work in school (l. 1).

Ex. (5)

```
1   Tea:  pourquoi est-ce que: vous travaillez à l'école vous.
          why        do        you  work       in school
2         (1.2)
3   Bar:  [pour a[pprendre?]]
          for  learning
4   Noé:  [pour a[pprendre?]]
          for   learning
5   (?):          [     (xx)][(xx)]
6   (?):                    [°non][c'est pas tr(hh)ès:: hehh]=
                             no  it's not  very
7   Car:                          [non pour les souvenirs.  ]=
                                   no for memories
8   Lis:  =ehehehh ·hh
9   Ang:  £--------------------------((until the end of line 11))--£
10  Bar:  £---------------------------((until the end of line 12))--£
11  Car:  (°°non non mais sincèrement°°.)=
            no no but honestly
12  Lis:  =£j(h)e travaille parce que je suis obligée£ c'est tout.
            I      work       because   I    have to       that's all
13  Ang:  £--------------------------(( until the end of line 19))--£
14  Lin:  £--------------------------(( until the end of line 25))--£
15  Pat:  £--------------------------(( until the end of line 25))--£
16        (0.5)
17  (?):  [°hehhh][hehehehhh°  ]
18  (?):  [°hehhh][hehehehhh°  ]
19  (?):          [HAHAhahahaha]
20  (?):  ·hhh [hhhe]
21  (?):       [hhhe]
22  Bar:  hehehahah
23  Lis:  £°mais chais pas°?
           but   I dunno
24        °(ça rend bien quoi°.)£ hh
          it sounds good actually
25        (1.6)
```

```
26 Car:   £----------------------£
27 Tea:   mhm mhm.
28        (0.3)
29        pis patricia tu travailles pourquoi?
          and patricia you work      why
```

The teacher's question (l. 1) clearly invites the students to offer their personal take on the issue at hand. Barbara and Noémie simultaneously provide the same answer (l. 3–4), marked as a candidate by rising intonation that displays uncertainty regarding the answer's relevancy. While another student produces what appears to be the start of a mitigated disagreement (see l. 6: lower voice, vowel lengthening, and laugh particles), Carine (l. 7), in partial overlap, offers a straightforward disagreement (no delayed turn-start, no dispreferred action turn-shape, no lower voice; see also the *no*-token in turn-initial position and the conclusive intonation). Interestingly, this first student who assertively expresses her opinion does it in a humorous way: Humor here is made accountable by the disjunction between the dispreferred nature of the ongoing action (disagreeing with the co-participants) and the preferred action turn-shape. The non-seriousness of Carine's turn is further displayed by its formatting as an overdone figurative phrase (Holt 2011). Her classmates make recognizable that they are treating Carine's previous talk as non-serious by laughing and smiling (l. 8–10; Holt 2013). In line 12, Lisa prolongs the humorous episode: Her smiley voice and laugh particles make her turn hearable as humorous. This hearing is further enhanced by the breach between the potentially delicate action (i.e., complaining) and the assertive turn-shape: Lisa produces a complaint in a straightforward manner (no turn-delay, no hesitation marker, and no lower voice) with a conclusive intonation (see also the conclusive "that's all"). Subsequently, by smiling (l. 13–15) and producing extended shared laughter (l. 17–22), the other classmates display their affiliation. Through humor, Carine and Lisa not only exert a higher degree of assertiveness (see the straightforward delivery of their complaints) but also augment the interactional saliency of their opinions, while supporting alignment and affiliation on the part of the co-participants. Since the teacher does not react and possibly because extended shared laughter disrupts the progressivity of the ongoing talk, Lisa closes the humorous episode (l. 23) by shifting to uncertainty (see the epistemic marker "I dunno," the smiling lower voice, and the final rising intonation). Moreover, by retroactively displaying uncertainty, Lisa softens the provocative nature of her assertion (see also the account "it sounds good actually," l. 24). After a silence (l. 25), the teacher produces a minimal ratification (l. 27) before resuming the activity by selecting another student as the next speaker (l. 29).

We observe a similar trajectory in the following excerpt. The class is discussing the difference between girls' and boys' behavior. Female students have just said that girls are quieter than boys. The teacher asks them whether they consider themselves more mature than male students (l. 1).

Ex. (6)

```
1   Tea:  (pis) vous êtes plus mûres les filles?=
           so   girls you are more mature
2   (?):  =[ouais.]
            yeah
3   (?):  =[OH ][oui::::.]
            oh   yes
4   Noé:          [AH OUI ] JUSTEMENT c'est ce que j'allais [dire. ]
                  oh yes exactly that's what I was going to say
5   Tea:                                                     [ouais.]
                                                             yeah
6         (0.2)
7   Noé:  ils ont pas grandi dans leur petite tête encore.
          they haven't grown up in their little head yet
8   All:  ((laugh: 1.2)) [((laugh))                      ]=
9   Noé:  £--------------------------((until the end of line 15))----£
10  Tea:                 [°huhu[huhuhuhuhuhuhuhuhuhuhuhuhu°]=
11  (?):                       [moi je trouve (d(h)e)-  ·hh]=
                                me  I  think
12  All:  =[((laugh))         ]
13  Tea:  =[°huhuhuhuhuhuhuhuhuh° ]
14  (?):  =[comme elle a dit ça eh?]
            how she has said that
15  All:                            [((laugh))          ]
16  Tea:                            [°huhuhuhuhuhuhuhu° ]
17  Noé:  mais [c'est ↑vrai.   ]
          but   it's   true
18  (?):       [(°xxxx) ↑fl(h)a]tteur°:=
                       complimenting
19  Noé:  =vous regardez un garçon et une fille c'est pas pareil,
          you  look at   a boy   and a   girl  it's not the same
20        enfin chais pas::,
          well  I  dunno
```

```
21          (0.3) >on est- on est< plus mûres quand même.=
                  we are- we are more   mature    PTR
22 Car:     =ils grandissent [plus tard.]
            they   grow up      later
```

Three students near-to simultaneously self-select and affirmatively respond to the teacher's question (l. 2–4). One of them, Noémie, takes the floor again (l. 7) and produces an overt negative assessment about boys. Again, the straightforward manner in which this delicate action (the boys are co-present in the class) is produced (no turn-delay, no hesitation, no uncertainty markers), combined with an extreme case formulation ("little head," l. 7; see Pomerantz 1986), makes the turn hearable as humorous. This is shown in the subsequent turns where the teacher and the other students jointly produce extended laughter (l. 8, 10, 12–13, 15–16). Noémie smiles (l. 9) and joins in the laughter (l. 12, 15). In line 14, a student comments on the unexpectedness of Noémie's formulation, in overlap with the class' choral laughter. Humor thus allows Noémie to overtly assert a critical opinion about a group some of her classmates belong to (the boys) while at the same time securing co-participants' affiliation—including from the very classmates that were part of the negatively assessed category, that is, "boys."

Interesting here is also the fact that, after co-participants' extended shared laughter, Noémie self-selects again (l. 17) and closes the humorous episode by shifting to more serious talk. She first reaffirms her position by means of her *mais c'est vrai* "but it's true" (l. 17). She then reformulates her opinion about boys' immaturity (l. 19) but downgrades it (l. 20), retroactively, displaying her uncertain stance (see Degoumois 2013, on "well I don't know" in turn-final position in French). Subsequently, she cautiously reformulates her opinion (l. 21), hedging it by means of the turn-final particle *quand meme* "still/anyway," while resorting to the type of generalized assessment that is typically used to initiate sequence-closing (see Drew and Holt 1998). Noémie thereby closes the humorous episode, re-engaging the progressivity of the talk that has been disrupted by extended laughter, while mitigating the competitiveness of her opinion. Another student, Carine, self-selects (l. 22) and reopens the sequence by seriously formulating her opinion while affiliating with Noémie.

Intermediate Summary

Just as when a specific student is invited by the teacher to offer his or her opinion, students who volunteer their opinion, in response to a general invitation by the teacher addressed to the whole class, mobilize both humor and displays of uncertainty to subtly balance between asserting their opinion and fishing for their classmates' affiliation and the teacher's acceptance. Yet, in the case of students volunteering their opinion, the trajectories of opinion formulations are organized differently than in the case of specific students being other-selected. Students volunteering their opinion first use humor to assert their views before shifting to uncertainty as a resource to close the humorous episode and to soften its potential inappropriateness. Since humor involves a sequential breach, it represents an efficient means for attracting recipients' attention. This makes it an efficient resource for accessing the floor in competitive environments, as shown in both excerpts (5) and (6). Furthermore, humor allows the students to take the risk of overtly asserting a delicate opinion in front of the class (a complaint about the obligation to work at school in Ex. 5; a critical assessment of boys' behavior in Ex. 6) while suggesting some non-seriousness and thereby minimizing disaffiliation on the part of their classmates. It is precisely because humor does not exactly define a stretch of talk as entirely non-serious but merely suggests some (undefined) degree of non-seriousness that it can efficiently be used for proffering delicate matters in an affirmative yet alignment- and affiliation-inviting way (see Holt 2013).

However, in the course of classroom interaction, teachers often do not usually treat humorous talk as relevant, which is evidenced by their refraining from providing a sequence-closing third after students' humorous responses (but see the teacher's affiliative laughter in Ex. 6). This lack of reaction on the part of the teacher seems to lead students to reconsider the legitimacy of their opinion—or rather of the way it is delivered—and thus to shift to the display of uncertainty, thereby retrospectively downgrading their commitment to their preceding talk. In doing so, students close the humorous episode and thereby restore the progressivity of classroom activities which has been disrupted by extended shared laughter.

Various resources that co-occur to mark uncertainty (lower voice, intra-turn delays, and epistemic disclaimers) thus function both as means for closing the humorous episode (see Pekarek Doehler 2016, for French *chais pas* "dunno" as a turn-exit device that can also initiate sequence-closing) and to downgrade students' commitment to what precedes (Weatherall 2011). Also, by switching from humor to uncertainty, the students indicate their understanding of the potential inappropriateness of their opinion formulation, thus displaying what they consider as institutionally legitimate ways of acting in the classroom.

Discussion and Conclusion

The Classroom and Beyond: On the Moral Order of Expressing Personal Opinions

The expression of personal opinions is ubiquitous to both ordinary conversation and institutional talk. It puts into play a moral order rather than an epistemic order. For one thing, opinions are not a matter of knowing or not knowing but a matter of having a view on some issue in the world. Therefore, although personal opinions cannot be judged as right or wrong, people may not be equally entitled to express an opinion on a given issue (think of friends offering their opinion on the conduct of your own children). For another thing, personal opinions—although we may see them as pertaining to individuals—call upon socially shared normative views regarding others and the world. As such, different opinions will not be equally assessed as "morally" (i.e., normatively) acceptable. This is why, in essence, the public display of personal views is always a potentially delicate matter.

This potentially delicate nature of expressing personal opinions may find itself strongly augmented in situations where group dynamics is at play. This is the case for the lower secondary classroom involving students at the age of puberty, for whom appreciation by peers as much as differentiation from peers are of primary importance (Brinthaupt and Lipka 2012, 4) as part of larger concerns with social group conformity or defiance, as well as dynamics of inclusion and exclusion (see also Harter 1999). When we observe students carefully balance between assertiveness and mitigation of their personal points of view, and when we observe them doing so in response to local interactional contingencies such as co-participants' laughter, disapproval, or silence, we see them deal exactly with those competing issues of conformity and differentiation with regard to their peers. In this sense, the interactional negotiation of personal opinions that we have scrutinized in this study not only reflects and structures group dynamics and more generally the institutional order but also is a central vector of young peoples' socialization while they move toward adulthood.

Humor and Displays of Uncertainty as Interactional Resources for Managing Personal Opinions in the Classroom

As documented in this study, the way in which students formulate personal opinions in the classroom shows their orientation to the delicate nature of that activity—an activity they subtly manage according to the local circumstances of the ongoing talk. Students succeed in offering opinion formulation in a way that is attended to and accepted by others, and they do so by mobilizing both humor and various resources to display uncertainty. As part of a range of systematic procedures (or methods, in the ethnomethodological sense; see Garfinkel 1967) that participants use for engaging in social interaction, the use of humor and displays of uncertainty are an integral part of people's interactional competence. Participants use these procedures in locally contingent ways: Students adapt opinion trajectories to how the teacher prompts them to express their views, as well as to how peers react to these views in the very course of the interaction. By displaying uncertainty after the teacher has selected a specific next speaker (exx. 3, 4), students react to the interactional "pressure" to provide a response by first announcing the problematic nature of the upcoming action. They then switch to humor and thereby express their opinion in an assertive way, while at the same time, displaying that assertiveness is too risky to be performed seriously. By contrast, when teachers elicit personal opinions without selecting a specific student as the next speaker (exx. 5, 6), the self-selected student first uses humor as a resource for gaining speakership and attracting co-participants' attention. By shifting subsequently to displays of uncertainty, the student closes the humorous episode and retroactively mitigates the provocative nature of his/her humorous talk.

While the use of mitigators in opinion expressions may not come as a surprise, the pervasive use of humor was not what we expected to find in the data. As shown in the analysis, it is precisely because humor does not exactly define a stretch of talk as entirely non-serious but merely suggests some (undefined) degree of non-seriousness (see also Holt 2013) that it works as an efficient means for proffering delicate matters in an affirmative- yet affiliation-inviting way. Navigating between humorous assertiveness and serious displays of uncertainty is thus a powerful device for managing the delicate nature of expressing personal opinions in the classroom—and possibly beyond. As part of the students' interactional competence, the contingent use of these resources allows them to satisfy the teacher's prompt for personal opinions, to respond to the educational task (i.e., assertively expressing a personal opinion), while managing moment-by-moment affiliation on the part of peers.

Throughout these points, the findings shed light on how personal opinions are interactionally organized and, in the end, collaboratively accomplished—a topic that has attracted practically no attention in research so far.

Legitimate Practices, the Institutional Order and How They Change Over Time

The findings also inform us about some facets of the complex institutional order that is talked into being through the interactionally managed expression of personal opinions in the classroom. On the one hand, the expression of personal opinions is called for by the institutional agenda both in explicit formulations pertaining to the curriculum[1] and as implemented in the local unfolding of social interaction (especially teachers' prompts). As documented in this study, students in the classroom manage to satisfy teachers' expectations while minimizing risks of disaffiliation on the part of their peers. Thereby, they ultimately augment the public acceptance of their conduct by peers in a way that also conforms to the institutional order at hand. On the other hand, as mentioned above, the offering of personal opinions is treated as a delicate matter in the lower secondary classroom, invoking a moral order that may be more or less shared among classmates (and teachers). Interestingly, this ensues in a specific type of tension in the data: While peers are concerned with the contents of opinions, the teacher seems to be concerned with *how* opinions are delivered. This is evidenced through the fact that peers overtly agree with or dismiss a student's opinion, while teachers remain agnostic in this regard. What teachers seem to orient to is students' conduct while delivering opinions. In particular, students' use of humor appears to be tacitly sanctioned, possibly because it routinely generates lengthy laughter by peers, and hence disrupts the progressivity of classroom interaction. It is tacitly sanctioned through the fact that teachers often do not respond to humor, refraining for instance from providing uptake after a student's delivery of a humorous response. The findings therefore also shed light on some facets of students' competence that are not treated as legitimate in the lower secondary classroom: Although humor represents an interactionally efficient means of eliciting alignment and affiliation by peers, it is often not oriented to as legitimate by the teacher.

Now, interestingly, processes of legitimization by which participants mutually indicate normatively expected ways of communicating in the classroom evolve from the lower to the upper secondary level and so do the corresponding targets of such interactional processes of legitimization. Although this was not the topic of this chapter, in a range of other studies we observe change in the participatory cultures between lower and upper secondary levels with regard to both the use of humor and the way personal opinions are enacted. At the lower secondary level (we studied students aged 13–14), humor most often causes a diversion of classroom activities that is sanctioned by the teacher, while at the upper level (we studied students aged 16–17) students' humor is instrumental in promoting the progressivity of ongoing activities (Petitjean 2015; see also Petitjean and Priego-Valverde 2013). In light of the above findings, this suggests that, between the lower and the upper secondary level of schooling, students adapt their conduct according to what is treated as legitimate in the classroom. This also applies to the expression of personal opinions: By contrast to what we have observed in the present study for the lower secondary classroom, at the upper secondary level, students regularly volunteer to assertively express their personal opinions, performing lengthy turns at talk with a straightforward turn-shape (Degoumois 2014a,b). This change not only indicates that students, over time, comply to the normative orders of the classroom as enacted through the teacher's implicit interactional sanctioning or legitimization; it also shows that, as they move from puberty to adulthood, students show increased assertiveness in how they publicly commit to their own opinions.

Acknowledgment We thank Esther González-Martínez and Adrian Bangerter for their thoughtful comments on an earlier version of this paper.

Notes

1. See http://www.plandetudes.ch for the school curricula of lower secondary schools in the French-speaking part of Switzerland.
2. See Appendix for a list of the transcription conventions.

Appendix: Transcription Conventions

The transcription of laugh particles is based on Jeffersonian conventions (Jefferson 1985; see also Hepburn and Varney 2013). When laughter is jointly produced by several participants, which is difficult to transcribe, we have used the comment ((laughs)), indicating its duration when it does not overlap with talk. When a participant smiles without speaking, we have transcribed smile by using the symbol £ in the line below the speaker's turn (in italics), indicating the person performing the smile and its duration.

(0.2)	Silence in tenths of a second
hello:	Sound stretch
?	Rising intonation
,	Continuative intonation
.	Falling intonation
partici-	Cut-off
=	Fast follow-up
↑↓	Rise or fall in pitch
bonjour	Accentuation
bonJOUR	Louder talk
bon°jour°	Softer talk
>bonjour<	Faster speech rate
<bonjour>	Slower speech rate
[ ]	Overlapping talk
(bonjour)	Uncertain transcription
(xxx)	Non-understandable segment
.h	Inhalation
h	Exhalation
£bonjour£	Smiley voice
bonj(h)ou(h)r	Infiltrated laugh particles
((writing: 1.0))	Transcriber's comment
PRT	Particle
All:	All students

References

Antaki, C., Houtkoop-Steenstra, H., & Rapley, M. (2000). "Brilliant. Next Question … ": High-grade assessment sequences in the completion of interactional units. *Research on Language and Social Interaction, 33*(3), 235–262.

Bourdieu, P. (1971). Le marché des biens symboliques. *L'année sociologique, 22*, 49–126.

Brinthaupt, T. M., & Lipka, R. P. (2012). Understanding early adolescent self and identity: An introduction. In T. M. Brinthaupt & R. P. Lipka (Eds.), *Understanding early adolescent self and identity* (pp. 1–21). New York: SUNY Press.

Clift, R. (1999). Irony in conversation. *Language in Society, 28*, 523–553.

Coulter, J. (1990). Elementary properties of argument sequences. In G. Psathas (Ed.), *Interaction competence* (pp. 181–203). Lanham, MD: University Press of America.

Degoumois, V. (2013). "Mais ça dépend parce que enfin je sais pas": la gestion interactionnelle des positionnements épistémiques en milieu scolaire. In *VALS-ASLA Conference*, Basel University, 13 May 2013.

Degoumois, V. (2014a). The expression of personal opinions in the classroom: Insights into teachers' implicit legitimization of students' competences. In *4th International Conference of Applied Linguistics and Professional Practice (ALAAP)*, University of Geneva, Geneva, 10–13 September 2014.

Degoumois, V. (2014b). An interactional practice for dealing with questions about personal opinion in classroom interaction: *je sais pas* ("I don't know") as turn-beginning and hedging device. In *4th International Conference on Conversation Analysis (ICCA2014)*, University of California, Los Angeles, 25–29 June 2014.

Drew, P., & Holt, E. (1998). Figures of speech: Figurative expressions and the management of topic transition in conversation. *Language in Society, 27*(4), 495–522.

Du Bois, J. W. (2007). The stance triangle. In R. Englebretson (Ed.), *Stancetaking in discourse: Subjectivity, evaluation, interaction* (pp. 139–182). Amsterdam: John Benjamins Publishing.

Garfinkel, H. (1967). *Studies in ethnomethodology*. Englewood Cliffs: Prentice Hall.

Glenn, P. (1991/1992). Current speaker initiation of two-party shared laughter. *Research on Language and Social Interaction, 25*, 139–162.

Goodwin, C., & Goodwin, M. H. (1987). Concurrent operations on talk: Notes on the interactive organization of assessments. *IPrA Papers in Pragmatics, 1*(1), 1–55.

Harter, S. (1999). *The construction of the self: A developmental perspective*. New York: Guilford Press.

Hay, J. (2001). The pragmatics of humor support. *International Journal of Humor Research, 14*(1), 55–82.

Hepburn, A., & Varney, S. (2013). Beyond ((Laughter)): Some notes on transcription. In P. Glenn & E. Holt (Eds.), *Studies of laughter in interaction* (pp. 25–38). London: Bloomsbury.

Holmes, J. (2000). Politeness, power and provocation: How humor functions in the workplace. *Discourse Studies, 2*(2), 159–185.

Holt, E. (2011). On the nature of "laughables": Laughter as a response to overdone figurative phrases. *Journal of Pragmatics, 21*(3), 393–410.
Holt, E. (2013). "There's many a true word said in jest": Seriousness and nonseriousness in interaction. In P. Glenn & E. Holt (Eds.), *Studies of laughter in interaction* (pp. 69–89). London/New York: Bloomsbury.
Hutchby, I. (1996). *Confrontation talk. Arguments, asymmetries and power on talk radio*. Mahwah: Lawrence Erlbaum.
Jacknick, C. (2013). "Cause the Textbook Says … ": Laughter and student challenges in the ESL classroom. In P. Glenn & E. Holt (Eds.), *Studies of laughter in interaction* (pp. 185–200). London/New York: Bloomsbury.
Jefferson, G. (1985). An exercise in the transcription and analysis of laughter. In T. A. Van Dijk (Ed.), *Handbook of discourse analysis* (Vol. 3, pp. 25–34). London: Academic Press.
Korobkin, D. (1988). Humor in the classroom: Considerations and strategies. *College Teaching, 36*(4), 154–158.
Lerner, G. H. (2013). On the place of hesitating in delicate formulations: A turn-constructional infrastructure for collaborative indiscretion. In M. Hayashi, G. Raymond, & J. Sidnell (Eds.), *Conversational repair and human understanding* (pp. 95–134). Cambridge: Cambridge University Press.
Mondada, L. (2009). The embodied and negotiated production of assessments in instructed actions. *Research on Language and Social Interaction, 42*(4), 329–361.
Mullan, K. (2010). *Expressing opinions in French and Australian English discourse. A semantic and interactional analysis*. Amsterdam: John Benjamins.
Myers, G. (1998). Displaying opinions: Topics and disagreement in focus groups. *Language in Society, 27*(1), 85–111.
Pekarek Doehler, S. (2016). More than an epistemic hedge: French *je sais pas* 'I don't know' as a resource for the sequential organization of turns and actions. *Journal of Pragmatics, 106*, 148–162.
Petitjean, C. (2015). Les pratiques humoristiques dans des interactions en classe de français. Transition de l'école obligatoire à l'école post-obligatoire en Suisse romande. *Langage et Société, 154*, 101–126.
Petitjean, C., & Degoumois, V. (2014). Humor in classroom interaction: How epistemic markers index students' not-so-funny practices. In *4th International Conference on Conversation Analysis (ICCA2014)*, University of California, Los Angeles, 25–29 June 2014.

Petitjean, C., & González-Martínez, E. (2015). Laughing and smiling to manage trouble in French-language classroom interaction. *Classroom Discourse, 6*(2), 89–106.

Petitjean, C., & Priego-Valverde, B. (2013). Pourquoi et comment faire de l'humour en classe ? Les représentations sociales de la compétence humoristique dans des interactions didactiques en Suisse romande. *Langage et Société, 144*, 41–63.

Pomerantz, A. (1984). Agreeing and disagreeing with assessments: Some features of preferred/dispreferred turn shapes. In M. Atkinson & J. Heritage (Eds.), *Structures of social action. Studies in conversation analysis* (pp. 53–95). Cambridge: University Press.

Pomerantz, A. (1986). Extreme case formulations: A way of legitimizing claims. *Human Studies, 9*(2–3), 219–229.

Priego-Valverde, B. (2003). *L'humour dans la conversation familière. Description et analyse linguistiques du fonctionnement de l'humour dans la conversation.* Paris: L'Harmattan.

Priego-Valverde, B. (2009). Failed humor in conversation. A double voicing analysis. In N. R. Norrick & D. Chiaro (Eds.), *Humor in interaction* (pp. 165–183). Amsterdam: John Benjamins.

Quéré, L. (1995). L'opinion comme événement interactionnel. In D. Véronique & R. Vion (Eds.), *Modèles de l'interaction verbale* (pp. 23–44). Aix-en-Provence: Publications de l'Université de Provence.

Sacks, H. (1992). *Lectures on conversation.* Oxford: Blackwell.

Schegloff, E. A. (2007). *Sequence organization in interaction: A primer in conversation analysis* (Vol. 1). Cambridge: University Press.

Schegloff, E. A., & Lerner, G. H. (2009). Beginning to respond: Well-prefaced responses to wh-questions. *Research on Language and Social Interaction, 42*(2), 91–115.

Sidnell, J. (2012). "Who knows best?": Evidentiality and epistemic asymmetry in conversation. *Pragmatics and Society, 3*(2), 294–320.

Waring, H. Z. (2013). Doing being playful in the second language classroom. *Applied Linguistics, 34*(2), 191–210.

Weatherall, A. (2011). I don't know as a prepositioned epistemic hedge. *Research on Language and Social Interaction, 44*(4), 317–337.

3

The Use of Personal Storytelling in Speech and Language Therapist–Adolescent Interactions

Geneviève de Weck, Audrey Sublon, and Gwendoline Fox

Introduction

This chapter studies the formal and interactional characteristics as well as the functions of personal storytelling (PS) co-produced during speech and language therapist (SLT)–adolescent interactions in a socio-interactionist approach. PS is defined as an interactional practice in which speakers express themselves using the first person describing an experience that they have lived; in terms of psychology of language (Bronckart 1996), PS is characterized as involved in the production context and disjointed from the ongoing social interaction. PS is also characterized by a chronological dimension (Revaz 1987) and is articulated around an expanded event that is worth telling (Labov 1972). It is frequently used

G. de Weck (✉) • A. Sublon • G. Fox
Center of Logopedics, Department of Language
Sciences and Communication, University of Neuchâtel, Neuchâtel,
Switzerland

S. Pekarek Doehler et al. (eds.), *Interactional Competences in Institutional Settings*, DOI 10.1007/978-3-319-46867-9_3

in daily life and in the context of school, work or therapy. It can thus be seen as a window into the interactional competences of adolescents with language impairments. The analysis of PS management allows for an understanding of its functioning and how it can be legitimized within this particular institutional frame.

After presenting the major functions of PS as described in the social sciences, this introduction focuses on impairments linked to storytelling and their consequences in adolescent speech. Finally, we present the speech therapy setting with particular attention to the space given to language practices.

Major Functions of Personal Storytelling

Several authors have highlighted different functions of storytelling. The *recalling* function (Labov 1972) appears to be inherent to PS, thus putting the speaker(s) in a position of detachment toward the lived event (Zittoun 2006; Ryekel and Delvigne 2010). PS enables the reconstruction of the event, which implies a reading of reality that gives to storytelling a *symbolization* function, and hence a *meaning construction* function (Zittoun 2006).

Consequently, storytelling explains the event (see, e.g., Abell 2004). For Bruner (1991), the human mind creates meaning either through narrative logic or by explanation. Applied to the field of feelings, storytelling enables the naming and understanding of lived emotions (Ryekel and Delvigne 2010). This dialectic between past and present also gives to storytelling a *continuity* function (Ehlich 1980; Ricoeur 1988; Bruner 2002; Zittoun 2006; Kohn 2008; Ryekel and Delvigne 2010). Conversely, as a testimony of experience, storytelling permits the comparison between what was and what is, and has thus a significant role in periods of change. PS therefore ensures the *connection between experiences* (Bruner 2002; Zittoun 2006; Kohn 2008). As a preferential locus to tell an unexpected event/situation, it constitutes (Bruner 2002) a preferential tool to *identify issues*. By soliciting a projection ability, it drives one to question what is possible and what could be, what concerns imagination and what could have been. For Ehlich (1980), PS helps to mobilize one's own capacities to change things. It therefore allows a connection between present and future. The construction of meaning and the continuity function also apply to collective settings, which make PS a process by which social representations of reality are constructed (e.g., Ricoeur 1988).

Following Bruner (1996), Perret-Clermont and Zittoun (2002), who go into the meaning construction function in depth, emphasize the role of the narrative mode for the *construction of identity*. Identity demands continuity from one sphere of life (family, school, leisure activities, speech therapy) (Zittoun 2006) to another: Storytelling highlights how adolescents cope with the plurality of their experiences and how they connect them in order to facilitate the dynamic construction of their identity.

As a general rule, appropriating discursive productions like storytelling constitutes an integration tool in human communication activities (Bronckart 1996) and in *socialization processes*. In that sense, storytelling plays a role in the creation and reinforcement of friendships (Miller et al. 1997; Bliss et al. 1998), or in the establishment of professional relations (Bangerter et al. 2011).

Personal Storytelling and Adolescents with Language Impairments

Specific language impairments (SLIs) are impairments of the structure of oral language that are not incidental to other pathologies. There is little documentation on this type of impairment in manuals about adolescence, but it is attested for this period in numerous studies (Conti-Ramsden et al. 2001; de Weck and Marro 2010; Clegg et al. 2005; Lindsay and Dockrell 2012). The SLIs encountered during childhood tend to evolve toward discursive and/or pragmatic impairments (de Weck and Rosat 2003; Jullien 2005; Reed et al. 2007; Wetherell et al. 2007a,b), which have negative repercussions on adolescents' literacy competences (Bishop and Clarkson 2003), their social, behavioral or emotional abilities (Conti-Ramsden and Botting 2008; Simkin and Conti-Ramsden 2009), or their professional life (Conti-Ramsden and Durkin 2012). It is therefore necessary "to provide ongoing intervention for SLI adolescents during their secondary school years" (Reed et al. 2007, 959). Speech therapists should also encourage them to express the difficulties encountered in their daily life (Botting and Conti-Ramsden 2008).

Specificities in Speech and Language Therapy and Interactional Competence

The speech therapy setting is characterized by its linguistic specificity, in particular by a focus on language impairments and competences. Speech therapy treatment is commonly defined as an ecological and functional context that enables the reuse of each patient's evolving language processes (Estienne-Dejong 1983; Rosenbaum 1997; Roth and Worthington 2011). With this aim, speech therapy practice is based on the patients' resources in order to help them access communicational autonomy in producing various types of discourse and in managing interactions outside of the speech therapy context. The intervention modalities can take the form of an individual follow-up, involving a therapist and his/her patient, or of a group follow-up, including several patients and therapists. Rosenbaum (1997) defines a speech therapy group as the pooling of each member's communicational competences that enables the start of change processes and the continuation of learning processes. The goals of therapy are usually known by the members. To reach them, sessions are composed of various activities focusing on a particular linguistic or interactional aspect.

In a socio-interactionist approach of speech therapy (de Weck 2005), language activities, which are considered as social practices depending on the production context, are at the heart of interventions given that they constitute for the therapists both the object of observation and a tool for intervention (de Weck 2003). As a consequence, participants are bound to co-produce different types of discourse upon the solicitation of either speaker (de Weck 2003). The proposed type is then accepted or not by the interlocutor, continued or not, modified, and often negotiated. This co-production requires several competences, notably on pragmatic grounds (Botting 2010). For instance, one should be able to appropriately introduce a storytelling according to the activities and objectives of the session, while taking into account the production context and the level of shared knowledge with the interlocutor (Wetherell et al. 2007a; de Weck and Marro 2010). These discursive and pragmatic competences are not always acquired during adolescence, especially if SLIs are involved.

Thus, the co-production of PS appears to be one of the discursive characteristics of speech therapy sessions (de Weck 2003). PSs are also important because of their psycho-affective and cognitive assets, and because they allow children to formulate their life story. According to McLean and Mansfield (2012), sharing personal experiences is a way for speakers to connect their own feelings and thoughts with events. This sharing thus gives others the opportunity to approve, challenge or help the construction of this story.

Yet, even if adolescents are conscious of their specific difficulties (Palikara et al. 2009), and even if they need support during their schooling and show their satisfaction when they benefit from a speech therapy follow-up (Simkin and Conti-Ramsden 2009), few studies describe the characteristics of an appropriate treatment for this age range. We thus propose to document speech therapy interventions intended for adolescents by examining the use of PS during treatment phases. This study aims to highlight the interactional characteristics and functions of PS, according to the description above. In general, we expect that the specificity of speech and language therapy treatments (i.e., their explicit focus on the language and resources of patients) will influence the functioning of PS as well as its legitimization within the interaction.

Method

In this part, we present the participants, the data collection and the different characteristics considered for analysis.

Participants

Our study sample is composed of three adolescent-SLT dyads and a therapeutic group involving adolescents with language impairments and SLTs.[1]

The dyads involve three different SLTs and three different adolescents: two females named Marine[2] and Barbara, and a male named Mathieu, respectively aged 12;07, 13;08 and 16;02. Marine has SLI. Barbara had severe difficulties in learning French as second language in the past and has a diagnosis of dyslexia-dysorthographia, and Mathieu has dysphasia in continuum with autistic disorders. The therapeutic group is composed of two SLTs and four male adolescents: Ralph (14;09), Alexis (15;05), Elliot (15;07) and Victor (16;01). They all have a diagnosis of dyslexia-dysorthographia; Elliot also has SLI, and Alexis has had a language acquisition delay when he was young.

Data Collection

We analyze SLT(s)–adolescent(s) interactions during therapy sessions. All interactions were audio-video recorded by the SLTs themselves during three months. They were asked to manage the therapy sessions as they usually do. There are eight sessions for Marine's dyad, six for Barbara's dyad and five for Mathieu's dyad. We thus have 19 therapy sessions (about 12 hours) for the individual setting. For the group setting, five therapy sessions were recorded (about 8 hours). The interactions were transcribed according to conventions presented in Appendix.

Analyses

In this section, different steps of the analyses are presented: storytelling identification, modes of story initiation, the participants' implication in the stories, link with the ongoing activity and story legitimation.

Storytelling Identification

The first step was to identify PSs, which are usually defined as accounts of personal events that occurred in the past, but we enlarged this definition to include the future. Storytelling comprises some temporally organized facts. Generally the events told were lived only by the storyteller, but in speech therapy, the participants can also tell shared events, that is, events experienced within the speech therapy framework. Moreover a storytelling must be composed of a minimum of five utterances, which can be produced by several participants (see Ex. 1). This minimum can be justified by the fact that the account cannot be expanded in less than five utterances.

Ex. (1): Dyad, Marine, session 2

MAR58-	**et puis pendant les vacances j'ai commencé déjà l(e) skate[3].** *and then during the vacation I already started skating*
SLT55-	**ah! bon? bin alors ça c'était euh madame X qui avait r(e) gardé? ou bien c'est toi qu'as fait toute seule?** *oh really? so was it Mrs. X who looked at it? or was it just you?*
MAR59-	**ben c'est mon- j'ai demandé à mon beau père s'il connaissait quelqu'un qui- qui avait un skate à m(e) donner. puis il a dit "oui"** *well...it is my- I asked my step-father if he knew somebody who- who had a skateboard to give me. and he said "yes"*
SLT56-	**mhm.**
MAR60-	**parce que son fils avant i(l) fai[t]ait- il faisait du skate.** *because his son he used to- he used to skateboard.*

In the corpus some utterances could not be defined as a PS, because the storyteller talks about a personal event in less than five utterances without developing it. We also considered these kinds of utterances and called them news announcements (NAs; see Ex. 2), as they could have turned into PSs if the interlocutor had developed the event told.

Ex. (2): Dyad, Barbara, session 1

SLT159-	(...) si tu lis pas bien les consignes Barbara forcément tu vas faire des erreurs que t'aurais pas faites autrement. *(...) if you don't read the instructions carefully Barbara you will necessarily make mistakes that you wouldn't do otherwise*
BAR153-	ouais. ouais. **j(e) pars p(eu)t-être pour l'Angleterre . / pendant UNE semaine.** *yes. yes. I may go to England. / for ONE week.*

SLT160- **avec ton école?**
with your school?

BAR154- **non. toute seule.**
no. on my own

SLT161- **mais moi j'ai pas envie de r(e)garder ça maintenant.**
but I don't want to look at that now

In total we identified 736 PSs representing 32.01% of the utterances of the interactions and 275 NAs representing 1.91% of the utterances. Put together, PSs and NAs constitute an important proportion of the utterances produced in the interactions. This means that the speech therapy institution is a privileged place to speak about one's own experience, which supports our aim to understand how the participants use PS (and NA) during the treatment.

Modes of Story Initiation

Two dimensions were observed for the initiation modes: the participant who initiates the PS or NA, and the way in which it is done. The *initiation* can be realized either by an *SLT* or by an *adolescent* (ADO) in two ways: PS and NA can be solicited or auto-initiated. When they are *solicited*, a participant asks somebody to tell a personal account: This request can be a *general* one (see Ex. 3) or a *specific* one concerning a particular event (see Ex. 4).

Ex. (3): Dyad, Mathieu, session 2

SLT36- **est-ce que toi tu as quelque chose à raconter d'important avant qu'on commence?**
do you have anything important to tell before we start?

Ex. (4): Group, session 6

VIC70- **c'était bien ton stage?**
did your internship go well?

When an account is *auto-initiated*, the storyteller has taken his/her turn *autonomously* without any suggestion from another participant (see Exx. 1, 2), or in *reaction* to another request than to tell a personal event (see Ex. 5).

Ex. (5): Dyad, Barbara, session 2

The SLT and Barbara talk about orthographic difficulties

SLT85- **comment on SAIT qu(e) c'est des mots qu(e) tu arrives pas**
how does one KNOW that these are words you cannot manage

BAR95- parce qu'en fait moi avec monsieur X en français on nous demande de lire une espèce de livre sur j(e) sais pas quelle euh …quelle personne mais euh (il) y a des mots un peu bizarres que nous on dit pas main(te)nant qui ab- euh comme euh j(e) sais pas euh "trouva"- euh "trouvasse" des choses un peu bizarres
because actually I with Mister X in French class we are asked to read a kind of book about I don't know which uh …which person but uh there are some words that are a little strange that we don't say nowadays which uh like uh I don't know uh "trouva" uh "trouvasse"[4] *things that are a little strange*

Implication of the Participants in Storytelling and News Announcement

This dimension captures whether the event was shared or not by the participants. Non-shared events are experienced by one participant only (see all previous examples), whereas shared experience involves all the participants of the dyad or of the therapeutic group (see Ex. 6).

Ex. (6): Group, session 2

SLT(B)736- **qu'est-ce qu'on a fait après Ralph ?**
what did we do after Ralph?

SLT(A)498-	**Alexis a lu.** *Alexis read*
ALE413-	**lu** *read*
SLT(A)499-	**très bien. ensuite troisième information. on a fait quoi après?** *very good. then third information. what did we do next?*
(...)	(...)
ELI418-	**on a joué à** *we played at*

Link with the Ongoing Activity

This analysis concerns the production context in which PSs and NAs are co-produced. After having identified the different activities observed in the therapy sessions (like welcome and greetings, session planning and activities structured on the oral or written language), the link between activities and PS/NA is described. Two types are defined: PS/NA is *linked* to the ongoing activity (see Ex. 6) or there is *no link* (see Ex. 2). In Ex. (6), the group is engaged in a free conversation activity at the end of the session, and the participants recall what they did during the session. In Ex. (2), the participants discuss how to successfully read instructions in a structured activity. In turn BAR153, the adolescent initiates an NA that has no link with the activity.

Legitimation of Storytelling and News Announcement

The last analysis captures the acceptance degree of PSs/NAs. Two cases are observed: PSs/NAs can be *accepted* (the following intervention is an acquiescence, a question or a commentary), or *not accepted* (the account can be ignored as in Ex. 7, RA242 / SLT(B)229 , or rejected as in Ex. 2, BAR154 / SLT161). The NA in Ex. 2 is rejected for planning reasons. In Ex. (7) Ralph's attempt is ignored because the participants are focusing on Alexis' experience.

Ex. (7): Group, session 3

Alexis did an internship where he was hazed. Ralph wants to speak about a similar experience he had.

RAL242-	**on m'a fait la même chose que toi.** *the same thing as you was done to me*
ELI113-	c'était pas rien. *it wasn't nothing*
RAL243-	**le p(e)tit gag .** *the small joke*
SLT(B)229-	est-ce que vous avez des questions à lui poser à Alexis concernant cette profession ? *do you have questions for Alexis concerning this profession?*
ALE177-	t'es y allé à la cuisine ? *did you go to the kitchen?*

Quantitative Analyses

The interactions were coded by our team according to the dimensions presented above. Team sessions were organized to discuss and resolve in common the analysis of unclear cases, but no inter-rater coding was done. Concerning the quantitative analyses, the distributions (in percentage) of the different dimensions' categories were calculated by taking into account the setting (dyads vs. group) in which PSs/NAs are co-produced. The chi-square test was used to compare the distributions between the adolescents and the therapists, the two settings, and NAs *versus* PSs. We also used the binomial test for some categories internally to test which option is favored.

Results

Quantitative results are presented in five subsections: the distribution of PSs and NAs in the dyads and the group, the modes of story initiation, the participants' implication with regard to the events evoked in the stories, the link between PSs/NAs and the ongoing activity, and their legitimation. Then, some extended examples are discussed in a qualitative way to identify some functions of PSs in the therapeutic context.

Storytelling and News Announcement in the Dyads and the Group

As Table 3.1 shows, PSs are more frequent than NAs in both settings. However both types of account are more frequent in the dyads than in the group (PS: $\chi^2 = 1063.5$, df = 1, $p < 0.001$; NA: $\chi^2 = 30.717$, df = 1, $p < 0.001$). The setting thus influences the production of PSs and NAs.

Table 3.1 Distribution (in percentage) of the utterances belonging to PSs and NAs according to the setting and for the whole corpus

	Personal storytelling		News announcement		
Setting	%	*N*	%	*N*	Total of utterances (*N*)
Group	25.37	6246	1.58	388	24624
Dyads	39.51	8628	2.29	499	21838
General	32.01	14874	1.91	888	46462

Modes of Story Initiation

Among the 736 PSs, 460 were initiated by the SLTs and 276 by the adolescents. Concerning the 275 NAs, 136 were initiated by the SLTs and 139 by the adolescents. The results on the mode of initiation are presented only for PSs, because NAs are always auto-initiated. The manner in which PSs were initiated differs between the SLTs and the adolescents (Table 3.2; $\chi^2 = 162.24$, df = 1, $p < 0.001$). In general the SLTs dominantly solicited PSs (62.61%) from their interlocutor, whereas the adolescents mostly auto-initiated their PSs (85.87%).

In the SLTs' distribution, solicitations are mostly specific in the dyads (binomial test: $p < 0.001$) and in the group (binom., $p < 0.001$). However in the group, there are more general demands produced compared to the dyads ($\chi^2 = 24.35$, df = 1, $p < 0.001$).

Table 3.2 Distribution (in percentage) of the ways PSs are initiated according to the initiating participant (ADO vs. SLT) for the different settings and the whole corpus (*GEN* and *SPE:* general and specific demands, *AUT* and *REA:* autonomous auto-initiations and auto-initiations in reaction)

		Solicited		Auto-initiated		
	Setting	GEN	SPE	AUT	REA	Total (*N*)
ADO	Dyads	0.00	18.18	53.64	28.18	110
	Group	0.60	10.84	68.67	19.88	166
	General	0.36	13.77	62.68	23.19	276
SLT	Dyads	4.73	53.72	34.46	7.09	296
	Group	21.95	48.17	25.00	4.88	164
	General	10.87	51.74	31.09	6.30	460
Total		6.93	37.50	42.93	12.64	736

As for the adolescents, their auto-initiations are mostly realized autonomously in the group (binom., $p < 0.001$) and in the dyads (binom., $p < 0.01$) rather than in reaction to another demand.

These results need some comments. First, the differences between the SLTs and the adolescents reflect the role of each participant in the therapy sessions. The SLTs have the responsibility to plan the sessions and to monitor their progress. In this social context, they solicit the adolescents to tell a personal event when they think it is useful or relevant for the progress of the activity. The adolescents' role as patients does not allow them to solicit the SLTs to tell a personal account. Second, although the setting of the therapy does not influence the way adolescents auto-initiated their PSs, they also used PS to react to a request to explain an element of the ongoing activity or discussion (see MAR48 and MAR50 in Ex. 8b below). It appears to be a specific resource for them, which is not the case for the SLTs.

Storyteller Implication in Storytelling and News Announcement

The results for PSs and NAs are presented in Table 3.3. In general the participants co-produced as many *PSs* about shared events as about non-shared events (binom., $p = 0.8538$). This means that about half of PSs

Table 3.3 Distribution (in percentage) of the shared and non-shared experiences in PSs and NAs according to the setting and for the whole corpus

		Personal storytelling			News announcements		
	Setting	Shared	Non-shared	Total (*N*)	Shared	Non-shared	Total (*N*)
ADO	Dyads	14.55	85.45	110	22.73	77.27	44
	Group	57.83	42.17	166	35.79	64.21	95
	General	40.58	59.42	276	31.65	68.35	139
SLT	Dyads	50.34	49.66	296	66.67	33.33	87
	Group	67.07	32.93	164	63.27	36.73	49
	General	56.30	43.70	460	65.44	34.56	136
Total		50.41	49.59	736	48.36	51.64	275

concern events taking place in the therapy sessions. But the adolescents initiate more PSs about non-shared events, whereas the SLTs tend to initiate more PSs about shared events (χ^2 = 16.439, df = 1, $p < 0.001$). The comparison of the two settings shows different profiles. In the group, the adolescents and the SLTs initiated PSs about shared events in a similar proportion (χ^2 = 2.6229, df = 1, $p > 0.05$), while in the dyads, there is a difference between the participants (χ^2 = 41.118, df = 1, $p < 0.001$): The adolescents dominantly initiated PSs about non-shared events (binom., $p < 0.001$), and the SLTs initiated as many PSs about shared events as about their own experiences (binom., $p = 0.9537$).

Regarding *NAs*, the SLTs and the adolescents show different trends (χ^2 = 30.084, df = 1, $p < 0.001$). The two-thirds of NAs initiated by the SLTs concern shared events, in both settings. They often consist in brief recalls of elements experienced in a previous session. In contrast, the adolescents initiated NAs about non-shared events in about two-thirds of cases; this appears more often in the dyads than in the group, but the difference is not significant (χ^2 = 1.8063, df = 1, $p = 0.179$).

Link with the Ongoing Activity

In general almost all the PSs and NAs are linked to the ongoing activity (93.18%). The PSs and NAs initiated by the SLTs all display this link in both settings. However, even if the vast majority of PSs/NAs initiated by the adolescents are linked to the activity (83.37%), some are not

(16.63%). The latter case tends to occur more in the group (19.16%) than in the dyads (12.34%) but not significantly (χ^2 = 2.7759, df = 1, $p > 0.5$). Thus, the setting does not influence the link with the activity. There are however more NAs without a link than PSs (χ^2 = 10.122, df = 1, $p < 0.01$).

Legitimation of Personal Storytelling and News Announcements

As shown in Table 3.4, a large majority of PSs and NAs are accepted. But their legitimation is influenced by three factors. First, the PSs/NAs initiated by the SLTs are more accepted than those initiated by the adolescents (χ^2 = 79.551, df = 1, $p < 0.001$). Second, the PSs are more accepted than the NAs (χ^2 = 51.436, df = 1, $p < 0.001$). Third, the PSs/NAs linked to the activity are more accepted than those with no link (χ^2 = 196.11, df = 1, $p < 0.001$).

Among the *PSs/NAs initiated by the SLTs*, only a few cases are not accepted. As for the *PSs/NAs initiated by the adolescents*, there is more variation. PSs are more accepted than NAs (χ^2 = 29.483, df = 1, $p < 0.001$). Moreover if PSs and NAs displaying a link with the activity are predominantly accepted, it is not the case for those that have no link.

Table 3.4 Distribution (in percentage) of PSs and NAs initiated by the adolescents, the SLTs and for the whole corpus, according to their legitimation and link with the activity

			Legitimation		
Storyteller	PS/NA	Link with the activity	Accepted	Not accepted	Total (*N*)
ADO	NA	No link	28.57	71.43	35
		Link	73.08	26.92	104
		General	61.87	38.13	139
	PS	No link	44.12	55.88	34
		Link	91.74	8.26	242
		General	85.87	14.13	276
	General		77.83	22.17	415
SLT	NA	Link	91.91	8.09	136
	PS	Link	97.39	2.61	460
	General		96.14	3.86	596
Total			88.62	11.38	1011

Some Functions of Personal Storytelling

In this subsection, two excerpts of PSs are commented in light of the quantitative results above to highlight some of their functions. In order to give a brief overview of the diversity of the activities carried out within the sessions, we present PSs co-produced during two different activities: one (Exx.8a, b) during an activity structured around written language (learning of indicative tenses) in one of the dyads, and the other (Exx.9a, b) during a free conversation activity in the group.

Ex. (8a): Dyad, Marine, session 1

SLT21-	**NOUS c(e) qu'on était en train d(e) faire.** *what WE were doing*
MAR24-	oui. *yes*
SLT22-	**c'était toi qu'avais d(e)mandé pour la conjugaison. hein?** *you're the one who asked for conjugation. aren't you?*
MAR25-	ouais. *yes*
SLT23-	alors attends voir / j(e) vais juste reprendre c(e) qu'on avait dit. *so wait a minute / I'll just recap what we said*
MAR26-	c'était écrit devant. *it was written in front*
SLT24-	voilà ici c(e) que t'avais toi écrit euh? dit. c'était améliorer la conjugaison les verbes de cinq sixième au présent imparfait et futur. *so here we have what you had written um? said. it was to improve the fifth sixth grade verb conjugation for the present imperfect and future*
MAR27-	mh.
SLT25-	**qu'est ce que TOI tu t(e) souviens?** on avait déjà écrit des choses ici. *what do YOU remember? we had already written some things here*
MAR28-	(je) sais plus. *(I) don't remember*

SLT26- **sur la conjugaison de quoi tu t(e) souviens de c(e) qu'on avait discuté ensemble?**
on the conjugation of what do you remember what we discussed together?

MAR29- ben que quand j'ai appri- quand j'(e) ferai des bonnes- là c'est juste un comment dire? c'est comme un exercice. et puis à la fin quand j(e) connais tout ces- presque tous ces verbes on f(e)ra un test.
well that when I learned- when I will do good- now it's just a how to say? it's like an exercise. and then in the end when I know all these- almost all these verbs we'll do a test.

SLT27- mhm. ouais.
mhm yes

MAR30- à la fin.
in the end

SLT28- si t'as besoin on peut faire comme ça. **mais qu'est-ce que TOI tu te rappelles de c(e)qu'on a fait ? sur la conjugaison ?**
if you need it we can do like that. but what do YOU remember about what we did? about conjugation?

MAR31- **ben je sais qu'on avait fait les verbes on avait- je sais qu'on avait fait les verbes sur l'ordinateur.**
well I know that we did verbs we did I know we did verbs on the computer

SLT29- **ouais** et puis on avait parlé -->
yes and we talked -->

MAR32- **oh! comment trouver le futur et le // imparfait.**
oh! how to find the future and the // imperfect

SLT30- **(il) y avait ça avec le futur et l'imparfait.**
that's it with the future and the imperfect

The therapist starts the activity by initiating the story of a shared experience (SLT21), recalling a structured activity done during a previous session following a request of the adolescent (SLT22): the learning of the construction of indicative tenses. The purpose of this storytelling is to define and introduce the activity, whose learning objectives are known by the adolescent and thematized (SLT22). In a second stage, the therapist uses the storytelling to focus attention on the content of their previous structured activity. She solicits the adolescent three times (SLT25, SLT26, SLT28) so that the latter recapitulates the elements that were addressed. The first solicitation leads the adolescent to admit that she forgot (MAR28), and in the second one she mentions an inappropriate content by projecting herself instead of recalling what they did. After the third solicitation, the adolescent's turns (MAR31, MAR32) constitute an appropriate answer concerning the previous activity: the study of the future and imperfect tenses. This answer is accepted (SLT29 and 30).

Ex. (8b)

SLT45-	**le futur on avait dit justement que le -r -->** *the future we precisely said that the -r -->*
MAR48-	**j'arrive pas trop- j'arrive pas trop à l'apprendre / c'est dur / encore.** *I can't really manage- I can't really manage to learn it / it's hard / still.*
SLT46-	d'accord. celui-là c'est les terminaisons où c'est encore un peu difficile? *ok. for this one the endings are still a bit difficult?*
MAR49-	((acquiescement)) c'est j(e) crois que j(e) me confonds avec le futur et le imparfait. *((acquiescence)) it's I think that I get confused between future and imperfect*
SLT47-	ah! puis c'est là où on avait dit que pour le futur tu peux utiliser le -r. **et puis?** *ah! that's when we said that for the future you can use the -r. and then?*
MAR50-	**nan c'est pas pour ça. j'a- la dernière fois quand je fais les tests.** *no that's not why, I- last time when I take the tests*
SLT48-	non c'est pas ça? *no that's not why?*
SLT49-	ouais. *yes*

MAR51- **j'étais en train d(e) dire "mais est-ce que c'est futur euh ? le verbe "entendre" si c'est ça la fin" d(e) temps en temps c'est flou encore le futur et l'imparfait pour moi.**
I was saying "but is it future hmm? the verb "to hear" if that is the ending" sometimes it's still hazy for me future and imperfect.

SLT50- **ouais. et puis c'était- le test c'était des phrases qui étaient écrites?**
yes. and it was- the test was made of written sentences?

MAR52- non. comment dire?
no. how to say?

The therapist asks the adolescent to tell her how they addressed the future construction (SLT45). The adolescent does not answer to that request directly; she talks about her difficulties to learn these tenses (MAR48). The therapist suggests that her difficulties lie in the use of endings (SLT46). The adolescent agrees (MAR49) and then states she does not master the distinction between the two tenses (MAR49). Then, again, the therapist invites her to recapitulate the content of their previous activity (SLT47), but the adolescent answers again by mentioning a personal experience (MAR50). This account initiated in reaction to the therapist's requests allows the adolescent to make explicit her difficulties in learning tenses at school. The therapist legitimates this account by inviting her to pursue with follow-up questions (SLT50). Following the adolescent's account, the therapist indicates that she understands her difficulties and engages in an attempt to resolve them.

Example (9) deals with a conversation about professional internship searches, which is a recurrent theme in this group.

Ex. (9a): Group, session 1

SLT(A)232- **moi j(e) voulais savoir si euh si i(l) y avait du nouveau par rapport à des s tages?**
I wanted to know if there is something new with respect to internships?

VIC230- ((non de la tête)).
((shakes his head no)).

SLT(A)233- Victor rien.

	Victor nothing
VIC231-	j(e) téléphone! ce soir. *I'll phone! tonight.*
RAL297-	**MOI moi j(e) veux parler !** *ME me I want to talk!*
SLT(A)234-	Elliot?
ELI291-	ben moi j'attends mon mail. *well I'm waiting for my email.*
(…)	(…)
SLT(B)407-	non. il était déjà revenu. **c'est Ralph qui a été faire des examens.** *no. he was back already. Ralph was the one who took exams.*
RAL300-	OUIIII *YEEEES*

The discussion concerns available communication media and the way to use them in order to obtain an internship, via telephone (VIC231) or via email (ELI291). Following SLT(A)232's intervention, which offers the adolescents the opportunity to express themselves about their experience as interns, RAL(297) auto-selects himself, but his speaking is momentarily ignored, and hence not legitimized at that moment. This comes later, after the therapist has talked to another adolescent (SLT(A)234) and when the other therapist SLT(B)(407) mentions the exams he took. This theme, linked to professional internships, becomes the topic of the conversation.

Ex. (9b)

SLT(B)411-	alors Ralph comment s'est passée cette épreuve / de tests? *so Ralph how did this test go?*
VIC234-	il a eu les réponses. *he had the answers.*
RAL303-	**ben c'était bien / hé bEN le matin ben j'ai dû m(e) réveiller à six heures du matin. j(e) me suis préparé tout ça . j(e) suis parti à la gare. j'ai pris l(e) train de →** *well it was good / so wELL in the morning well I had to wake up at 6 AM. I got ready and stuff. I went to the station. I took the train of →*
VIC235-	ouah!.

	wow!
VIC236-	**tout seul?**
	all on your own?
RAL304-	ouais / j'ai pris l(e) train de mh comment ça s'app(elle) de mouais j(e) crois de de Villexxx. ouais. j'ai pris c(el)ui de l- le train de Villexxx. j'ai d(e)mandé si il allait à Bu- i(l) passait par Buixxx. i(ls) m'ont dit "oui". euh j'ai acheté les bill- j(e) me suis acheté un billet euh pour un enfant quoi un réduit.
	yes / I took the train mm how is it called I think coming from Villexxx. yes. I took this one the train coming from Villexxx. I asked if it was going to Bu- was going through Buixxx. they told me "yes". uh I bought a ticket uh for children well at reduced rate.
ALE182-	Lausanne.
	Lausanne
SLT(B)412-	mhm.
	mhm.
RAL305-	j(e) suis allé. ben j'ai pris le b- train / j'a-i ça a pas pris trop longtemps pour arriver là-bas. / ensuite quand j(e) suis- quand j(e) suis descendu ben j'ai sorti la carte euh dans mon p(e)tit sac. et je m- j'ai r(e)gardé i(ls) d- sur la carte i(ls) disaient "*passez sous le passage sous voie*". ben j(e) suis passé. euh après ils m'ont dit de conti- de passer par le chemin de tatata tout ça. et puis ben euh j(e) suis arrivé.
	I went. well I took the train / I- it didn't take very long to arrive there. / then when I got- when I got off I took the map from my little bag. and I looked on the map it said "take the underpass". so I went. uh then it said to carry- to go through the lane of tatata and stuff. and then well uh I was there.
SLT(A)238-	**t'as fait tout tout seul ?**
	you did everything alone?
RAL306-	mhm.
	mhm.
SLT(A)239-	**wouah ! bravo !**
	wow! congratulations!

RAL(303) starts his account about his day, by recounting his travel from home to the exam location. The therapists legitimate this story by letting him continue. VIC236's question shows that he is astonished that RAL went to his exam on his own, which suggests that in his own mental representations, he would expect an adolescent to be accompanied to go somewhere that requires a train journey. The therapist reuses this question and puts forward Ralph's ability to be autonomous (SLT(A)238). The account thus constitutes an opportunity for the adolescent to mention what he is capable of doing outside of the group therapy, and for the therapist to emphasize the described skill. She makes this skill apparent to the other adolescents since she congratulates the adolescent (SLT(A)239). In this excerpt, the establishment of links between experiences and the comparisons allowed by this enable a collective construction of representations about a professional environment's expectations that can serve as references for the adolescents.

More generally, the two excerpts presented show that the SLTs' solicitations allow the starting of activities and that co-produced accounts serve meaning construction about linguistic knowledge or individual paths, through requests to recall the content of previous structured activities or through the sharing of professional experiences. By doing so, the SLTs offer the adolescents a discursive space that they can use, among other things, to express their learning difficulties. As a result, these co-produced PSs enable the establishment of a common ground of understanding between speech therapists and adolescents and to construct collective representations. PS is therefore likely to bring relevant elements to plan and guide therapy.

Discussion and Conclusion

This study examined the space given to PS during speech therapy sessions in two settings (dyadic and group) and proposed a description of some of its characteristics and functions. We expected an influence of the speech and language therapy's specificities on the functioning of PSs even if we would observe some of the functions described in the literature. To answer this, we first conducted a quantitative analysis of the characteristics of PSs, then a qualitative analysis based on two excerpts. These analyses broadly confirmed our expectations, in particular the existence of some specificities in the speech therapy institution.

During the identification phase of PSs, we observed that certain utterances referred to events that were not developed. These NAs were integrated in our analyses. They are less frequent than PSs, but they also constitute a source of information on the expectations concerning "talking about oneself" during speech therapy sessions. For example, even if they are equally auto-initiated by the adolescents and the SLTs, the implication varies according to the participants: The adolescents' NAs mainly concern non-shared experiences while those of the SLTs rather refer to shared experiences and can constitute brief reminders. Consequently, the SLTs' NAs are principally centered on activities performed during the sessions. The non-shared implication of some of the adolescents' NAs, which are then not linked to the activity, explains why they are not always encouraged by the SLTs, who generally ignore them. It seems that the adolescents interpret this absence of reaction as an indication that carrying on their account is inappropriate. Conversely, when an adolescent tells an experience that displays a link with the activity, acceptance utterances are observed. Event reports are thus only legitimized by the SLTs when they give meaning to the ongoing activities. In this case, they may develop to form a PS.

Concerning the characteristics of PSs more specifically, it appears that they constitute an important part of the interactions in both settings. The PSs are often initiated by the SLTs, who encourage the adolescents to give accounts of shared events, as well as non-shared events. Those initiated by the adolescents predominantly concern non-shared events and are often found in free conversation activities (because they are centered on conversational exchange) and in language-based activities, principally in the form of summary-accounts concerning activities or learning experiences. Most PSs are thus linked to the ongoing activity, and hence legitimized. Those that are not legitimized are mostly unrelated to the activity. These analyses enabled us to shed light on the specificities of PSs co-produced during speech therapy sessions. First, these accounts represent a substantial part of the discursive productions of the participants. Speech therapy sessions therefore enable interactional practices where the participants talk about themselves. Second, half of these accounts concern experiences shared by the dyads or the group. This shared implication allows the participants to center on the ongoing activities and thus plays an important role in the sessions' dynamics. Accounts of shared experiences concerning ongoing activities therefore appear to be a characteristic feature of speech therapy sessions. Finally, we could observe an inverted tendency, linked to the participants' roles, between the adolescents and the SLTs concerning the manner with which they initiate an account: While the SLTs strongly solicit the adolescents, the latter tend to auto-initiate their accounts.

Among the functions identified, *meaning construction* is central, regardless of the activity. As described by Bruner (2002) and Ryekel and Delvigne (2010), it has several subfunctions that can be observed in both settings, like knowledge acquisition, experience sharing and linkage, the collective establishment of a state of understanding, or explaining encountered difficulties.

As for *knowledge acquisition*, PSs serving linguistic or communicational learning were distinguished from PSs that contribute to the participants' representations of topics linked to adolescence. The adolescents used them to consolidate their knowledge or to give meaning to their professional experiences. As shown by Bruner (2002), Kohn (2008) and Zittoun (2006), PS thus permits one to detach oneself from an experience, to integrate it and to understand it, while symbolizing it for the other participants.

By this, PS also takes on a function of *experience and knowledge sharing*, thus offering the opportunity to *establish links between experiences and compare them*. First, the fact that adolescents hear their peers' (for the group) or their therapist's (for the dyads and the group) PSs activates their ability to connect experiences with their own life. Moreover, the peers' remarks, supported by those of the therapists who emphasize certain aspects of PSs, solicit the adolescents to reflect on the institutional expectations of professional environments concerning communication issues. Establishing connections between experiences therefore helps adolescents understand and collectively elaborate representations about the interactional requirements of professional settings. The transformative power of PS (Ricoeur 1988) can thus be seen during speech therapy in the construction of knowledge. For example, in the group, sharing an experience can constitute a common ground to understand interactional behaviors expected during adolescence, like for instance what procedure to follow in order to obtain an internship, how to interact efficiently on the telephone, or how to highlight one's skills. Second, by considering experiences within their time frame, it is possible to link the past with the present, as well as with potential future projects. This activates the *continuity* function between past and present (Ehlich 1980; Ricoeur 1988; Bruner 2002; Zittoun 2006; Kohn 2008; Ryekel and Delvigne 2010), which allows adolescents to give meaning to their own therapy pathway and to the formulation of their projects; they can therefore reflect on their integration in the professional world. This meaning construction necessarily contributes to the sense of personal continuity, which is fundamental during adolescence, given that it contributes to the subjects' positioning toward their learning. Thus, when adolescents produce a PS, they also define themselves in their projects, their abilities and their confrontation with knowledge (Perret-Clermont and Zittoun 2002).

PSs co-produced on the initiative of the therapists also constituted efficient resources for the adolescents, especially *to point out and make explicit the difficulties* encountered during their learning. It appears to be easier for them to explain or to answer questions using storytelling, which shows their capacity to efficiently invest the discursive space provided by the therapists.

Given that storytelling provides a state of joint understanding between the adolescents and the therapists, it constitutes a tool to guide, or even *to plan the therapy*. Indeed, when an activity is initiated, mentioning learning contents that have been already addressed or sharing professional experiences make it possible for the participants to jointly get involved in the activity. Then, according to the needs identified by the therapists during the co-production of the account, the content and the planning of the activity can be adapted. This function seems to be specific to speech therapy, as envisaged in a socio-interactionist approach (de Weck 2003, 2005), which focuses on people's resources and competences, in order to ensure the progress of, and to give them autonomy toward, their learning.

To conclude, this first study on the interaction competences of adolescents with language impairments shows that they appropriately use their storytelling competences: In the large majority of cases, they take into account the interaction context (setting, activity) when they initiate

PSs, and the content of their stories is legitimized by the therapists. This competence constitutes a resource that serves different illocutionary purposes (explanation, illustration, answer to a question). The adolescents therefore appear to master the question of when to initiate a storytelling.

However, given that the results concern adolescents whose linguistic knowledge is fragile, it appears necessary to further examine their storytelling competence and to enlarge our study to other pragmatic-discursive levels. It would be interesting to see how they manage the co-construction of storytelling, the way in which they give information, or how the status of the interlocutors (peers vs. therapist) influences storytelling in the group. In other words, an in-depth study of the discursive quality of these PSs seems necessary. Furthermore, given that other types of discourse are also produced depending on the type of activity, within the speech therapy institution or in other institutional settings, it appears that an analysis of these types of discourse would be relevant in order to have a larger overview on the interaction competences of the adolescents of our study.

Moreover, the speech therapy objective to ensure adolescents' interactional and linguistic autonomy should be extended outside of this particular institution. It would thus be interesting to examine how they invest their production competences in other social and professional environments that are not centered on language, which necessarily display other types of interactional expectations and legitimization processes compared to speech therapy. To do so, it would be interesting to examine how storytelling occurs, as well as other types of discourse, and to see to what extent positive interaction experiences produced during therapy constitute an effective preparation for the adolescents to transfer their competences to other contexts.

Finally, and more generally, this study raises trans-disciplinary questions. If one considers the example of the planning function of storytelling, which we linked to the particular institutional setting of speech therapy, it seems legitimate to ask whether it is also relevant in other settings that share some of the characteristics of speech therapy (centered on learning). We can hypothesize that this function is also used at school, especially in classes with a limited number of students, which host children or youth with important learning difficulties, or to a smaller extent, in professional training settings, to guide discussions between referring professionals and apprentices.

Notes

1. The authors would like to thank the speech therapists who volunteered for our research, as well as the adolescents who kindly accepted to be recorded during their therapy sessions. Informed consent was obtained for all participants, and we ensure the confidentiality and protection of the data collected. Thanks also to the students who participated in the transcription of the video recordings.

   This study was conducted in the subproject "Interactional Competences: Social representations and interactional practices in speech and language therapy," under the direction of Prof. G. de Weck, of the IC-You project funded by the Swiss National Fund, grant number CRSII1_136291.
2. The names of the adolescents were modified in order to guarantee their anonymity.
3. Bold characters indicate the target elements.
4. The book in question is a play by Molière; "to find" is used in an old literary form of conjugation.

Appendix: Transcriptions Conventions

The transcription conventions of the speech therapy subproject of IC-You come from different sources (LEAPLE 2001; de Weck 2002; FNRS project "Interaction mère-enfant en situation logopédique" (no. 100012-111938 obtained in 2006) directed by G. de Weck et A. Salazar Orvig). The symbols used are presented here.

Utterance Delimitations:	
.	assertions
!	exclamations
¡	orders
?	questions
-->	oral starts (when the participant starts saying a word or utterance while expecting that the interlocutor ends it)
Verbal Productions:	
an: (underlined)	overlap
AAA:	accentuation
(e):	elision
/:	one second pause

References

Abell, P. (2004). Narrative explanation: An alternative to variable-centered explanation? *Annual Review of Sociology, 30*, 287–310.

Bangerter, A., Mayor, E., & Pekarek Doehler, S. (2011). Reported speech in conversational narratives during nursing shift handover meetings. *Discourse Processes, 48*, 183–213.

Bishop, D. V. M., & Clarkson, B. (2003). Written language as a window into residual language deficits: A study of children with persistent and residual speech and language impairments. *Cortex, 39*(2), 215–238.

Bliss, L. S., McCabe, A., & Miranda, A. E. (1998). Narrative assessment profile: Discourse analysis for school-age children. *Journal of Communication Disorders, 31*(4), 347–363.

Botting, N. (2010). 'It's not (just) what you do, but the way that you do it': Factors that determine narrative ability in atypical language learners. *Developmental Medicine & Child Neurology, 52*(10), 886–887.

Botting, N., & Conti-Ramsden, G. (2008). Emotional health in adolescents with and without a history of specific language impairment (SLI). *Journal of Child Psychology & Psychiatry, 49*(5), 516–525.

Bronckart, J. P. (1996). *Activités langagières, textes et discours. Pour un interactionnisme socio-discursif.* Paris: Delachaux et Niestlé.

Bruner, J. (1991). The narrative construction of reality. *Critical Inquiry, 18*, 1–21.

Bruner, J. (1996). *L'éducation, entrée dans la culture. Les problèmes de l'école à la lumière de la psychologie culturelle.* Paris: Retz.

Bruner, J. (2002). *Pourquoi nous racontons-nous des histoires?* Paris: Retz.

Clegg, J., Hollis, C., Mawhood, L., & Rutter, M. (2005). Developmental language disorders a follow-up in later adult life. Cognitive, language and psychosocial outcomes. *Journal of Child Psychology & Psychiatry, 46*(2), 128–149.

Conti-Ramsden, G., & Botting, N. (2008). Emotional health in adolescents with and without a history of specific language impairment (SLI). *Journal of Child Psychology & Psychiatry, 49*(5), 516–525.

Conti-Ramsden, G., Botting, N., Simkin, Z., & Knox, E. (2001). Follow-up of children attending infant language units: Outcomes at 11 years of age. *International Journal of Language & Communication Disorders, 36*, 207–219.

Conti-Ramsden, G., & Durkin, K. (2012). Postschool educational and employment experiences of young people with specific language impairment. *Language, Speech & Hearing Services in Schools, 43*, 507–520.

de Weck, G. (2002). Options théoriques et choix méthodologiques pour l'étude des capacités discursives des enfants d'âge préscolaire. *Revue Parole, 22–24*, 143–174.

de Weck, G. (2003). Pratiques langagières, contextes d'interaction et genres de discours en logopédie / orthophonie. *Travaux neuchâtelois de linguistique, 38–39*, 25–48.

de Weck, G. (2005). L'approche interactionniste en orthophonie-logopédie. *Rééducation Orthophonique, 221*, 67–83.

de Weck, G., & Marro, P. (2010). *Les troubles du langage chez l'enfant: description et évaluation*. Issy-les-Moulineaux: Masson.

de Weck, G., & Rosat, M. C. (2003). *Troubles dysphasiques. Comment raconter, relater, faire agir à l'âge préscolaire*. Paris: Masson.

Ehlich, K. (1980). Der Alltag des Erzählens. In K. Ehlich (Ed.), *Erzählen im Alltag* (pp. 11–27). Frankfurt/M.: Suhrkamp.

Estienne-Dejong, F. (1983). *Une logothérapie de groupe*. Paris: Editions universitaires.

Jullien, S. (2005). Introduction de référents topiques dans des dialogues d'adolescents dysphasiques : le cas de la construction présentative clivée. *Travaux neuchâtelois de linguistique, 41*, 49–68.

Kohn, M. (2008). Je récite l'homme : du récit dans la psychanalyse. *Cliniques méditerranéennes, 77*, 205–214.

Labov, W. (1972). *Language in the inner city*. Philadelphia: University of Pennsylvania Press.

LEAPLE. (2001). *Conventions de transcriptions*. Unpublished manuscript, Paris.

Lindsay, G., & Dockrell, J. (2012). Longitudinal patterns of behavioral, emotional, and social difficulties and self-concept in adolescents with a history of specific language impairment. *Language, Speech, & Hearing in School, 43*, 445–460.

McLean, K., & Mansfield, C. (2012). The co-construction of adolescent narrative identity: Narrative processing as a function of adolescent age, gender, and maternal scaffolding. *Developmental Psychology, 48*(2), 436–447.

Miller, P., Wiley, A., Fung, H., & Liang, C. (1997). Personal storytelling as a medium of socialization in Chinese and American families. *Child Development, 68*(3), 557–568.

Palikara, O., Lindsay, G., & Dockrell, J. (2009). Voices of young people with a history of specific speech and language difficulties in the first year of post-16 education. *International Journal of Language & Communication Disorders, 44*(1), 56–78.

Perret-Clermont, A. N., & Zittoun, T. (2002). Esquisse d'une psychologie de la transition. *Education permanente, 1*, 12–15.

Reed, V. A., Patchell, F. C., Coggins, T. E., & Hand, L. S. (2007). Informativeness of the spoken narratives of younger and older adolescents with specific language impairment and their counterpart with normal language. *Clinical Linguistics & Phonetics, 21*(11–12), 953–960.

Revaz, F. (1987). Du descriptif au narratif et à l'injonctif. *Pratiques, 56*, 18–38.

Ricoeur, P. (1988). *Time & narrative*. Chicago: University of Chicago Press.

Rosenbaum, F. (1997). *Approche transculturelle des troubles de la communication—Langage et migration*. Paris: Masson.

Roth, F. P., & Worthington, C. K. (2011). *Treatment resource manual for speech-language pathology*. Delmar: International.

Ryekel, C., & Delvigne, F. (2010). La construction de l'identité par le récit. *Psychothérapies, 30*, 229–240.

Simkin, Z., & Conti-Ramsden, G. (2009). "I went to a language unit": Adolescents' views on specialist educational provision and their language difficulties. *Child Language Teaching & Therapy, 25*(1), 103–122.

Wetherell, D., Botting, N., & Conti-Ramsden, G. (2007a). Narrative in adolescent specific language impairment (SLI): A comparison with peers across two different narrative genres. *International Journal of Communication Disorders, 42*(5), 583–605.

Wetherell, D., Botting, N., & Conti-Ramsden, G. (2007b). Narrative skills in adolescents with a history of SLI in relation to non-verbal IQ scores. *Child Language Teaching & Therapy, 23*(1), 95–113.

Zittoun, T. (2006). *Transitions. Development through symbolic resources*. Greenwich, CT: InfoAge.

4

Shaping Participation in Vocational Training Interactions: The Case of Schisming

Vassiliki Markaki and Laurent Filliettaz

Introduction

This chapter focuses on vocational training interactions, namely typical experiences faced by young people when they perform their transition from school to work and progressively become involved in professional practice. Vocational training depends on early career choices and has long-lasting effects in young people's lines of work (Schoon and Silbereisen 2009). As we argue here, the vocational training period can also be seen as an experience of high density and of change, not only in terms of professional knowledge and skills but also in terms of interactional competences: learning workers are faced with new and sometimes unexpected institutional requirements regarding how to behave and how to participate in social interactions; they are also involved in complex

V. Markaki (✉)
Ecole Normale Supérieure of Lyon, Lyon, France

L. Filliettaz
University of Geneva, Geneva, Switzerland

S. Pekarek Doehler et al. (eds.), *Interactional Competences in Institutional Settings*, DOI 10.1007/978-3-319-46867-9_4

legitimation mechanisms, in which their contributions to interactions are constantly evaluated and assessed according to such requirements (de Saint-Georges and Filliettaz 2008; Filliettaz 2011, 2013; Losa et al. 2014).

The legitimation and acquisition mechanisms of these aspects of interactional competences will be investigated here in a specific empirical context, that of the vocational training of students learning the profession of early childhood educators. In the Swiss vocational education system, early childhood educators are trained at the tertiary level, in what is called higher vocational education. Students move back and forth between periods of being taught in vocational schools and periods of practical training in preschool child care institutions. During their practicums, students are supervised by mentors, who assist them during their first days at work and make sure they meet the pedagogical objectives required by the curriculum. It is precisely the setting of the practicum and the specific interactions afforded within such workplace contexts which will be of interest here. Highly complex and constantly changing participation formats emerge in such contexts, where students engage in educational activities involving children while being supervised by their mentors, and from which they are expected to learn.

From that perspective, the chapter examines the sorts of interactional competences required from students as they engage in complex forms of participation combining educational and training purposes. By using audio-video data of multiparty interactions involving students, children and mentors during practicums, the study shows that participation issues are mobilized as a practical and situated resource useful to display the participants' hybrid orientations, to highlight situated evaluations and establish mutual understanding all along the vocational training experiences.

In the chapter, we focus on a series of particular cases in which mentors make the decision to intervene, and therefore to guide or shape children's behavior, during a session carried out by the student. Such interventions do not interrupt the student's activity and lead to the emergence of two distinct but not impermeable interactional spaces. This particular and complex participation framework, known as "schisming," is recurrently observed in vocational training interactions and seems to contribute to overcome practical issues within multiparty settings. Our study investigates how schisming constitutes a particular sequential phenomenon where participants reorganize interaction and co-construct a social and cognitive interactional space, thus enabling a shared understanding of the specific training context at stake.

The chapter begins with a brief overview of the literature dedicated to guided learning at work and emphasizes the role of language and communication issues, as well as interactional competences, in connection with vocational and professional education practices. Methodological aspects are then presented, including the context of investigation, the sorts of data collected and the specific interactional phenomenon under scrutiny. In an empirical section, interactional data are presented and analyzed, from the perspective of complex participation formats and the emergence of schisming. In a concluding section, the properties of schisming in interaction are established and connected with vocational learning issues, as well as with more general considerations regarding the transition of young people from school to work.

Guided Learning at Work as Interactional Accomplishment

The Connections Between Guided Learning and Work

The connections between learning and work have been under particular scrutiny in a context where an increasing number of vocational training programs are engaging students not only with theory and school-based practices but also with practicum experiences taking place in workplace settings. Various properties of learning experiences as they emerge in the condition of professional practice have been highlighted in the literature (Billett et al. 2014).

First, recent literature in the field of workplace learning has stressed the importance of guidance in the process of learning in and from practice (Billett 2001a,b; Fuller and Unwin 2003). Workers do not only learn by conducting specific tasks individually; they learn when adequate resources are made available to them and when more experienced workers are able to share their knowledge and skills and to assist them in their practice. Based on a socio-constructionist framework, these studies stress the dual and reciprocal mechanisms through which social resources are provided to learning workers, who have to engage with these resources individually. Only then, through reciprocal participatory configurations, may learning arise from practice, according to Billett (2001a,b).

Other scholars also emphasize various aspects of the complex nature of learning processes as they occur in workplace contexts. One first aspect of complexity lies in the specific activity systems that underlie training experiences at work, and which combine simultaneously work production tasks and learning purposes. As pointed out by specialists in vocational didactics (Mayen 2015), actions, as they are enacted in vocational training situations, are not only "productive," in the sense that they consist in a transformation of the production context. They are also "constructive," in the sense that they are oriented to the subject itself, and may affect and expand the repertoire of resources available to participants. Moreover, learning, as it occurs in the conditions of professional practice, should not be limited to epistemic or cognitive dimensions. It also involves identity transformations and a process of becoming a member of a community of practice, as illustrated by the various empirical examples presented in Lave and Wenger (1991).

Another property of guided learning experiences at work lies in its dynamic and transformative nature. Closely aligned to Lave and Wenger's model of progressive and "legitimate peripheral participation" (Lave and Wenger 1991), the research undertaken by Kunégel on apprenticeship in car mechanics shows for instance that the relations between mentors and apprentices are not stable and fixed (Kunégel 2011). They evolve in time and take the shape of different recurrent and recognizable formats, based on specific interactional patterns. For instance, in the preliminary phase of "familiarization," apprentices work in close collaboration with their mentors, whereas later on, once they have acquired expertise, they engage in more independent and autonomous forms of actions. From there, a constant process of accommodation is required from both mentors and apprentices to adapt the "interactional scenario" to each specific step in the apprentices' learning trajectory.

The Connections Between Guided Learning at Work and Interactional Competences

Because of the prominence of a constructivist and situated approach in the literature described above, much of the discussion on trainee evaluation focuses on interactional competences. Increasingly, research on interaction envisages guided learning processes as being interrelated to communication and interactional issues (Greeno 2011; Koschmann 2011). Research results show that these processes are deeply shaped by the ways participants talk to each other, display a mutual orientation and engage in complex and multimodal coordination processes (Filliettaz 2010; Zemel and Koschmann 2014). Among the contributions of a growing conceptual and empirical literature on *professional interactions*, the following, mainly issuing from *interactional sociolinguistics*, are of particular interest for the study of vocational training.

First, it should be noted that, in an increasing number of professions, language use and interactional skills are not peripheral ingredients of professional practice, but lie at the center of what is expected from workers when performing their work. Such a reinforcement of social requirements related to literacy skills has sometimes been referred to as a "linguistic turn" by sociolinguists (Boutet 2008; Heller 2003; Holmes and Stubbe 2003), who have stressed and described the growing importance of semiotic means in contemporary workplaces. From there, becoming a skilled worker requires not only the mastery of specific knowledge and skills but also an ability to perform speech acts in a certain way, to respond to humor adequately, to engage in small talk in a suitable manner, and to use specific contextualization cues in a way that is relevant to specific professions. In brief, becoming a competent worker is, to some extent, displayed through the acquisition of interactional competences perceived as relevant in the context in which they are enacted.

Language use, communication and interaction also contribute to vocational education, not so much concerning the contents of what has to be learnt, but rather to the means through which learning may occur. In the conditions of work, learning occurs through participation in interaction, which means that interactional properties may serve as resources for learning. This can be observed for instance in specific interaction patterns, different from explicit teaching, that may emerge in the course of work production tasks, and that may display an "instructional component" from the perspective of the participants (Koschmann et al. 2007; Koskela and Palukka 2011). This can also be observed in the ways the participants' specific contributions to interactions may be ratified, ignored or corrected, depending on their local contextual relevance. Mondada (2006) describes for instance how the production of questions by junior surgeons during surgery may be adequate or inadequate depending on the progress of the surgery. She also describes how expert surgeons respond differently to such questions, depending on the relevance of the point in time in which they emerge in the sequential organization of the interaction.

These studies stress the interest of a close description and understanding of the mechanisms of social interaction to grasp how guided learning may arise in the conditions of professional practice. By focusing on interactions as they are accomplished during periods of practicum in the workplace, our project is concerned with the ways students manage the complex participatory configurations involving groups of children and the co-presence of one or more professionals within day-care centers. Previous research on that matter shows that this is a critical outcome in terms of professional development and training (Filliettaz et al. 2014). Our own research is designed as a contribution to this field.

Data and Method

In this section we present the empirical context of our research and introduce the key methodological entries concerning the data collection. We also identify and define a relevant phenomenon that shapes our analytical lens to explore vocational training through guided interactions at work.

Empirical Context

As mentioned before, we focus here on vocational training interactions within early childhood educational settings. Early childhood education, as a paradigmatic illustration of a service encounter, addresses key interactional issues in terms of consumer-delivered services, as well as in terms of professional training (Monette et al. 2013). Educators in the field of early childhood perform professional tasks through constant social interactions, with children, colleagues, parents or other stakeholders involved in the care system. Interestingly very few studies explore effective interactional practices in these settings and even fewer consider vocational training interactions as their prime object of investigation (Rémery and Markaki 2016).

In Switzerland, vocational education programs for early childhood educators are positioned at the tertiary level, and belong to higher professional education. Training lasts three years and takes the form of a combination between teaching sessions provided by higher vocational colleges and practical experiences gained in various child care institutions. Students alternate between periods of courses taught by vocational teachers, and periods of practicum where they develop a practical expertise by working in various child care institutions. Within such work institutions, students are supervised by "mentors." Mentors are certified and experienced professionals, hired as educators within care institutions, and who, in addition to educational tasks toward children, are in charge of providing guidance to students during their practicum. The provision of such guidance may take the form of a joint contribution to educational activities carried out by the student, or a contribution to pedagogical interviews during which more explicit advice may be delivered.

The research project was invited and supported by the Early Childhood Education Service of the Geneva city council, in a context of deep changes in the training curriculum of early childhood educators, and, more generally, a perception of a lack of recognition of the specific and complex skills underlying the profession of early childhood educator.

Data Collection

Our research project consisted of carrying out a longitudinal fieldwork and investigating the trainee's paths at different moments and in different settings, within the three-year vocational training program. Three first-year volunteer students and their respective mentors agreed to participate in our study. In collaboration with different day-care centers in Geneva, we observed and video-recorded 18 hours of the students' practicum training during the first year and 16 hours of their practicums during the last year of their training program.

Audio-video recordings were used as the main empirical observation device, set up in order to record, replay and describe the mentor/trainee's interactional practices at work through detailed transcriptions (Appendix: Note—the transcription conventions used in this study are described at the end of the chapter) and to discuss findings with participants and other researchers (Heath and Luff 2006). Video ethnographic analyses gave us the possibility to focus on micro-sequences as social multi-semiotic accounts of the multimodal organization of interactions between educators, mentors, students and children. Thus, we have compared similar activities and/or similar interactional sequences at different moments of the training program and with different participants (Filliettaz et al. 2014; Markaki and Rémery 2016).

Data Analysis and Identification of a Relevant Recurrent Phenomenon

In order to uncover the practical problems students face when they engage in complex participation configurations, a video analysis of naturally occurring data is of particular interest. But are all these configurations comparable? And if not, how can we proceed to establish relevant distinctions? To answer these questions, we started by identifying interactional events within video data such as arguments, assessments and interventions The present study takes as its starting point the participatory configuration through which students, mentors and children accomplish joint actions. More specifically, we are interested in the particularly observable moments when the mentor intervenes to correct a child's action during a task conducted by the student. Mentors' interventions are considered both as a collaborative accomplishment between the mentor, the student and the children, and as an interactional device through which the mentor impacts and questions in a more or less straightforward manner the student's ongoing activity. Within such configurations, we look at the ways the student aligns or not with these interventions, and more generally, how the student, together with the mentor, project, shape and reorganize their activity with the group of children following these interventions.

Fine-grained transcripts of talk and other non-verbal features, such as intonation, gestures, gazes and body orientation, were produced and aligned to video recordings of the mentors' intervention sequences. This video analysis-transcription combination enabled the access to both the situated ways in which the participants interact and their frequency (Psathas and Anderson 1990; Schegloff 1993; Hepburn and Bolden 2013).

To hold sequential ingredients of such *student's orientation to mentor's interventions* constant in our analysis, we established a collection of occurrences (Schegloff 1993; Mondada 2013) where the mentor's intervention consists in a direct address to a child or a group of children different from those addressed by the student. Within this collection, another narrower collection of sequences was defined, including all situations where parallel conversations emerged.

Parallel Conversations or Schisming

In our data a great number of situations emerge where interventions initiated by mentors result in parallel conversations and produce what has been referred to as *schisming* (Egbert 1993, 1997; Traverso 2012). Schisming can be defined as a specific interactional pattern emerging within multiparty settings, when four or more participants (professionals and children) build together complex interactional participatory configurations with two or more co-occurrent conversations (Filliettaz 2014; Filliettaz et al. 2014).

The interactional phenomenon of parallel conversations has already been described in the literature as something specific to multiparty conversations revealing a practical way for participants to orient toward a momentary reorganization of the topical development of their talk without interrupting the main topic of discussion (Egbert 1993, 1997; Grosjean 2001; Traverso 2004). These studies also mention how these parallel conversations influence each other in such a way that the interactional boundary between them should be considered as porous. Indeed, Egbert (1997) shows how participants to parallel conversations are sensitive to the ways discussions evolve next to one another. This fundamentally interactive character of parallel conversations reveals intricate coordination processes between interactants and the incorporation of a mutual understanding of what is happening.

In relation to vocational training settings, this observation raises important questions regarding the students' situated learning experience. Following Dewey's (1938) and Lindeman's (1926) perspectives, any kind of experience in a more or less formal educational setting may act as a learning opportunity. But how can the description of specific interactional practices such as *schisming* inform us about the students' learning experiences?

Filliettaz and others have shown how interactional configurations give different participation opportunities to students at work and how the structure of subsequent participation frameworks is sensitive to mentors' and students' situated interpretative engagement within vocational training interactions (Filliettaz 2011; Filliettaz et al. 2014; Filliettaz and Rémery 2015; Rémery and Markaki 2016; Markaki and Rémery 2016). According to these research results, we consider parallel conversations as specific participation formats that both structure and reveal the ways the participants organize the ongoing monitoring of concurrent interactional productions while at the same time they interpret and negotiate the situated meaning of the unfolding interaction.

In other words, on the one hand, we highlight dynamic *interactional configurations* between participants (educators, students and children) through fine-grained descriptions of the ways the participants mobilize and shape frameworks within interactions in terms of sequential, spatial and temporal arrangements (Goffman 1981; Filliettaz et al. 2014). On the other hand, and mainly following Sacks's (1974, 1992) and Goodwin's work on members' local interpretation work (1981, 1986, 1995), we observe that these *interactional configurations* provide students with situated *interpretative templates*, that is frameworks for the interpretation of the unfolding activity (Goodwin 1984), through various syntactic, intonational and other pragmatic resources, which, as we will show in our data, the professionals use to induce, sustain and complete parallel conversations.

Our analysis depicts the emergence of two parallel conversations or the co-occurrence of two conversations and the reconfiguration of the participation framework following the mentors' interventions. These conversations are held simultaneously by the student and the mentor with two different children or groups of children. To investigate the conditions in which these parallel conversations or *schisming* emerge (Sacks et al. 1974; Egbert 1997), we look into the sequential organization around these conversations and more particularly into: (a) the *schism-inducing procedures*, namely the moment when a conversation begins to split up into two parts, (b) the specific ways parallel conversations are maintained and mutually adjusted, and finally, (c) the moment when the two parallel talks merge back into a single conversation again. The sequential organization of schisming raises important analytical questions about the interactional organization of the unfolding activity. These questions guided our analysis and are summarized in Fig. 4.1.

In other words, we propose to examine students' guided learning experiences in close connection with the ways mentors participate and intervene in students' educational activities. We will show that these interventions

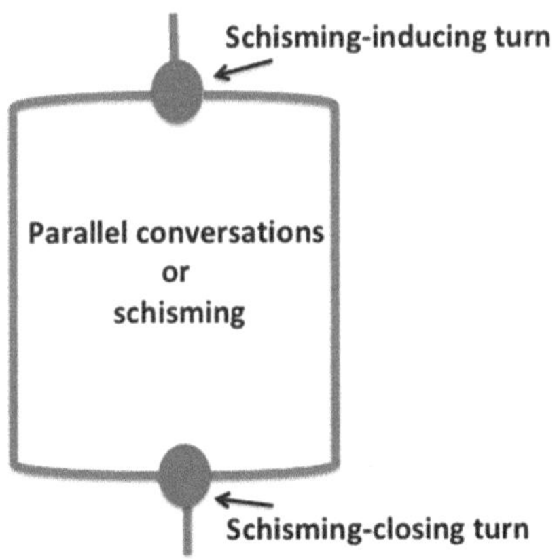

Fig. 4.1 Key issues on schisming within vocational training (see also Egbert 1997)

operate as a template that students may use to organize their own activity and make sense of the mentors' contributions to the interaction.

Analysis

In what follows, we illustrate various aspects of the unfolding of parallel conversations in vocational training interactions by referring to excerpts of data available in our collection. We will consider the sequential outline of the schisming organization presented in Fig. 4.1, which is relevant to the participants from direct observation: first the *schisming-inducing procedures*, then the accomplishment and maintenance of two *parallel interactional sequences*, and finally the *closure of schisming* and the return to a single conversation.

The Activity Before the Emergence of Schisming

In excerpt (1a) below, the student leads a modified version of the card game called "Memory Game," with a group of six children aged below two She shows a card to the participants, who, in turn, are expected to recognize the drawing depicted on the card and then to identify the matching card located on a table through a pointing gesture. Identification of the drawing followed by pointing shows that the child has identified the second part of the pair. Recognition, identification and pointing constitute therefore three separate and successive actions children are expected to perform when playing the game. The consecutive accomplishment of these three actions is not spontaneous and arbitrary; it is shaped by the rules of the game and has to be learned by the children as such. These actions are thus invited by distinct requests performed by the student. In excerpt (1a), we focus on the identification and pointing actions of Natalia's turn to play: Natalia has just recognized the drawing on the card ("a cup of coffee") and the student asks her to find (identify and show) the card with the same drawing on the table. Screenshots used in our excerpts show interactional key moments, indicating the participants' names/functions (the participants' names have been made anonymous by using pseudonyms). Screenshots have been aligned to the transcriptions with a specific sign (see transcription conventions) showing their position within the turn at talk (Table 4.1).

In this first turn (see l. 1–3), the student fixes her gaze toward Natalia and performs a request in two parts to identify the card on the table ("where is the cup of coffee"—*she looks at Natalia*, followed by "here"—*she points to and looks toward the cards on the table*).

In educational settings, requests project the kind of knowledge and correlated action(s) that educators expect children will acquire and be able to mobilize later when they are alone in more or less similar contexts (Gardner and Forrester 2009; Filliettaz 2011). From an interactional perspective, this situated knowledge could be described as a series of embedded and observable actions. Thus, the targeted knowledge at stake through the student's request could be illustrated here by the child's capacity to take the floor both verbally or non-verbally, in order to respond to the request, to point to the right card but also to align to a verbal and/or non-verbal other-selection, to exhibit a good understanding of the rules of the game and so on.

1 2	STU: nat	*+hEh h .h (0.4) elle est où la ***+hEh h .h (0.4) where is the** **looks at Natalia------------->* +looks at the student-------->* tasse de café* **cup of coffee*** ----------->*	
3		#*ic[i **#*he[re** **points and looks towards cards on table-->* **#fig4.2**	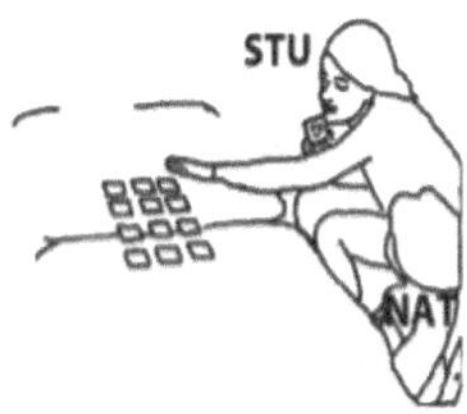 #fig4.2

Table 4.1 Ex. (1a)

Interestingly, Natalia does not orient her gaze toward the table and still fixes her gaze at the student at the end of the first part of her request (see l. 1–2 and fig. 4.2). The extension of this first request and the production of a deictic ("here," see l. 3) both display the student's monitoring of Natalia's focused attention and index the wrong direction of her gaze. The deictic is accompanied by a circular gesture over the cards, marking out the position of the cards on the table, as well as by the student's shifted visual gaze toward them (see l. 3).

By doing so, the student embodies a possible way for Natalia to initiate her answer: While looking at the cards, she points toward the "cup of coffee" card on the table. In other words, she initiates a self-repair of the requested action, and she does so by demonstrating a possible way to repair, in other words, by imitating a large part of the action to accomplish, which is a rather frequent case in adult-preschool children interactions (Forrester 2008; Gardner and Forrester 2009).

Schisming Induction

The mentor is present during the card game and mainly endorses a bystander role. But during Natalia's turn to play, she momentarily shifts her participation status by inviting more explicitly Natalia to look at the cards on the table (l. 4). The placement of the mentor's turn designs her intervention as a co-animation rather than a competition regarding the student's activity. The mentor orients to the pragmatic construction of the student's request: her question ("where is the cup of coffee"), followed by the deictic word ("here"). She intervenes only on the deictic part of this request, with the terminal overlapping reformulation ("you look here"). This *terminal overlap* (Jefferson 1984) is not treated by the student and the children as problematic (Table 4.2).

The mentor reformulates the deictic word "here" by a new request ("look here") and directly selects Natalia as an addressed recipient through the personal pronoun "you." She also indicates immediately after the pronoun the expected type of action to be performed ("look"), and the point in space where the action should take place ("here"). Interestingly, she points toward the cards on the table.

3	STU: ic[i he[re	
4	MEN: [#$°tu regardes £ici/° [#$°look £here/° men £points towards cards>	
5	LOA: [#$elle est [là:/ [#$it's [there:/ loa $points towards the card #fig4.3	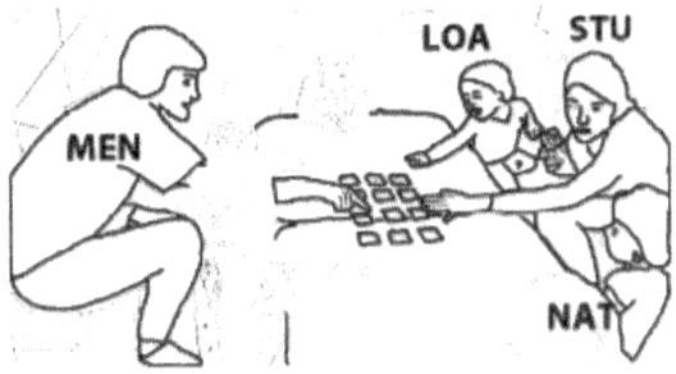 #fig4.3

Table 4.2 Ex. (1b)

On the one hand, she aligns and contributes to the student's effort to direct Natalia's attention on the cards located on the table. On the other hand, by doing this in overlap of the student's request, she makes available a slightly different manner to perform a repair initiation. Her action orients to Natalia's rather passive posture and projects an embodied answer as a relevant next turn. The direct request allows the mentor to show the need to be more explicit with Natalia and to focus repair on the action part of the answer rather than on its speaking part.

At the same time, Loane, another child taking part in the "Memory" card game and who is observing the interaction between the student and Natalia, gazes at the student's right hand in motion, self-selects once the student's hand points toward the cards on the table, and gives the answer by talking ("it's there:/") and pointing to the card depicting the "cup of coffee" (see l. 5 and Fig. 4.3).

Interestingly, both the student and the mentor do not react ostensibly to Loane's answer. Although Loane started to point to the card of the cup of coffee before the mentor's pointing, the mentor neither interrupts her turn nor abandons her pointing gesture. Her posture projects an intent to continue the unfolding answer-question sequence with Natalia.

The student's subsequent orientation implements this preference for progressivity initiated by the mentor (see l. 4–6; Liddicoat 2007): Her focus quickly switches from Natalia to the mentor and then again to Natalia (l. 6) before aligning to the mentor's projected action consisting in reformulating repair in more explicit terms (see l. 6 and l. 9) (Table 4.3).

While the student is suggesting to Natalia to stand up, Natalia repeats Loane's answer and points toward the card on the table (l. 7). Just after Natalia's repetition, the mentor addresses Loane directly and reacts to her interrupting answer by producing a *schisming-inducing turn* (SIT) ("Loane do you remember what we said," see l. 8), implementing the first moments of the parallel conversation per se. She designs a question that elicits a particular answer from Loane while the student continues to interact with Natalia. Egbert defines *SIT* as:

> inducing a second conversation rather than as a contribution to the already ongoing conversation … sequentially, the speaker of the SIT breaks away from the ongoing conversation by initiating a new sequence type. With respect to its topical connection or action type, the SIT also breaks away from the preceding talk in that it introduces a shift in topic or action. (Egbert 1997, 3)

In our collection of parallel conversations, SITs are recurrently formatted as being "non-interrupting implicatives," namely as new action types subordinated to the student's activity.

The mentor's question "Loane do you remember what we said" (l. 8) breaks the contiguity between actions and introduces a shift in activity.

5	LOA: [elle est [là:/ **[it's [there:/**	
6	STU: *(.)[tu* peux [te £ lever ***(.)[you* can [£ stand up** stu *1.Ment*looks at Natalia---->> men -points towards cards£	
7	NAT: [+elle est là **[+it's there** nat +points towards the card	
8	MEN:[Loane tu te souviens ce qu'on a **[Loane you remember what we said/**	STA: [si tu veux tu peux te lever **[if you want you can stand up**
9	dit/	

Table 4.3 Ex. (1c)

With that question, the next action, which is not related to the preceding task of identifying the correct card, becomes relevant and offers Loane an opportunity to report on the principles of turn-taking in games that the group has discussed earlier.

Interestingly the mentor's intervention does not interrupt the student's activity. In the interaction the question occupies a slot following the syntactic completion point of the "where is the cup of coffee"/"Natalia's answer" sequence (l. 7). At the same time, it introduces a new action in overlap with the ongoing activity. The mentor's intervention pattern, that is, "enter the floor at a sentential completion point" and "launch a new parallel action with a different recipient identified by his/her name," seems to increase the clarity of her projected intervention, launches the schisming and facilitates the coordination between the two professionals in order to manage the maintaining of parallel activities.

In what follows, we provide a second excerpt from our collection of the emergence of parallel conversations illustrating how gaze, gestures and body orientations seem to be central and how they allow a better understanding of the conditions in which schisming emerges in interaction (Markaki and Filliettaz 2015; Goodwin 2000). The following interaction took place with a different mentoring dyad. In this excerpt, non-verbal resources (head nods and gazes) are used by the participants to accomplish the schisming induction. The incipient of the SIT is thus displayed before the participants start to speak (Jefferson 1984).

In excerpt (2) transcribed below, the student (Beatrix) and the mentor are sitting side by side looking at the group of children (fig. 4.4). The activity consists in distributing the children into two groups: one that will do a painting activity with the student and one that will go to the playground with another educator. In the excerpt, the student asks the child Celia whether she wants to come with her (l. 1), before mentioning the painting activity (l. 2) (Table 4.4).

During the student's invitation to Celia ("so Celia do you wanna come/"), Celia starts to move toward the dyad composed of the mentor and the student (see l. 1) and performs a non-verbal agreement to the student's request. Following Celia's embodying agreement, the student shifts her gaze, and thus her focus of attention, from Celia to the group of children, displaying her orientation to the relevance of identifying the

1	STU	#*alors celia/]>> $ t- ça t' d- << tu veux venir/%$ **#*so celia/]>> $ t- do y' d- << you wanna come/%$**	
	stu	**looks at Celia-------------------------------- -%1. group of children->*	
	cel	*$moves forward-------------------$nods---------------->*	
		 *#fig4.4*	
2			STU %faire$de la peinture%xxx% **%do $ to do painting %xxx%**
	cel	*-----$moves towards the mentor---->*	*stu -1. group of children---*
	men	*%1.Cel,nods--%*	*----------------------------*
3	MEN	alors celia% tu t'asseois près de beatrix **so celia % seat yourself near beatrix** *%points toward the student--->*	*----------------------------> *

Table 4.4 Ex. (2)

next child to call for the painting activity (l. 1). By shifting her gaze, the student does not appear to perceive the fact that Celia has stopped her move and performed a head nod. Head nods produced at this point in time, after an embodied agreement marker, may be treated as an interactional trouble, revealing a problematic understanding of the request. The mentor's head nod (l. 2), combined with a direct request ("seat yourself near Beatrix," l. 3), reveals the trouble and resolves it by directing the child to the place where she should wait while the student is simultaneously pursuing her activity of calling the next child.

Interestingly the discursive accomplishment of the SIT addressed to Celia is produced with no overlap here. However, in terms of actions, the mentor engages in a focus of attention that is designed to be different from the second complementary part of the student's question ("to do painting"). By shifting her focus on Celia, the mentor defers a repair sequence regarding Celia's trajectory. And by avoiding an overlap, she initiates an action that is not competing with the student's activity and induces the possibility of maintaining parallel conversations (mentor/Celia; student/next child).

To sum up on that short excerpt, we identify the same kind of construction as before: The mentor "enters the floor at a sentential completion point" and "launches a new parallel action with a different participant than the one who the student is taking care of, identified by his/her name."

Schisming Maintenance

Schisming maintenance has very interesting interactional implications for professionals. Indeed, it allows them to accomplish with different participants simultaneous activities, which, otherwise, would conflict with one another. From that perspective, schisming provides a collaborative interactional space where participants can (re)organize actions within multiparty settings. In terms of competencies, schisming maintenance constitutes a step forward, away from the mentor's close supervision, in the student's growing capacity for independent practice within practicum.

In order to study the features of the schisming sequence per se, and how it is maintained, we return to excerpt (1) and the "Memory" card game. At this stage, two parallel conversations unfold between two dyads: The mentor interacts with Loane while the student remains oriented to Natalia (Table 4.5).

As already mentioned before, the mentor modifies the participation framework by engaging in a parallel conversation while the student is engaged in the pursuit of the game with Natalia (l. 8). In doing so, she orients to the social rule of the game, requiring that the participants have to play in turn and remain silent while other participants have the right to play (see l. 8–12). In other words, the mentor changes the focus of interaction, from playing the game recalling the rules, so that Loane can align with such rules and let Natalia play. The student, in turn, explains to Natalia the sequence of actions she may take after having identified the card. She also encourages her to stand up by slightly pushing her in the back (see l. 8–12 and fig. 4.5b).

Remarkably, the mentor and the student simultaneously shape the overall overlapped first part of two different sequences: The mentor performs a new question on the topic of the rules (l. 8); the student performs

	 #fig4.5a	 #fig4.5b
8	MEN: #Loane tu te souviens ce qu'on a **#Loane you remember what we** **#fig4.5a**	STU: #si tu veux tu peux te lever **# if you want you can stand up** **#fig4.5b**
9	dit/ on joue seulement quand **said/ one just plays when**	si tu veux. et tu peux **if you want. and you can**
10	c'est son tour **it's one's turn**	PREndre la carte\ **TAKe the card**
11	sinon on fait shu::t (.) **otherwise one does shu::sh (.)**	
12	d'accord/ **okay/**	
13	PAO: elle est là **it's there**	
14	STU: voi:[la\ (.) bravo Natalia **he:[:re it is\ (.) congratulations Natalia**	

Table 4.5 Ex. (1d)

a request that pursues her activity with Natalia (l. 9). They do so in a similar manner, based on the conversational preference principles to both explicitly minimize the correcting of the other's action and use direct and not mitigated forms of talk-in-interaction production (Heritage and Pomerantz 2012).

It should also be noted that there is an interdependence between the two parallel interactions: While the two professionals are physically engaged in interactions with different children, their verbal exchanges are both produced in low voice and adjust to the other conversation.

The Closure of Schisming

In our main example (see l. 8–12), it is the mentor who not only initiates the SIT but also makes a move toward the closure of the parallel conversation. This closing procedure is performed by producing a minimal form of post-expansion after the request was granted ("okay," l. 12) and before the student's activity is coming to an end (l. 14). Minimal post-expansion is frequently mobilized in talk-in-interaction as a means to convey the appreciation that the response to the requested action was appropriate (Schegloff 2007).

Interestingly, when another child taking part in the card game (Paolo) self-selects himself and produces the answer to the student's question in line 13 ("it's there"), after Natalia's turn, his turn is not corrected, neither by the student nor by the mentor. This may be due to the fact that Paolo's non-solicited response takes place after, and not before, the designated player's turn. This indicates that professionals seem to orient to the consequences of children's actions as more or less important depending on the sequential organization of the unfolding activity (for more information about the conditional relevance linking an initiating action and its response see Schegloff and Sacks 1973).

Discussion and Conclusion

To sum up, participants mobilize parallel conversations in educational settings to manage multiple children at the same time. In the data, schisming is not problematic since the mentors and students are able to ensure sufficient interactional density with their interlocutors (mutual focus of attention, sequential contiguity, activity's progressivity, etc.) while at the same time they avoid a competitive overlap or the activity's interruption, mainly by monitoring and adjusting the parallel conversations (turn-taking, voice volume, complementarity of actions, etc.).

From the empirical analysis of our collection (of which we have detailed here two occurrences), it appears that schisming, or the emergence of parallel conversations, both offer participation opportunities and constrain participants. Indeed, our detailed analysis presented above illustrates the fact that the mentor provides the student with crucial resources that she uses to adjust and maintain the implementation of a parallel conversation. The mentor provides interpretative templates to the student, by inducing schisming with no overlap, or launching a new action designed as a repair to an unsolicited turn taken by a participant to the game.

Reciprocally, the student needs to understand, adapt and thereby collaborate in the realization of an elaborated participation configuration within multiparty settings. In that particular example, the student seems to succeed in holding her position within such a complex participation framework: She does not turn her activity into a competitive one and does not interrupt herself nor changes the key features of her talk (e.g., intensity and turn design). In other words, she mobilizes specific interactional competences to keep her engagement constant toward the children while the mentor performs distinct and complementary contributions to the ongoing educational activity.

These results are not only relevant from the perspective of the description of participation in multiparty settings. They also inform about the institutional requirements and mechanisms of legitimation in and through interaction itself. The excerpts of data presented here illustrate how the institutional context of early childhood education produces specific expectations and constraints regarding the rules of turn-taking in educational settings with preschool children. Within settings such as a card game, only designated players have the right to take their turn, whereas other participants must take an observer's position. These rules are in no way transparent and self-evident for children. They have to be noticed and learned by them and are part of the educational purposes underlying the activity. As such, these rules are both enacted in interaction and brought to the attention of children.

Learning to become an educator is not external to such aspects of interactional competence. As shown in our example, leading an educational activity requires an ability to perform the rules in a way that is accessible to the targeted audience. It requires from educators that they make these rules salient. In our example, the student is not the only participant entitled to prompt children to legitimate forms of participation. As shown in the analysis, the mentor assists her in such learning in many different ways. She self-selects herself as a legitimate speaker when children encounter difficulties in taking their turn. She prompts the student to ask questions in specific ways or to elicit specific actions from participants. She reformulates explicit rules while the student moves to the next step of the game.

From there, it appears that the induction, maintenance and closing of schisming can be seen as a powerful resource not only for educating children in multiparty configurations but also for training newcomers in the profession of early childhood educator. It is precisely in and through the accomplishment of parallel conversations that the mentor establishes the local contextual conditions that make it possible for the student to carry out her activity. And it is also through such parallel conversations that resources are made available to the student to help her in her activity. Here is a good example, we believe, of the hidden and subtle ways "transmission" may occur in interaction, beyond explicit content-knowledge production (Filliettaz and Rémery 2015).

To conclude, what did we learn here about the issue of transitions from school to work and the role of interactional competences and institutional requirements faced by young people? First, what is remarkable here is the high level of complexity underlying vocational training interactions. When learning a new profession in the conditions of practice, newcomers in the field of early childhood education encounter distinct and specific participation configurations. As stressed by our analysis, they take part in interactions gathering a large number of participants, endorsing numerous and distinct action roles. Moreover, they engage in situations, which are shaped not only by educational purposes (i.e., bringing children to learn interaction rules) but also by training objectives (i.e., learning how to teach interaction rules). And finally, they have to adapt to constant changes in the ways participation evolves within such dynamic environments.

Another interesting result of our data and analysis relates to the positions young people may hold with respect to institutional demands and legitimation mechanisms in social interactions. Prior to work and vocational training experiences, young people may predominantly hold the position of "targets" of specific institutional requirements. Their contributions to interactions are often categorized as legitimate or not, by teachers, parents or representatives of specific institutions. What is remarkable in the context of the vocational training of early childhood educators is that students are not only placed in the position of being taught, trained, guided or educated. When interacting with children, they are themselves producing and reproducing the rules belonging to the institution and also become "sources" of legitimation processes. It is precisely the experience of becoming a source of legitimation in interaction that may constitute a key ingredient of vocational training practices, and that could be seen as an important milestone in the journey from school to work. Describing the conditions in which parallel conversations emerge in vocational training interactions only unveils a limited portion of such mechanisms. But we believe it illustrates in a promising way how guided learning experiences may be fruitfully investigated through the lens of a detailed analysis of social interactions.

Appendix: Transcription Conventions

Talk and multimodal details have been transcribed according to the following conventions. See Jefferson (2004) and Mondada (2014).

[ ]	overlap (onset & end)
(.)	micro-pause (< 0.2 seconds)
(2.0)	pause in seconds
/ \	rising/ and falling\ intonation
(she)	uncertain transcription
the:	sound stretch
xxx	incomprehensible segment
=	latching
°here°	low volume
PRE	increased volume
ter-	cut-off
>> <<	faster tempo
* *	descriptions of embodied actions (gestures, gazes, etc.) are delimited between two identical symbols (one symbol per participant): ++,$$,££,%%,...
- -->	movement or gaze continuing in the following lines
#	indicates the exact point within a turn at talk where a screen shot (figures) has been taken

References

Billett, S. (2001a). *Learning in the workplace: Strategies for effective practice*. Crows Nest: Allen and Unwin.

Billett, S. (2001b). Learning through work: Workplace affordances and individual engagement. *Journal of Workplace Learning, 13*(5), 209–214.

Billett, S., Gruber, H., & Harteis, C. (Eds.). (2014). *International handbook of research in professional and practice-based learning*. Dordrecht: Springer.

Boutet, J. (2008). *La vie verbale au travail: des manufactures aux centres d'appels*. Toulouse: Editions Octarès.

de Saint-Georges, I., & Filliettaz, L. (2008). Situated trajectories of learning in vocational training interactions. *European Journal of Psychology of Education, 23*(2), 213–233.

Dewey, J. (1938). *Expérience et éducation*. Paris: Armand Colin.

Egbert, M. 1993. *Schisming: The transformation from a single conversation to multiple conversations*. PhD SDUSDU, Det Humanistiske Fakultet Faculty of Humanities, Institut for Design og Kommunikation Department of Design and Communikation.

Egbert, M. (1997). Schisming: The collaborative transformation from a single conversation to multiple conversations. *Research on Language and Social Interaction, 30*(1), 1–51.

Filliettaz, L. (2010). Guidance as an interactional accomplishment: Practice-based learning within the Swiss VET system. In S. Billett (Ed.), *Learning through practice: Models, traditions, orientations and approaches* (pp. 156–179). London: Springer.

Filliettaz, L. (2011). Asking questions ... getting answers: A sociopragmatic approach to vocational training interaction. *Pragmatics and Society, 2*(2), 234–259.

Filliettaz, L. (2013). Affording learning environments in workplace contexts: An interactional and multimodal perspective. *International Journal of Lifelong Education, 32*(1), 107–122.

Filliettaz, L. (2014). Learning through interactional participatory configurations: Contributions from video analysis. In A. Rausch, Ch. Harteis, & J. Seifried (Eds.), *Discourses on professional learning* (pp. 317–339). Springer Netherlands.

Filliettaz, L., & Rémery, V. (2015). Transmettre le travail par les mises en forme langagières de l'activité. In R. Wittorski (Ed.), *Comprendre la transmission du travail* (pp. 47–81). Nîmes: Editions Champ Social.

Filliettaz, L., Rémery, V., & Trébert, D. N. P. (2014). Relation tutorale et configurations de participation à l'interaction: analyse de l'accompagnement des stagiaires dans le champ de la petite enfance. *Activités, 11*(1), 22–46.
Forrester, M. A. (2008). The emergence of self-repair: A case study of one child during the early preschool years. *Research on Language and Social Interaction, 41*(1), 99–128.
Fuller, A., & Unwin, L. (2003). Learning as apprentices in the contemporary UK workplace: Creating and managing expansive and restrictive participation. *Journal of Education and Work, 16*(4), 407–426.
Gardner, H., & Forrester, M. (Eds.). (2009). *Analysing interactions in childhood: Insights from conversation analysis*. Chichester: Wiley-Blackwell.
Goffman, E. (1981). *Forms of talk*. Philadelphia, PA: University of Pennsylvania Press.
Goodwin, C. (1981). *Conversational organization: Interaction between speakers and hearers*. New York: Academic Press.
Goodwin, C. (1984). Notes on story structure and the organization of participation. In M. Atkinson & J. Heritage (Eds.), *Structures of social action* (pp. 225–246). Cambridge: Cambridge University Press.
Goodwin, C. (1986). Audience diversity, participation and interpretation. *Text, 6*(3), 283–316.
Goodwin, C. (1995). Seeing in depth. *Social Studies of Science, 25*(2), 237–274.
Goodwin, C. (2000). Action and embodiment within situated human interaction. *Journal of Pragmatics, 32*(10), 1489–1522.
Greeno, J. G. (2011). A situative perspective on cognition and learning in interaction. In T. Koschmann (Ed.), *Theories of learning and studies of instruction* (pp. 41–72). New York: Springer.
Grosjean, M. (2001). De la parole plurielle au polylogue effectif. Les relèves inter-équipes à l'hôpital. *Bulletin vals-asla, 74*, 57–81.
Heath, C., & Luff, P. (2006). Video analysis and organisational practice. In H. Knoblauch, S. Bernt, J. Raab, & H.-G. Soeffner (Eds.), *Video-analysis. Methodology and methods*. London: Peter Lang.
Heller, M. (2003). Globalization, the new economy and the commodification of language. *Journal of Sociolinguistics, 7*(4), 473–492.
Hepburn, A., & Bolden, G. B. (2013). The conversation analytic approach to transcription. In J. Sidnell & T. Stivers (Eds.), *The handbook of conversation analysis* (pp. 57–76). Boston: Wiley-Blackwell.
Heritage, J., & Pomerantz, A. (2012). Preference. In J. Sidnell & T. Stivers (Eds.), *The handbook of conversation analysis* (pp. 210–228). Boston: Wiley-Blackwell.

Holmes, J., & Stubbe, M. (2003). *Power and politeness in the workplace*. London: Longman.
Jefferson, G. (1984). Notes on some orderlinesses of overlap onset. In V. D' Urso & P. Leonardi (Eds.), *Discourse analysis and natural rhetoric* (pp. 11–38). Padua: Cleup Editore.
Jefferson, G. (2004). Glossary of transcript symbols with an Introduction. In G. H. Lerner (Ed.), *Conversation analysis: Studies from the first generation* (pp. 13–23). Philadelphia: John Benjamins.
Koschmann, T. (Ed.). (2011). *Theories of learning and studies of instructional practice*. New York: Springer.
Koschmann, T., LeBaron, C., Goodwin, C., Zemel, A., & Dunnington, G. (2007). Formulating the triangle of doom. *Gesture, 7*(1), 97–118.
Koskela, I., & Palukka, H. (2011). Trainer interventions as instructional strategies in air traffic control training. *Journal of Workplace Learning, 23*(5), 293–314.
Kunégel, P. (2011). *Les maîtres d'apprentissage. Analyse des pratiques tutorales en situation de travail*. Paris: L'Harmattan.
Lave, J., & Wenger, E. (1991). *Situated learning: Legitimate peripheral participation*. Cambridge: Cambridge University Press.
Liddicoat, A. J. (Ed.). (2007). Adjacency pairs and preference organization. In A. J. Liddicoat (Ed.), *An introduction to conversation analysis* (pp. 105–124). London: Continuum.
Lindeman, E. (1926). *The meaning of adult education*. New York: New Republic.
Losa, S., Duc, B., & Filliettaz, L. (2014). Success, well-being and social recognition: An interactional perspective. In M. M. Bergman (Ed.), *Success and well-being in education and employment* (pp. 69–98). Dordrecht: Springer.
Markaki, V., & Filliettaz, L. (2015). Les schismes dans les activités tutorales: une approche multimodale. In *Communication. Séminaire IC-YOU*, Neuchâtel, May 6, 2015.
Markaki, V., & Rémery, V. (2016). Documenter l'activité tutorale en situation de travail: Pour une approche du « travail en acte ». In *Sociologie et sociétés, numéro thématique sur "Le travail au prisme de l'activité"*, coordonné par H. Eckert & M. Vultur, XLVIII, No. 1, 143–167.
Mayen, P. (2015). Vocational didactics: Work, learning, and conceptualization. In L. Filliettaz & S. Billett (Eds.), *Francophone perspectives of learning through work: Traditions, conceptions and practices* (pp. 201–219). Dordrecht: Springer.
Mondada, L. (2006). La compétence comme dimension située et contingente, localement évaluée par les participants. *Swiss Journal of Applied Linguistics, 84*, 83–119.

Mondada, L. (2013). The conversation analytic approach to data collection. In J. Sidnell & T. Stivers (Eds.), *The handbook of conversation analysis* (pp. 32–56). Boston: Wiley-Blackwell.

Mondada, L. (2014). Conventions for multimodal transcriptions. Retrieved February 2, 2016, from http://mainly.sciencesconf.org/conference/mainly/pages/Mondada2013_conv_multimodality_copie.pdf

Monette, D., Sullivan, T., & DeJong, C. (2013). *Applied social research: A tool for the human services*. Belmont: Cengage Learning.

Psathas, G., & Anderson, T. (1990). The "practices" of transcription in conversation analysis. *Semiotica, 78*(1–2), 75–100.

Rémery, V., & Markaki, V. (2016). Travailler et former: l'activité hybride des tuteurs. In *Education Permanente, « Le tutorat aujourd'hui »*, coordonné par S. Mahlaoui & A.-L. Ulmann, No. 206, 47–59.

Sacks, H. (1974). An analysis of the course of a joke's telling in conversation. In R. Bauman & J. F. Sherzer (Eds.), *Explorations in the ethnography of speaking* (pp. 337–353). Cambridge, UK: Cambridge University Press.

Sacks, H. (1992). Lectures on conversation. In G. Jefferson (Ed.), *Introductions by Emanuel A. Schegloff* (Vol. 2). Oxford: Blackwell.

Sacks, H., Schegloff, E. A., & Jefferson, G. (1974). A simplest systematics for the organization of turn-taking for conversation. *Language, 50*(4), 696–735.

Schegloff, E. A. (1993). Reflections on quantification in the study of conversation. *Research on Language and Social Interaction, 26*(1), 99–128.

Schegloff, E. A. (2007). *Sequence organization in interaction: A primer in conversation analysis* (Vol. 1). Cambridge, UK: Cambridge University Press.

Schegloff, E. A., & Sacks, H. (1973). Opening up closings. *Semiotica, 8*(4), 289–327.

Schoon, I., & Silbereisen, R. K. (Eds.). (2009). *Transitions from school to work: Globalization, individualization, and patterns of diversity*. Cambridge, UK: Cambridge University Press.

Traverso, V. (2004). Interlocutive "crowding" and "splitting" in polylogues: The case of a meeting of researchers. *Journal of Pragmatics, 36*(1), 53–74.

Traverso, V. (2012). Ad hoc-interpreting in multilingual work meetings. In C. Baraldi & L. Gavioli (Eds.), *Coordinating participation in dialogue interpreting* (pp. 149–176). Amsterdam: John Benjamins.

Zemel, A., & Koschmann, T. (2014). "Put your fingers right in here": Learnability and instructed experience. *Discourse Studies, 16*, 163–183.

5

Taking the Initiative in Job Interviews: Extended Responses to Questions and Storytelling

Adrian Bangerter and Paloma Gosteli-Corvalan

Social Interaction in Job Interviews

Job interviews are institutionalized social interactions between recruiters and candidates, with the official goal of determining the fit between a candidate and a job. Interaction in job interviews typically consists of recruiters asking candidates questions (and, in some parts of the interview, of candidates asking recruiters questions). Candidates' answers are used to assess their suitability for a particular job. The job interview thus differs from other institutional interactions described in this book because of its explicitly evaluative character (Button 1987). It is one of the most widely used personnel selection methods (Ryan et al. 1999) and much is known about its psychometric properties (Melchers et al. 2015), that is, how well it can measure candidates' relevant personal characteristics. This wealth of knowledge contrasts with the paucity of research on the actual conduct

A. Bangerter (✉) • P. Gosteli-Corvalan
University of Neuchâtel, Neuchâtel, Switzerland

S. Pekarek Doehler et al. (eds.), *Interactional Competences in Institutional Settings*, DOI 10.1007/978-3-319-46867-9_5

of social interaction in job interviews (but see Ragan and Hopper 1981; Komter 1991; Kerekes 2007). In other words, we know little about how candidates are expected to behave, or, more specifically, about what kinds of interactional behavior are warranted and how candidates and recruiters conduct themselves in this respect. This is a significant issue—understanding these phenomena better would have both theoretical implications for social interaction in institutional settings and practical implications for both candidates and recruiters. Candidates could gain from better knowledge about how to talk (what to say, for how long), what kind of questions they are allowed (or expected) to ask and so on. Recruiters could gain from understanding how the interview conversation contributes to creating a basis for their evaluation of the candidate, and how their impressions of the candidate may partly emerge from the collaborative give-and-take of interview conversation, including their own actions.

In this chapter, we propose that one major expectation of candidates in job interviews is that they "take the initiative." That is, candidates are expected to take an active role in the interview conversation, by responding proactively to questions and creating or seizing opportunities to present themselves favorably. We explore this expectation by first describing scientific research in work and organizational psychology on impression management in job interviews as well as the popular literature giving advice to job candidates. Both bodies of literature diffuse similar normative expectations about how candidates should "take the initiative" in interview conversations to present a positive image of themselves.

The question arises, however, as to whether candidates are able and willing to "take the initiative," especially for inexperienced job candidates, for example, young people who are confronted with an interview for an apprenticeship position or a first job. Such candidates have little or no direct experience with job interviews. Moreover, their prior interactions with institutional representatives are largely confined to school settings, where their main experience of participating in question-answering activities derives from the classroom. Importantly, the organization of classroom question-answering activities is highly scripted (Mehan 1979), with initiative-taking incumbent on the teacher (Cazden and Beck 2003; Degoumois et al. this volume; but see Petitjean 2013). In this chapter, we thus examine varying extents to which young candidates do or do not "take the initiative" for an extended turn-at-talk in the job interview, that is, a turn that goes beyond a minimal answer to a recruiter's question, typically using the answer as an opportunity to volunteer additional information to project a positive image of oneself. We examine a gamut of cases ranging from very brief and hesitant responses to cases where candidates aptly use the context afforded by a recruiter's question to initiate extended talk to effectively further self-presentational goals. We focus especially on the case of storytelling as a particularly challenging extended-turn activity and examine the role of recruiters as more or less active participants and facilitators of candidates' initiative-taking. By taking initiatives, candidates demonstrate their ability to recognize and respond appropriately to the normative expectations of the interview situation.

Impression Management in the Interview: Personnel Selection Research

The scientific study of social interaction in job interviews is at its most advanced in work and organizational psychology, in the subfield of personnel selection. Traditional concerns have revolved around determining psychometric properties of personnel selection procedures, especially predictive validity, defined as the correlation between applicants' performance at the selection procedure and their subsequent performance on the job (Schmidt and Hunter 1998). A prominent finding is that structuring the job interview increases its predictive validity. There are several ways to increase structure (Campion et al. 1997), including standardizing questions asked of candidates or standardizing how interviewers evaluate responses (Huffcutt and Arthur 1994).

In recent years, interest for social interaction processes in job interviews has increased (Levashina et al. 2014). Much research focuses on self-presentation (Goffman 1959) and *impression management*, defined as "conscious attempts to control the images that are projected in ... social interactions" (Schlenker 1980, 6). Impression management involves linguistic and nonverbal behaviors as well as manipulation of one's physical appearance or extended actions like rendering a favor (Schneider 1981). Impression management strategies can be assertive or defensive

(Stevens and Kristof 1995). Assertive strategies involve "proactive image construction" (Stevens and Kristof 1995, 588), whereas defensive strategies involve "reactive image repair" (Stevens and Kristof 1995, 588). Two prominent examples of assertive impression management are self-promotion and ingratiation. Self-promotion involves producing "positive statements to describe oneself, one's future plans, or one's past accomplishments" (Stevens and Kristof 1995, 589). Using assertive impression management tactics improves interviewer evaluations (Levashina et al. 2014). These findings suggest that interviewers *expect* candidates to use impression management in their responses, with perceptions of "honest" impression management being related to positive evaluations and perceptions of "deceptive" impression management (e.g., *faking*, Levashina and Campion 2007) being related to negative evaluations.

Research in personnel selection employs quantitative methods (experimental studies, questionnaire measures or content analysis) to study the prevalence of impression management (e.g., Stevens and Kristof 1995; Roulin et al. 2014). However, it remains unclear how various tactics like self-promotion are (linguistically and bodily) implemented. In other words, how do candidates actually go about self-promotion? Is self-promotion realized in a single utterance or is it best characterized as a collaborative sequence? What role do interviewers play in facilitating candidate self-promotion? The wording of questionnaire items can reveal some of the implicit assumptions about what constitutes evidence of a tactic. Kristof-Brown et al. (2002, 35) measured self-promotion with the following four items: (1) "During the interview I demonstrated my knowledge and expertise," (2) "I described my skills and abilities in an attractive way," (3) "I took charge to get my point across" and (4) "I described my skills and experience." It is notable that these descriptions remain rather abstract and that they also involve potentially complex actions on the part of the candidate (e.g., "taking charge" or "demonstrating") that may go beyond producing single statements in response to an interviewer's question.

One self-promotion tactic that has received some discussion in the literature is storytelling. Stevens and Kristof (1995) found that candidates often told stories to illustrate their accomplishments. Storytelling may become more frequently expected from candidates with the advent of behavioral interview questioning (Roulin and Bangerter 2012), a method focused on eliciting candidates' accounts of their past behavior in job-related situations. Nonetheless, one study found that candidates told stories in response to behavioral questions less than 25 percent of the time (Bangerter et al. 2014). Many candidates, especially inexperienced ones, may be unsure how to go about telling a compelling story. Ralston et al. (2003) thus proposed criteria for evaluating stories, like internal consistency, relevance, detail or whether candidates' actions depicted in the story express their essential values. They suggested using such criteria to train candidates in the art of storytelling. Other insights may come from conversation-analytical studies of storytelling, which emphasize its special nature relative to the turn-taking rules that govern conversation, requiring additional interactive work to make the story mutually recognizable as a story and to align with the project of telling. This is often accomplished via prefaces (Sacks 1974; Mandelbaum 2013). In job interviews, some stories may be explicitly solicited by an interviewer's question (e.g., a behavioral question), while others may emerge as part of a candidate's extended response. Thus, similar to self-promotion, the case of storytelling suggests that effective impression management often goes beyond responding to a question and may sometimes require extended action by the candidate or even collaborative pre-sequences between the candidate and interviewer.

Taking Control of the Interview: The Advice Literature for Candidates

Advice on how to behave in job interviews is widely available. Thousands of books and websites advise candidates on preparation, the best answers to specific questions or how to deal with delicate situations. The content (and probably the quality) of this so-called advice literature varies widely. While one finds concrete models of good and bad responses (purportedly based on what recruiters expect), there is little indication about how to create or use opportunities to position those answers. Nonetheless, one recurrent theme is the recommendation for candidates to play an active, if not controlling, role in the interview conversation. To circumscribe this theme in detail, we reproduce several quotes from a selection of advice literature books:

> The job interview belongs to you; it is yours to control, yours to win, or yours to blow. (Powers 2005, 75)

> Learning how to use success stories effectively cannot be overemphasized… It takes some skill to weave success stories into an interview… You will have to take the initiative to find openings for your success stories. Even if your interviewer asks you a question that can be answered with a simple yes or no, resist the urge to give a one- or two-word answer. (Learning Express 2006, 69)

> From the outset of the meeting, maintain as much control as possible. This can begin by initiating the opening greeting and showing that you are proactive and confident. (Ferrone 2006, 38)

> Your objective is to create a give-and-take dialogue. (Ferrone 2006, 40)

> The goal is to create an exciting, stimulating 50–50 percent business conversation throughout the interview. (Ball and Ball 1996, 97)

> The most appealing candidates are those who take some initiative during the interview. You need to provide complete answers… You need to demonstrate depth of knowledge and abilities by going beyond short and superficial answers. You need to ask questions as well as respond to those asked of you. At least 50 percent of the conversation should be carried by you. If the interviewer is doing 70 to 80 percent of the talking, you will sense the interview is probably not going well! (Krannich and Krannich 1999, 95)

> Be as proactive as possible in an interview, asking intelligent and alert questions. View the situation as a two-way process, with a give-and-take between the parties… Always keep the conversational ball rolling: Don't answer questions with just "yes" or "no", or utter meaningless clichés… Respond to questions fully but cogently—speak no longer than two minutes at a time. (McDonnell 1995, 75)

These quotes describe expected behaviors at three levels of abstraction. The most abstract level concerns impressions of the candidate's personality that should be conveyed by the candidates' behavior (e.g., appearing "proactive" or "confident"). The second level of abstraction concerns general descriptions of conversation in the interview (e.g., "maintain as much control as possible," "demonstrate depth of knowledge and abilities"). The most concrete level of description concerns specific conversational moves (e.g., "initiating the opening greeting"). It is notable that the expectations formulated focus mainly on candidate behaviors. The potential role of the interviewer in facilitating or hindering candidates' "taking the initiative" is de-emphasized.

While these quotes specify how specific conversational moves can be employed to achieve desirable interview conversations (and how these in turn contribute to conveying impressions about the candidate), it seems questionable whether candidates are capable of attaining such expectations, especially young or inexperienced candidates, and especially if the role of the recruiter in co-creating such conversational outcomes remains unclear. As a result, it is important to examine actual interview conversations to gauge the extent to which young candidates are capable of using job interview questions as occasions to engage in self-promotion, and, more importantly, how these occasions play out interactionally.

Our Study

Corpus and Current Analysis

Our data come from a corpus of naturally occurring job interviews with young people (Gosteli-Corvalan in preparation). The corpus was collected with the goal of observing storytelling activities. Storytelling, defined as the collaborative activity of relating a unique past event experienced by one or more conversational participants, is a good example of initiative-taking in conversation, because would-be narrators have to jointly coordinate with interlocutors on aspects like establishing the relevance of the activity, suspending turn-taking rules (Mandelbaum 2013), crafting the progression of the story, positioning it as a relevant answer to the interviewer's question and returning to the next item on the agenda. In what follows, we use examples from this corpus to describe varying degrees of initiative-taking, focusing on the interplay between opportunities for extended talk created by the recruiters and ways candidates do or do not use them (examples were selected from collections of various interactional phenomena like storytelling, humor or reported speech that were built during initial analyses of the corpus; see Gosteli-Corvalan in preparation). But first we describe the interviews and our transcription conventions.

Interviews, Videorecordings and Transcription

The corpus comprises 26 videorecorded job interviews. Recordings took place in three organizations (two municipalities and one private enterprise) in French-speaking Switzerland. Candidates were in their last year of school and applying for an apprenticeship position, or were students applying for an internship or first job (Table 5.1). They were interviewed by nine recruiters (four women) who were human resource (HR) specialists, line managers (C1) or training managers (TM). Depending on the interview, between one and three recruiters were present. After having secured the organizations' agreement to participate, each candidate was approached before the interview, informed about the study and asked for their consent to videotape the interview.

Recordings were made via a discreetly positioned video camera augmented by an external microphone, affording a view of all participants, typically from the side. Recordings total a little more than ten hours. The shortest interview lasts 12 minutes, and the longest 49 minutes (mean duration 24 minutes). All interviews were initially transcribed in their totality. Subsequently, excerpts included in various collections were used to illustrate initiative-taking in the current chapter; these were transcribed in detail according to the Jefferson (2004) system and using the Transana software package. In this chapter, we have translated the

Table 5.1 Distribution of candidates by organization, position and gender

	Apprenticeship		Internship		First job	
	Male	Female	Male	Female	Male	Female
Municipality 1	–	–	–	2	1	–
Municipality 2	1	11	–	–	2	–
Private enterprise	9	–	–	–	–	–

original French conversation to English. To save space, we do not represent the original French talk (French-language transcripts are available upon request).

Taking the Initiative

We identified three "levels" of initiative-taking in the corpus, *minimal*, *limited* and *extended*. We describe the characteristics of these levels and illustrate them via representative excerpts. This taxonomy is not claimed to be representative of job interviews in general. However, it may serve as a useful initial characterization of candidate's initiative-taking in job interviews with young people. Note that the levels of initiative-taking are defined independently of the presence or absence of storytelling activities. Typically, stories will correspond to cases of extended initiative-taking, but this is not necessarily so.

Minimal Initiative-Taking

This level is characterized by extensive facilitative activity by recruiters and low responsiveness by candidates. To encourage candidates to participate in the conversation, recruiters ask repeated questions. This typically involves an initial, open-ended question followed by more specific questions. Recruiters may also summarize candidates' responses or produce continuers (Goodwin 1986). Candidates respond very briefly, do not expand beyond the scope of the question, often pause before response initiation and make little effort to display the relevance of their answers to the business at hand. As a result, recruiters often end up speaking more than the candidates do.

A first illustration is Excerpt (1). The male candidate (CA) is applying for an apprenticeship position in Municipality 2. He is interviewed by a female HR manager and a female TM (who does not participate in the excerpted sequence). The sequence starts with HR explaining how many apprentices will be chosen for the position (l. 2, 6) and asking CA why he feels he should be one of them (l. 8–9).

Ex. (1)

```
      (1.1)
HR:   we will have to choose an a- three apprentices?
      (0.2)
CA:   mhm?
      (0.2)
HR:   for next year,
      (0.6)
HR:   so now for you why do you think you are the candidate we should
      choose.
      (0.5)
HR:   why is it that we have to take ↑you in and not .h necessarily
      the other apprentices that we will receive >well< the other
      persons we will receive.
      (2.2)
CA:   uh
      (1.6)
CA:   ((throat clearing))
      (1.9)
CA:   first I am someone who i:s- who really has a lot of
      motivation,
      (1.9)
CA:   I ha:ve great responsibilities,
      (4.5)
HR:   when you say great responsibilities what is the: the greatest
      responsibility you had until now to undertake.
      (2.2)
HR:   since you still have done some [little&
CA:                                  [mhm
HR:   &jobs like that what is the most important thing to manage you
      have been given.
      (0.5)
CA:   °most important°
      (1.0)
HR:   in your eyes.
      (2.0)
CA:   m::
      (6.6)
CA:   ah I- once with uh my uncle at the restaurant of château de
      (xxxx) I had to watch all the restaurant by myself.
      (0.5)
CA:   and he left.
      (0.2)
CA:   and I had to do the closing also.
      (1.2)
CA:   ((sniffs))
      (1.7)
HR:   °mhm?°
      (3.3)
HR:   we:ll I'm sorry I just interrupted you because I built a
      little on uh great responsibilities .h so okay motivation,
      great responsibilities,
      (0.6)
```

```
HR:   and th-
      (1.3)
HR:   and then.
      (3.4)
CA:   always in a good mood,
      (3.8)
CA:   and uh
      (1.4)
CA:   always one hundred percent in what I undertake.
```

HR's initial question meets with a brief silence (l. 10), after which she rephrases it (l. 11–13). CA answers after an extended bout of silence and disfluency (l. 14–18). He prefaces his answer (l. 19) with "first," suggesting he is about to enumerate a list. But after producing two reasons, he stops speaking, and 4.5 seconds of silence ensue (l. 23). HR invites him to give an example of the greatest responsibility he has undertaken (l. 24–25). After 2.2 seconds of silence, HR reformulates the question (l. 27, 29–30), thereby also displaying her construal of CA's answer as insufficient. CA repeats part of the question (l. 32) and proceeds to initiate an answer (l. 38), but not after producing another filler (l. 36) and 6.6 seconds of silence (l. 37). His answer is a brief story that is lacking in detail (l. 38–39, 41, 43), and punctuated with further pauses (l. 40, 42, 44, 46). HR treats it as insufficient by producing a continuer (*mhm*, l. 47). CA declines the invitation to continue (3.3 seconds of silence in l. 48), upon which (l. 49) HR apologizes for "interrupting" him (a conspicuously inappropriate and possibly ironic choice of words, given CA's long silences throughout the excerpt), explains why she asked for an example of his responsibilities and lists the two items he mentioned, thereby inviting him to continue his list (l. 50, 51). This invitation is also extended in lines 53–54, where HR also produces a hand gesture (circular movement with an open palm extended upwards), indicating she is interested in hearing more elements. After 3.4 seconds of silence (l. 56), CA proceeds to enumerate two more items.

Excerpt (1) illustrates an extreme case of lack of initiative-taking, whereby repeated attempts by the recruiter to engage the candidate in conversation meet with delayed, hesitant and limited responses. In Excerpt (2), the candidate is more responsive but displays little awareness of the (ir)relevance of her responses to the interview agenda. The female CA is applying for an apprenticeship position in Municipality 2, and is interviewed by the HR manager and C1. The sequence begins with HR asking a question about whether CA has visited the municipality's website.

Ex. (2)

```
HR:   .h >have you< visited our website.
      (0.8)
CA:   yes?
HR:   yes?
      (0.7)
CA:   uh yes yes hh.
HR:   wha::t strikes you what did you li :ke what didn't you
      li:ke wha:t
CA:   u:h well [what I lik-
HR:            [WHAT emerges out of your visit to our website.
CA:   I liked because it was well indicate:d a:ll that it didn't
      have too complicated words.
HR:   mhm?
CA:   that were uh to expla:in uh what was what?
      (1.8)
C1:   what did you look at in particular?
CA:   u:h actually I did +almost everything ((laughing))+
      no I mainly went i::n towards the municipal council the
      council uh
      (0.6)
CA:   general,
      (1.2)
CA:   u::h
      (1.8)
CA:   what was there- I think there were the rights al[so,
C1:                                                   [mhm?
      (1.4)
CA:   all (x) this section?
HR:   one councillor can you give me a name?
      (0.2)
HR:   >like that< uh without without THINking.
CA:   mister weiner?
HR:   mister weiner.
```

CA answers "yes" to HR's question (l. 3). Her response is treated as insufficient by HR, who produces another "yes" with rising intonation as a continuer (l. 4), whereupon CA repeats her original answer without elaborating (l. 6). HR then asks additional questions about how CA may have experienced the website (l. 7, 8, 10), suggesting potential response alternatives (e.g., "what strikes you," "what did you like," "what didn't you like"). CA states that she liked the website because it was well indicated and did not use "too complicated words" (l. 11–12, 14) to explain things.

She uses format-tying (Goodwin 1990) (l.9–10) to display the fittedness of her response to the question. However, neither recruiter reacts to the response, but C1 asks CA if she looked at any specific aspect of the website (l. 16), a question unrelated to the response, thereby an indirect construal of the response as irrelevant. CA initially claims she looked at everything, but then laughs and lists some general aspects (the municipal council, the general council, citizens' rights; l. 18–19, 21, 25). HR asks CA if she can name one of the municipal councilors (l. 29, 31), whereupon CA obliges (l. 32).

In Excerpt (2), then, CA is a bit more responsive. She initiates her answers quicker and volunteers more information, but only after repeated invitations by HR. Her answers are brief, vague and bland (e.g., her mention of the website not using "too complicated words"), and marked by rising intonation (l. 3, 14, 33), indicating uncertainty about the appropriateness of her response (a correction-invitation device, Sacks 1992). Her answers are treated as irrelevant by the recruiters, who repeatedly ask for more precise information.

Limited Initiative-Taking

This level is characterized by similar recruiter initiatives in questioning. For example, recruiters ask questions and prompt candidates for more information. However, here, candidates give more extended answers and use subtle opportunities offered by recruiters to expand on them, thus reacting responsively to minimal prompting and obviating the need for recruiters to reformulate questions.

In Excerpt (3), CA (male) is applying for an apprenticeship position in the private enterprise. He is interviewed by a male TM. The excerpt starts with TM explaining why he asked a previous question about CA's family background (l. 1–6) and then asking a question (l. 7–8) about CA's motivation to enter the field in which the position is advertised.

Ex. (3)

```
TM:  .h I like to know a >little< bit what the family does it- it
     allows me to have a very small snapshot of the environment
     you >come from<,
     and uh it allows me to .h to >build< on uh
     (0.7)
```

```
TM:   my n↑ext question,
      finally what makes u:h you want to >enter< into this field of
      technics.
      (0.7)
CA:   well in fact I like things like electronics and things like
      mechanics, a↓nd I- since I did sev- se- several (xx) indeed
      several internships before I came here uh as an automatician,.h
TM:   yes?
CA:   it's exactly this aspect between mechan- °well° there is less
      mechanics but between mechani:cs and electronics that pleased
      me.
      (0.5)
CA:   as a profession.
TM:   okay and th↑at you ha:d the opportunity to- to see it,
      to experience it .h when.
CA:   I cou:ld do an internship at the ASLN as an automatician
      and at Jobin also,
TM:   okay?
CA:   and otherw↑ise once I had °a nintendo nine- from about nineteen
      eighty that did n↑ot work so I tried to open it to see what was
      wrong,
      (0.4)
CA:   °and finally I found and then uh (xx) managed to make it work
      again°.
      (0.2)
TM:   what was the problem with this nintendo?
CA:   >there was< a piece of dust which had settled on the
      motherboard, so it needed to be sprinkle:d °>well< not
      sprinkled but° sprayed on with a special product a:nd
      (0.8)
CA:   >after that it worked<.
TM:   it >worked again<.
      (1.0)
TM:   excell↑ent?
```

CA answers by invoking his attraction to things mechanical and electronics, before mentioning his several internships and finally his interest for the intersection between mechanics and electronics as a profession (l. 10–12, 14–18). TM then builds on this response by asking (l. 19–20) CA when he had the opportunity to notice this interest. CA initially answers by enumerating his internships (l. 21–22). TM produces "okay" with a rising intonation (l. 23), thereby inviting CA to provide an extended response (Bangerter and Clark 2003). CA then expands (l. 24–30) on his answer by recounting a story of a time when he repaired an old game console. The expansion allows him to bring forward an additional demonstration of his motivation by illustrating his curiosity and precocious skill with repairing electronic devices. This individuating information is validated as particularly relevant by TM (l. 39). However, the emergence and development of this story remain contingent on prompting by TM, especially when he asks a specific question about the problem with the console (l. 31), giving CA the cue to describe in detail what he did to solve the problem.

Excerpt (4) also involves a male CA applying for the same position as in Excerpt (3) and being interviewed by the same recruiter (TM). The excerpt also starts at a similar point as in Excerpt (3), with TM explaining why he questions candidates about their family background (l. 2–8). In this case, CA has previously indicated his father is a janitor and his mother is a salesperson. This leads TM to surmise that there are no links to the domain of technics in his family (l. 10).

Ex. (4)

```
1          (3.1)
2    TM:   °very well° >I like< asking what=do::: the relations do,
3          .h the family it allows=me to get a small very quick snapshot
4          .h u:h
5          (0.5)
6    TM:   of the background from where you come,
7          u:h to see a little bit .h if there are links with the domain
8          in which we are here today so technics,
9    CA:   °okay°
10   TM:   uh there there wouldn't really be any,
11         (0.2)
12   CA:   u:h well be[fore my&
13   TM:              [that-
14   CA:   &dad was a locksmith
15   TM:          o[kay
16   CA:            [my grandfather too,
17         (0.3)
18   TM:   your granddad too?
19   CA:   yeah actually it was my grandfather's company then my dad took
20         it over,
21         (1.9)
22   CA:   so we are pretty good with our hands in my family we [(x)
23   TM:                                                        [there.
24         (0.5)
25   TM:   there is a link.
26   CA:   yes so let's just say:
27         (0.4)
28   CA:   doing nothing uh
29         (0.2)
```

CA: and there are power outages and calling an electrician that's
not our st↓yle.
(0.2)
CA: there we >always< try uh to find the solution ourselves?
(1.8)
TM: °great° so there <there is an interesting link>
CA: with technics yes
TM: with the world of=technics of=mechanics and a little bit
of electricity.
CA: uh yeah a bit of electricity I do a little bit of that.

CA rapidly contradicts this conclusion by volunteering the additional information that his father used to be a locksmith, and his grandfather as well (l. 12, 14, 16). This information is treated as relevant by TM (l. 18), and CA further volunteers that his father took over his grandfather's company (l. 19–20). After a brief pause (l. 21, TM is nodding and taking notes during this time), he continues with a statement about how manual ability runs in his family (l. 22). TM treats this information as highly relevant (l. 23–25) to the issue of the link between CA's family background and the world of technics, even to the point of interrupting CA to express this idea. CA continues by explaining how his family's "style" is to actively solve manual or technical problems by themselves (l. 26–33). TM expresses pleasure at this discovery (l. 35, "great") and reintroduces the topic of the link. Both CA and TM produce a collaborative sequence describing the exact nature of that link (l. 36–39).

In this excerpt, CA reacts to a misconstrual by TM in a proactive manner. He is able to discern the potentially negative implications of "there not being a link" between his family background and the domain of technics, and volunteers information to demonstrate that there actually is such a link. But TM also plays an active role in facilitating the emergence of this information by indicating the relevance of the information volunteered. With this guidance, CA is able to switch the topic from the issue of what his father previously did to his family history and then to personal characteristics of family members (which are more directly suggestive of CA's own putative manual ability and his potential fit with the position) and thus engage in effective self-promotion.

Extended Initiative-Taking

This level is characterized by minimal prompting by the recruiter beyond an initial question. Candidates respond quickly and at length to the question, and are at pains to demonstrate the relevance of their answers to their question asked and to illustrate how they exemplify desirable characteristics of the candidate, thereby creating their own opportunities for self-promotion. They also deal with obstacles (e.g., interruptions, potentially damaging questions) and turn them to their advantage. During this activity, the recruiter plays a supporting role, either in producing continuers or positive assessments, or concurring with the conclusions drawn by the applicant.

In Excerpt (5), a female CA for an internship position in Municipality 1 is being interviewed by an HR manager, a male C1 and a female C2. The excerpt starts with HR asking CA to produce an example of one of her achievements.

Ex. (5)

```
          (1.4)
    HR:   do you have an example to give me of >something< that you have
          achiev[ed
    CA:         [well
    HR:   EVEN something private uh >maybe<
    CA:   yes,
    HR:   °not necessarily°
    CA:   well for example uh in high school,
          (0.4)
    CA:   I had to complete a : chosen assignment actually we had a
          choice,
          .h and I chose to work on uh the financial aspect of walt
          disney's movies,
          (0.9)
    CA:   .h so at the beginning actually my teachers we[re
    HR:                                                 [it's a family
          passion [walt disney huh.
    CA:           [((laugh))
    C1:   oh really?
          ((laughter))
    C2:   ↑okay?
    HR:   don't start mister [(xxx) on the subject&
    CA:                      [((laugh))
    HR:   &because uh you are uh the whole weekend uh ((laugh))
    CA:   no so uh actually it's uh my teachers at the beginning they .h
```

```
26          they had a little: well they didn't really think that I would
27          succeed in::
28          (0.4)
29    CA:   in f- well in finishing this assignment because just to find an
30          interview it would be uh difficult,
31    HR:   °that's for sure yeah°
32    CA:   and then they let me do it anyway to see uh what would happen,
33          (0.7)
35    CA:   so I did succ- >well< I succeeded in <contacting< u:h
36          di- walt disney the walt disney company in the united states,
37          (1.0)
38    CA:   I went also to: disneyland paris to contact them and do an
39          interview,
40          (1.1)
41    CA:   and in [the e-
42    HR:          [>they- they< accepted to receive you&
43    CA:   yes.
44    HR:   &in pa- in paris.
45    CA:   yes.
46    HR:   yeah okay?
47          (0.6)
48    HR:   °mhm°?
49          (0.8)
50    CA:   and in the end indeed we:ll
51          (0.5)
52    CA:   my:: teachers indeed >well< they were really very st-
53          satisfied and I got- I got a grade of six.
54    HR:   okay.
```

It is noteworthy that CA already starts responding (l. 4) in overlap with the end of HR's question. She starts to tell a story about a project she completed in high school. She persists in the narration in the face of a humorous interruption by HR (l. 16–17, 22, 24), who points out that the subject of Walt Disney is a passion of the candidate's father (who works in the same municipality as the recruiters and who is known to all of them), and that once started on the topic, he can talk about it "the whole weekend." She even closes this humoristic episode herself by producing "no" at the beginning of her turn in l. 25 (as a means of transitioning back to a serious mode of talk; Schegloff 2001). She describes (l. 25–30) the initial skepticism of her teachers about her ability to complete the project, thereby indirectly suggesting its ambitious nature. This is a typical Labovian (Labov and Waletzky 1967) complicating action, which frames the protagonists' actions as particularly impressive or heroic. HR aligns with this construal (l. 31). CA then describes the actions she undertook to complete her project (l. 35–41) as well as the outcome

(l. 50–53), where the teachers were satisfied and she received the highest grade (six) for her work. During this development, HR interrupts again (l. 42–44) to express her surprise that CA was able to secure an interview at Disneyland in Paris, indirectly marking this as a noteworthy accomplishment and thereby participating in the framing of the story as particularly impressive.

Throughout this performance, CA deploys a range of practices to display the relevance of her narrative to the recruiter's question. For example, she uses format-tying (Goodwin 1990) in echoing HR's "an example" (l. 2) by her own "for example" (l. 8). The temporal structure of the story progression is well marked ("at the beginning," "and then," "in the end"), and there is a clear linkage between the initial situation, CA's actions and the very positive final outcome. The recruiters play a minimal role in this sequence, but HR markedly validates CA's framing of the story as an impressive performance. It is also worth noting that CA manages to produce her own swift responses while managing the delicate issue of overlapping speech and digressions by the recruiter.

In Excerpt (6), CA is a male candidate for an ambulance driver position in Municipality 2. He is interviewed by the relevant head of department (SE) and a C1 (who does not participate in the excerpted sequence). The excerpt is near the end of the interview. The participants had started to wrap up (SE was informing CA about when he would next be contacted), but SE raises "a last question" (l. 1) from his notes concerning the fact that CA is a volunteer firefighter in his free time. The excerpt starts with SE asking CA whether this activity might potentially interfere with his work in the position he is applying for.

Ex. (6)

```
SE:   uh just do you think >that is a last question now< I: am
      seeing now (xxx) framed,
      uh the your activity as a volunteer firefighter is it
      compatible uh with a profession uh like like here with
      irregular schedules school and all that
CA:   mhm
SE:   in parallel?
CA:   simply because it is volunteer firefighter you know.
SE:   yeah
CA:   so I clearly told to my boss
SE:   yeah
```

CA: in volunteer there is volunteer right.
SE: yeah
CA: if I don't have the time I well I don't do it I don't put myself .h
SE: okay
CA: well
SE: yeah
CA: so there are professionals for that and oh no the voluntary work doesn't take priority over uh
SE: okay
CA: well after .h i:f if you come if I come from home to go to work
SE: m
CA: and then I see a traffic accident I stop
SE: yeah
CA: well I will stop anyway
SE: m m
CA: even if I am late for work
SE: yeah
CA: well you know
SE: mhm
CA: I can't I think that Hugo- Hugo already told me he already did that so uh
SE: mhm
CA: now I think it can only be a plus on the one hand the fact that I've seen uh .h many things it allows me maybe to
SE: yeah
CA: impro- >well< not improve but you can always make your contribution you know
SE: mhm
CA: I think there is no perfect system and
SE: mhm
CA: and me on the one hand back home they are happy because that makes someone who has a nearly professional activity
SE: m m
CA: so h well I don't know well .h the other day we made a call in a in the nursing home where I live,
SE: m
CA: well it was me who was the boss well the guys found there was a bit of change you know because
SE: m
CA: not used to have an oxygen bottle under the stretcher,
SE: m
CA: not used to .h eh don't you see you are putting on the pressure cuff while you got a perfusion,
SE: mhm
CA: well
SE: m
CA: you see me these are things I'm happy because you see before uh
SE: yeah
CA: I wouldn't have °realized that°
SE: mhm

```
CA:   °°there°°.
SE:   okay.so rather positive rather:
CA:   in both directions what's more.
SE:   not contradictory okay.
CA:   (xxx)
SE:   but priority indeed to the professional service which is which
      is rather logical [continues]
```

As in Excerpt (5), it is noteworthy that CA replies rapidly. The sequence is almost entirely composed of talk by CA, with participation by SE limited to the production of continuers until the end of the excerpt. In this interactional space, CA deploys several arguments. First, he states that the voluntary status of this activity makes it clearly second priority (l. 8–20). Next, he produces a caveat to that claim by stating that he would stop to help in a traffic accident even if it made him late for work and that a colleague of his already working for the municipality had done the same (l. 22–34) (CA has been working in the municipality on a temporary basis and thus knows other colleagues). Next, he states (l. 36–42) that his volunteer activity is actually an advantage because he has gained in experience and increases the potential professional contributions he can make (while hedging his choice of words, i.e., taking back "improvement" in favor of "contribution"). He then brings evidence of this by stating that his firefighter colleagues back home are happy because of his professional experience (l. 44–45). He then volunteers a specific example concerning a recent intervention of the firefighters at a nursing home where he was the leader of the intervening group. He claims that his leadership was important because he was able to detect and correct beginners' errors made by his colleagues (i.e., not having an oxygen bottle ready and inappropriately applying a pressure cuff over a perfusion in a patient) (l. 47–56). He ends by stating that he is happy because of the things he has learned through this experience (l. 60–63). The excerpt ends (l. 66, 68, 70–71) with SE describing the conclusions to be drawn from CA's extended turn-at-talk, namely that his volunteer activity is "positive" and does not "contradict" his professional activity, which takes priority. During this, CA is at pains (l. 67) to emphasize the mutual positive influence of his volunteer and professional activities.

In this excerpt, then, CA takes the initiative to dispel doubts about a potential drawback of his candidacy. In an extended turn, he turns the question to his advantage by initially claiming that his professional responsibilities have priority over his volunteer activity and then moving on to demonstrate how this activity actually constitutes a positive aspect of his candidacy. A particularly illuminating aspect of this demonstration is his enumeration of shared technical knowledge or "tricks of the trade" (the oxygen bottle under the stretcher, knowing that one does not apply a pressure cuff over a perfusion) that allow him to indirectly create a sense of professional community between himself and the recruiters. During his turn, he displays a sensitivity to potential alternative interpretations of his claims by revising his choice of words and introducing a caveat. Both CA and SE collaborate in building a conclusion about the advantages of his volunteer activity for his candidacy.

Conclusions

In this chapter, we investigated the extent to which young candidates new to the job market take initiatives in job interviews. We found that recruiters play an important role in creating opportunities for candidate's initiative-taking, and use several different means to do so, including asking open questions, prompting via follow-up questions, and using continuers and assessments to align with candidates' talk. Young candidates do not always exploit such opportunities, and we documented three types of initiative-taking in our data: minimal, limited and extended.

Minimal initiative-taking is characterized by extensive facilitation by recruiters (e.g., repeated questioning, summarizing responses, continuers) and little responsiveness by candidates. Candidates respond hesitantly and well within the scope of the question, pause abundantly and seem unconcerned about making their answers relevant. Many features of minimal initiative-taking resemble those of how secondary school pupils formulate personal opinions in the classroom (see Degoumois et al. this volume). Minimal initiative-taking may thus indicate young candidates' difficulties of emancipating themselves from interactional scripts related to classroom settings. Limited initiative-taking is also characterized by active recruiter questioning, for example, prompts for more information. But candidates give more extended answers (recruiters do not need to reformulate questions because of candidates' more proactive behavior) and those answers are treated as relevant and built on by recruiters' further questions. This leads in turn to more disclosure by candidates, for example, storytelling as in Excerpt (3). The outcome is thus a more successful collaborative activity of candidate self-promotion. Extended initiative-taking is characterized by minimal recruiter activity. Candidates respond quickly and extensively to questions, demonstrate the relevance of their answers and illustrate how they exemplify desirable characteristics, thus driving their own self-promotion. They also deal deftly with potential obstacles (e.g., interruptions, delicate questions, overlapping talk). Recruiters defer to the candidates' active role, producing continuers or positive assessments, or concurring with conclusions drawn by the applicant. While storytelling can potentially co-occur with all levels of initiative-taking, extended storytelling seems to increase over levels of initiative-taking (compare the extent of the storytelling activities in excerpts (1) (minimal initiative-taking), (3) (limited initiative-taking) and (5) (extended initiative-taking)).

Our findings have implications for understanding of impression management in job interviews. Previous studies of impression management in work and organizational psychology tend to view it as a performance by the candidate that can be more or less well detected by the recruiter (e.g., Roulin et al. 2014). However, our analyses suggest that, like any conversational behavior, initiative-taking is a collaborative activity in which recruiters play an important role. Our findings also have implications for training both candidates and recruiters (Ralston et al. 2003). In workshops, candidates could benefit by learning to recognize typical opportunities recruiters provide for them to take initiatives, and recruiters could be trained to more aptly produce such occasions. The realism conveyed by actual conversational data may provide a useful complement to the role-play techniques typically used in this kind of training. Such training initiatives might be combined with the CARM (conversation analytic role-play method, Stokoe 2014) interventions developed for applying conversation analysis to training communication skills. CARM uses metaphors like "racetracks" (a metaphor for goal-directed interaction), "slots" (opportunities for inserting talk) and "obstacles," all of which are very much related to issues of initiative-taking.

Further research should pursue analyses of initiative-taking, perhaps by studying interviews with more experienced candidates to document potentially different phenomena or the empirical distribution of different kinds of initiative-taking. Based on the training implications outlined above, it is important to evaluate such interventions to assess whether they enable more competent initiative-taking. Another potentially interesting direction would be to analyze cases where initiative-taking is not supported by recruiters, for example, when candidates' extended responses are treated as not relevant by recruiters.

References

Ball, F. W., & Ball, B. B. (1996). *Killer interviews*. New York: McGraw-Hill.

Bangerter, A., & Clark, H. H. (2003). Navigating joint projects with dialogue. *Cognitive Science, 27*(2), 195–225.

Bangerter, A., Corvalan, P., & Cavin, C. (2014). Storytelling in the selection interview? How applicants respond to past behavior questions. *Journal of Business and Psychology, 29*(4), 1–14.

Button, G. (1987). Answers as interactional products: Two sequential practices used in interviews. *Social Psychology Quarterly, 50*(2), 160–171.

Campion, M. A., Palmer, D. K., & Campion, J. E. (1997). A review of structure in the selection interview. *Personnel Psychology, 50*(3), 655–702.

Cazden, C. B., & Beck, S. W. (2003). Classroom discourse. In A. C. Graesser, M. A. Gernsbacher, & S. R. Goldman (Eds.), *Handbook of discourse processes* (pp. 165–198). Mahwah, NJ: Erlbaum.

Ferrone, R. (2006). *Don't blow the interview*. New York: St Martin's Griffin.

Goffman, E. (1959). *The presentation of self in everyday life*. Oxford: Doubleday.

Goodwin, C. (1986). Between and within: Alternative sequential treatments of continuers and assessments. *Human Studies, 9*(2), 205–217.

Goodwin, M. H. (1990). *He-said-she-said: Talk as social organization among Black children*. Bloomington: Indiana University Press.

Gosteli-Corvalan, P. (in preparation). *Organisation interactionnelle des récits conversationnels par des jeunes candidats lors d'un entretien d'embauche*. PhD, University of Neuchâtel.

Huffcutt, A. I., & Arthur Jr., W. (1994). Hunter and Hunter (1984) revisited: Interview validity for entry-level jobs. *Journal of Applied Psychology, 79*(2), 184–190.

Jefferson, G. (2004). Glossary of transcript symbols with an introduction. In G. Lerner (Ed.), *Conversation analysis: Studies from the first generation* (pp. 13–31). Amsterdam: John Benjamins Publishing.

Kerekes, J. A. (2007). The co-construction of a gatekeeping encounter: An inventory of verbal actions. *Journal of Pragmatics, 39*(11), 1942–1973.

Komter, M. (1991). *Conflict and cooperation in job interviews: A study of talk, tasks, and ideas*. Amsterdam: John Benjamins.

Krannich, C. R., & Krannich, R. L. (1999). *Dynamite answers to interview questions*. Manassas Park: Impact Publications.

Kristof-Brown, A., Barrick, M. R., & Franke, M. (2002). Applicant impression management: Dispositional influences and consequences for recruiter perceptions of fit and similarity. *Journal of Management, 28*(1), 27–46.

Labov, W., & Waletzky, J. (1967). Narrative analysis. In J. Helm (Ed.), *Essays on the verbal and visual arts* (pp. 12–44). Seattle: University of Washington Press.

Learning Express. (2006). *Job interviews that get you hired*. New York: Learning Express.

Levashina, J., & Campion, M. (2007). Measuring faking in the employment interview: Development and validation of an interview faking behavior scale. *Journal of Applied Psychology, 92*(6), 1638–1656.

Levashina, J., Hartwell, C. J., Morgeson, F. P., & Campion, M. A. (2014). The structured employment interview: Narrative and quantitative review of the research literature. *Personnel Psychology, 67*(1), 241–293.

Mandelbaum, J. (2013). Storytelling in conversation. In J. Sidnell & T. Stivers (Eds.), *The handbook of conversation analysis* (pp. 492–508). Chichester: John Wiley and Sons.

McDonnell, S. (1995). *You're hired! Secrets to successful job interviews*. New York: Macmillan.

Mehan, H. (1979). *Learning lessons: Social organization in the classroom*. Cambridge, MA: Harvard University Press.

Melchers, K. G., Ingold, P. V., Wilhelmy, A., & Kleinmann, M. (2015). Beyond validity: Shedding light on the social situation in employment interviews. In I. Nikolaou & J. K. Oostrom (Eds.), *Employee recruitment, selection, and assessment: Contemporary issues for theory and practice* (pp. 154–171). Hove, UK: Psychology Press.

Petitjean, C. (2013). Social representations of turn-taking in classrooms: From compulsory to post-compulsory schooling in French-Speaking Switzerland. *Classroom Discourse, 5*(2), 138–157.

Powers, P. (2005). *Winning job interviews*. Franklin Lakes: Career Press.
Ragan, S. L., & Hopper, R. (1981). Alignment talk in the job interview. *Journal of Applied Communication Research, 9*(2), 85–103.
Ralston, S. M., Kirkwood, W. G., & Burant, P. A. (2003). Helping interviewees tell their stories. *Business Communication Quarterly, 66*(3), 8–22.
Roulin, N., & Bangerter, A. (2012). Understanding the academic–practitioner gap for structured interviews: "Behavioral" interviews diffuse, "structured" interviews do not. *International Journal of Selection and Assessment, 20*(2), 149–158.
Roulin, N., Bangerter, A., & Levashina, J. (2014). Interviewers' perceptions of impression management in employment interviews. *Journal of Managerial Psychology, 29*(2), 141–163.
Ryan, A. M., McFarland, L. A., Baron, H., & Page, R. (1999). An international look at selection practices: Nation and culture as sources of variability in practice. *Personnel Psychology, 52*(2), 359–391.
Sacks, H. (1974). Some consideration of a story told in ordinary conversations. *Poetics, 15*(1–2), 127–138.
Sacks, H. (1992). The correction-invitation device. In G. Jefferson & E. Schegloff (Eds.), *Harvey Sacks: Lectures on conversation* (pp. 21–25). Oxford: Blackwell.
Schegloff, E. A. (2001). Getting serious: Joke → serious 'no'. *Journal of Pragmatics, 33*(12), 1947–1955.
Schlenker, B. R. (1980). *Impression management: The self-concept, social identity, and interpersonal relations*. Monterey, CA: Brooks/Cole.
Schmidt, F. L., & Hunter, J. E. (1998). The validity and utility of selection methods in personnel psychology: Practical and theoretical implications of 85 years of research findings. *Psychological Bulletin, 124*(2), 262–274.
Schneider, D. J. (1981). Tactical self-presentations: Toward a broader conception. In J. T. Tedeschi (Ed.), *Impression management theory and social psychological research* (pp. 23–40). New York: Academic Press.
Stevens, C. K., & Kristof, A. L. (1995). Making the right impression: A field study of applicant impression management during job interviews. *Journal of Applied Psychology, 80*(5), 587–606.
Stokoe, E. (2014). The Conversation Analytic Role-Play Method (CARM): A method for training communication skills as an alternative to simulated role-play. *Research on Language and Social Interaction, 47*(3), 255–265.

6

Newcomer Nurses' Telephone Calls to Porters and Doctors: Inquiring and Reporting as Vehicles for Requests

Anca-Cristina Sterie and Esther González-Martínez

Introduction

The hospital is a spatially distributed workplace with "myriad interactions" (Atkinson 1995, 34) taking place between professionals looking to coordinate their lines of action to provide patient care (Strauss 1988). When starting their first job at a hospital, young nursing graduates take on a new work assignment that is impossible to reproduce in the classroom environment and for which ordinary practical competences are indispensable yet insufficient (Barenfanger et al. 2004). They must make numerous telephone calls to many different members of the hospital personnel for care-coordination purposes. In the framework of the Sinergia IC-You project, we thus conducted a study on newcomer nurses' telephone conversations with other personnel in an acute-care hospital in French-speaking Switzerland.[1] Based on conversation analysis (Sacks et al. 1974) of a corpus of audio-recorded calls, this chapter

A.-C. Sterie • E. González-Martínez (✉)
Department of Social Sciences, University of Fribourg,
Fribourg, Switzerland

S. Pekarek Doehler et al. (eds.), *Interactional Competences in Institutional Settings*, DOI 10.1007/978-3-319-46867-9_6

sheds light upon this routine yet understudied work interaction. We examine in particular the conversational organization of nurses' requests to their interlocutors, which constitute the main activity in most of the calls. According to Schegloff (2007, 75–76), some first pair parts enact their own action—for instance, questioning or telling—while also serving as vehicles or formats for another action, for instance, requesting.[2] This chapter examines two vehicles that nurses use to make requests to porters and doctors, their most frequent telephone interlocutors at the hospital. The nurse conveys a request to a porter by inquiring as to his ability to carry out a transportation action. His or her request explicitly mentions the specific action to be accomplished as well as the person expected to carry it out—two items that are not included when the nurse reports a problematic situation with a patient to a doctor as a way to request his intervention in addressing it. The discussion bears on what the differential use of these vehicles for requests tells us about the interactional competences newcomer nurses call upon in the workplace.

Methods and Data

The setting of our research was a middle-sized acute-care hospital in the French-speaking part of Switzerland. Over a six-month period, we audio-recorded telephone calls between the two landlines of two nurse stations in the Surgery Department and 155 telephone numbers corresponding to 19 hospital departments. We thus collected 374 calls made or received by three young nursing graduates who were in their first year of employment at the hospital.[3] In their calls, the three newcomer nurses were in contact with 56 telephone numbers corresponding to 14 hospital departments. The nurses' interlocutors were various, ranging from their own nursing colleagues in Surgery and other departments, physicians and other health providers (like pharmacists, dieticians and social workers), to domestic, transportation, technical and administrative staff, among others. We supplemented the recordings with ethnographic fieldwork (in situ observations, informal interviews, documentation collection) in ten hospital departments, in which the nurses' main interlocutors worked, including the Surgery Department. The newcomer nurses have the most phone contact with the doctors of the Surgery Department and with Porter Services. Indeed, 34% of their calls are made between the telephone used by a newcomer nurse in his or her station, and a doctor of the Surgery Department; 14% are made with the main number of Porter Services.[4] Most calls are nurse-initiated (83%); nurses are the callers in 90% of all calls with doctors and 100% with porters. Overall, calls are short; on average, their length is 56 seconds, including the ringback tones. However, the length of the call varies depending on the interlocutor, those with doctors being on average longer (50 seconds) than those with porters (23 seconds).[5]

In most of the calls (76%), the dialing results in a connection with a single number in which one single conversation between two interlocutors accomplishing one single main activity takes place (González-Martínez and Sterie 2014). Monofocal calls (Wakin and Zimmerman 1999), in which participants rapidly transact a single business, are thus the most common form of hospital telephone communication in our corpus. Moreover, a request, in which the nurse asks his or her interlocutor, more or less overtly, to do something, is the most frequent main activity. Out of a total of 352 identified main activities, 333 are indeed requests.[6]

We transcribed the calls using the Jeffersonian conventions (Jefferson 2004) and analyzed them with a conversation analytic approach (Sacks et al. 1974) to examine how interlocutors produce and handle requests through specific organizations of talk-in-interaction. Analysis shows that requests are implemented through many different actions serving as vehicles for them (Schegloff 2007); we have grouped them into two categories: (1) inquiring (trying to find out something) and (2) telling (asserting a state of facts). In this chapter, we analyze the two most frequent vehicles nurses use to produce requests. First, an inquiring action: "inquiring as to the recipient's ability to carry out a specific action." Second, a telling action: "reporting a problematic situation with a patient."[7] The first one is pervasive in nurses' requests to porters, while the second is regularly in play when nurses address requests to doctors, and mainly in calls to them.

Conversation Analytic Studies on Requests

Conversation analytic research considers requests to be actions in which one participant asks another, more or less overtly, to do something (Curl and Drew 2008). A request initiated in first position makes relevant the production of a turn in second position that grants or rejects the request

(Schegloff 2007). The request activity thus portrays the recipient as having a say in the future conduct (Craven and Potter 2010). Studies distinguish between immediate requests, which demand immediate satisfaction during the conversation itself, and deferred requests, which require satisfaction at a later time (Houtkoop 1987; Lindström 1999; Schegloff 2007; Steensig and Heinemann 2014). Due to the fact that a requested deferred action cannot be achieved in the immediate interactional context in which the request is made, responses generally include specific components with which the recipient grants the request and displays his or her commitment to achieving the deferred action (Lindström 1999).

Conversation analysis contributes a new approach to the issue, inherited from speech act theory (Searle 1975), in terms of the formats—characterized by varying degrees of directness, explicitness or transparency—through which requests are achieved (Drew and Couper-Kuhlen 2014). It highlights the "double actionhood" (Levinson 2013, 127) or "double-barreled"-ness (Schegloff 2007, 76) of some first pair parts in the sense that they enact their own action—for instance, questioning or telling—while also serving as vehicles or formats for another action, for instance, requesting. In his or her response, the recipient of the first pair part deals with its double function, orienting both to the vehicle and to the action implemented through it, regularly in this order and in successive components (Schegloff 2007, 75–76). When the preference structures of both actions are cross-cutting, one of the actions being implemented may come to dominate (Schegloff 2007, 76–77).

The format of the request can be a display of the speaker's status regarding his or her epistemic (Heritage and Raymond 2005; Heritage 2012) or deontic rights (Stevanovic 2011; Stevanovic and Peräkylä 2012) to request something of the interlocutor. Analysts also explore the relationship between the format through which the request is conveyed and the speaker's display of both his or her entitlement to make the request and his or her orientation to the contingencies involved in granting the request (Curl and Drew 2008); the grammatical, syntactic and prosodic features of the format are crucial. Vinkhuyzen and Szymanski (2005) distinguish, for instance, between self-oriented declaratives that provide the recipient with several response possibilities and other-oriented interrogatives that are a more constraining format. Heinemann (2006) argues that the use of negative interrogatives, versus positive interrogatives, displays strong entitlement to produce a request. Asmuß (2007) shows that requests done as statements display an orientation to contingencies while negative interrogatives treat the request as unproblematic. Lindström (2005) argues that imperatives, questions and statements display different degrees of entitlement for the speaker to request a specific task. Curl and Drew (2008) distinguish between two request formats: an interrogative format using modal verbs (can/could you) and a declarative format in which the modal verb is prefaced by "I was wondering if you." According to the authors, the latter displays a speaker's lower entitlement to make the request and his or her awareness of unforeseen contingencies associated with its granting.

Studies have also shown that tellings taking the form of reports of problematic events may be heard as conveying a request (Zimmerman 1984; Robinson 2001; Curl 2006; Kendrick and Drew 2014). In calls to emergency services, for instance, some callers produce reports and descriptions of a problem or trouble with no mention of what is requested to be done in its regard. However, such formats project, and are responded to by, a next action through which the call taker grants/rejects a request for assistance (Zimmerman 1992). Producing a report on a problematic event that does not explicitly mention something to be done by the interlocutor reduces the opportunities for displaying entitlement or the epistemic and deontic status to produce a request. As such, the speaker can be seen as not going on the record as requesting a specific responsive action (Drew and Couper-Kuhlen 2014).

Two Vehicles for Requests

Porters are in charge of transporting patients and objects, such as medical equipment, records, blood tests or fragile medicine containers, from one location inside the hospital to another. In our data, nurses contact porters by dialing the main number of the hospital's Porter Services department, which corresponds to a cellphone carried by one of the porters on duty; the call is automatically transferred to the number of another porter's cellphone if not answered within ten seconds. Each call contains a deferred request for a specific future action, with explicit mention of the action requested and the person who is to carry it out. The request is granted during the call, when the porter commits to fulfilling the requested transportation action, and is satisfied afterwards, when the porter carries the transportation out. In this chapter, we will first examine "inquiring as to the recipient's ability to carry out a specific action," which is the vehicle for requests pervasive in calls to porters.

The newcomer nurses are also in contact by telephone with doctors of different ranks, but mostly with interns and residents that they contact directly by dialing the number of the doctor's cellphone. Requests to doctors adopt various forms: Some are immediate requests, others deferred; some include explicit mention of a specific requested action and the person who is to carry it out, others do not (Sterie 2016). The second part of this chapter is dedicated to the illustration and analysis of requests to doctors implemented through a report on a problematic situation with a patient, and in which the nurse does not mention a specific action to be carried out that could address the situation, nor the person that could carry it out. The report vehicles a request for, *ad minima*, the doctor to tell the nurse how to address the problematic situation; this is what we call the doctor's intervention. In this sense, the implemented action is an immediate request to be granted during the call. The request is granted if the doctor intervenes by telling the nurse how to address the situation, which can consist sometimes of simply stating that there is no need to take further action. The request is rejected if the doctor refuses to intervene due to not being in a position to tell what is to be done (for instance, because currently off duty or not being the person in charge). These requests are however much more complex than those two response possibilities suggest because some reports can be formulated to make relevant not just a granting response—in the sense of the doctor intervening to tell what to do—but a specific type of granting response—in the sense of the doctor designating a specific remedial action to address the problematic situation. For instance, the doctor can tell the nurse to ignore the situation (*vs.* doing something urgently), to administer a specific drug to the patient (*vs.* a doctor coming to visit him or her) or to have a doctor visiting the patient immediately (*vs.* later in the day). The doctor can thus produce a granting response that will match, to varying extents, what the nurse's report projected, with varying degrees of obliqueness, in terms of the action to be taken to address the problematic situation. When the report projects specific remedial action, the request is granted in full if the doctor confirms the projected remedial action as the way to go to address the problematic situation; this would be the case, for instance, if the report projects that a doctor's visit is due and the doctor indeed states that he or she is coming to visit the patient. The request is only partially granted if the doctor designates a remedial action other than the one projected by the report; this happens if, for instance, the report projects the administering of medication as a remedial action but the doctor designates a visit instead. To summarize, if the doctor tells the nurse what to do, the request is granted at least *ad minima*. In cases in which the request projects a specific remedial action to be taken during the call, for instance, a verbal order for medication, the request is fully granted and satisfied when the doctor produces the verbal order. However, in the event in which the request projects a specific remedial action to be taken after the call, for instance, a doctor's visit, the request is fully granted when the doctor commits to the visit during the call and fully satisfied when the visit is actually achieved.

In the following parts of this section, we will analyze two excerpts corresponding to two calls initiated by different nurses: Call 1 consists of a request to a porter and Call 2 a request to a doctor.[8]

Inquiring as to the Recipient's Ability to Do Something

In Call 1, Leandra, a newcomer nurse working in Surgical Unit 4, calls the main number of the hospital's Porter Services; Leonard, a porter, picks up the phone; the call lasts 17.28 seconds.[9] In the central phase of the call, the nurse asks the porter to transport a patient from his room to the Radiology Department (l. 1–3). An action consisting of inquiring as to the porter's ability to carry out a specific transportation action serves as a vehicle for the request.

Ex. (1): Call 1 C179

```
1  Lea:  °<oui salut Leandra en U quatre <est-ce que tu peux
          yes hi Leandra in U four can you
2         venir chercher monsieur Ferrari au vingt-trois fenêtre
          come pick mister Ferrari up in twenty-three window
3         pour l'amener en: radio s'il te ↑plaît
          to take him to X-ray please
4         (0.4)
5  Leo:   tu me le prépares ↓j'arri[ve ]
          you get him ready for me I'm coming
6  Lea:                            [mer]ci (.) ciao
                                    thanks bye
```

In line 1, following her self-identification and bypassing a possible point of completion of her turn, the nurse moves straight from the opening of the telephone conversation to its central phase and the business of the call. In lines 1–3, the nurse addresses a request to the porter, delivered in an "interrogative single utterance format" (Zimmerman 1984). The nurse inquires as to the porter's ability to carry out a specific transportation action. The question has a positive format and is initiated by the French interrogative marker *est-ce que*, which literally translates to "is it that", and projects the turn as interrogative. The marker is followed by the subject pronoun *tu* ("you"), referring to the porter, plus the corresponding form of the modal verb *pouvoir* ("can") in the present tense. Such a conventional format for requests displays the nurse's knowledge with regard to the activity to be done, her entitlement to make the request and have it granted, and an orientation to possible contingencies as being low (Curl and Drew 2008). This format is also associated with requests benefitting the requester (Thompson et al. 2015). In this case, the nurse enlists the porter's participation in a patient-related activity, which is not directly to her own personal benefit, but falls under her professional responsibility.

The initial "Can you" formula is followed by several components that are recurrently found in nurse-porter requests for patient transportation. These are delivered using ellipsis and abbreviations, forming a very compact but information-rich request. The request is uttered in one go, in the same turn-at-talk, without the porter intervening while in progress. An initial component signals a requested independent travel action ("to come") to be performed by the porter. A second component indicates the action expected from the porter upon his arrival at the care unit ("to pick someone/something up"). Together, these components form an expression ("to come pick someone/something up") that projects an activity having an ulterior purpose. They also display the request as being made for a deferred action (Lindström 1999) to be achieved in the future. A third component indicates the target of the action expected from the porter upon his arrival at the care unit: a "mister Ferrari." The nurse does not mention his status as a patient, but this information is made available through the next, and forth, component, in which she signals the transportation starting point. Indeed, after the person's name, the nurse provides his location in the care unit: She utters a patient room number followed by the detail "window", which singles out a specific bed inside the room. The reference is time-saving and elliptic in the sense that the nurse does not use the word "room" to specify what the number refers to. A fifth component voices the specific requested transportation action: to take (*amener*) someone somewhere. The final component provides the transportation destination point: the X-ray Department. The nurse adds a please token, in turn-final position, which contributes to marking her turn as a request. In a particularly streamlined fashion, the nurse thus accomplishes a request in this turn, in which the recipient is asked to carry out a specific future action.

Porters routinely produce granting responses to nurses' patient transportation requests, and this is foreshadowed by the fact that they pick up the call. And in most calls, they do so immediately after the request, in the next turn-at-talk. This is the case in Call 1, in which, following the request, Leo produces a granting response (l. 5). The response is short although it includes several components. The first one is an unrelated clause, in the sense that it is morphosyntactically independent from the request (Thompson et al. 2015), containing instructions for the nurse to prepare the patient ("you get him ready for me", l. 5). The patient's preparation in view of transportation entails a set of tasks including informing the patient of the transportation, removing the bed bars, unplugging tubes and cables (the drips, the bell), installing mobile devices like the oxygen cylinder, ensuring that the medical file is available and clearing the space around the bed. If any of these activities are not done before the porter's arrival, the nurse needs to be contacted, which is time-consuming, or the porter may need to do it himself, which may be against standard practices and procedures. Thus, in the first component of his response, Leo displays his orientation to the request's satisfaction being contingent on the completion of these tasks by the nurse prior to his arrival. The patient's preparation is referred to as benefitting the porter ("get him ready for me") or, rather, benefitting the progress of the requested transportation. The porter uses an expression (*tu me le prépares*) employed habitually in the French language to refer to objects being prepared—the word *le* can mean "him" or "it"—which somewhat objectifies the person to be transported. It thus conveys a routine activity that centers on the transportation action instead of on the patient transported. The reference to preparatory action projects the idea that the request will be complied with, but also delays the actual and more explicit granting.

The response is completed with a second component, a graded clausal (Thompson et al. 2015) through which the porter grants the nurse's request ("I'm coming", l. 5) and commits to its future satisfaction. The porter portrays himself as being in the process of taking travel action for a rapid fulfillment of the request. The absence of explicit time details in the nurse's request is thus treated by the porter as conveying a request for an action to be achieved in the very near future.

The nurse acknowledges the porter's granting response with a "thanks" token (l. 6), which marks the request-granting status of his response, accepts it and functions as a sequence-closing third (Schegloff 2007). This is produced in overlap with the final bits of the porter's response and constitutes a rapid uptake and move to closure once the request is granted. The nurse then produces an informal terminal greeting ("bye", l. 6).

To sum up, in Call 1, the nurse produces an interrogative turn that enacts an inquiring with regard to the ability of the recipient (the porter) to carry out a specific action (can you do X). The inquiring is the vehicle for a request that explicitly designates the action to be performed (a specific transportation) and the person to carry it out (the porter). The design of the turn displays the nurse's entitlement to address the porter and ask him to perform the transportation. It conveys the nurse's ownership of a coordination activity required for patient care and only limited orientation to contingencies associated with the porter's ability to grant the request. The porter grants the request and commits to its rapid satisfaction, presenting himself as already involved in travel oriented to a swift start of the transportation. Nevertheless, he also claims ownership of the transportation, assigning a preparatory activity to the nurse, to be performed in anticipation of his arrival in the unit.

Reporting a Problematic Situation with a Patient

In Call 2, Amaryse, a newcomer nurse working in Surgical Unit 4, calls Fabien, a resident doctor in her department, on his cellphone; the call lasts 1 minute 24 seconds. In the central phase of the call (l. 2–31), the nurse conveys a request for the doctor's intervention through a vehicle action consisting of reporting a problematic situation with a patient (l. 2–8). The doctor grants it by telling her how to address the situation. The doctor states that the patient will receive a visit and gives a verbal order for medication (l. 11, 24–29). In the excerpt, we have omitted nine lines of the original transcript corresponding to an interrogative series regarding the patient's existing medication, which takes place in the middle of the doctor's response.

Ex. (2): Call 2 C69

```
1  Fab:   salu:t Amaryse
          hi Amaryse

2  May:   euh: ↑moi j't'appelle pour madame Carlot.
          uh I I'm calling you about  Ms. Carlot

3  May:   ·hhh [parce] qu'elle se plaint que:: au niveau d'sa cicatrice=
          because she complains that in regard to her scar

4  Fab:        [oui  ]
               yes

5  May:   =c'est dur comme du béton: qu'ça y fait mal, ·hh [et pis ]=
          it's hard as concrete that it hurts her and then

6  Fab:                                                    [(ouais)]=
                                                             yeah

7  May:   =que: sa jambe gau:che elle a va- pas mal de douleurs: (pis)
          that her left leg she has va quite a lot of pain and

8         elle a d'la peine à la bouger [toute seule. ]
          she has trouble moving it by herself

9  (Fab:)                               [(°↓d'accord°)]
                                              all right
```

```
10        (0.7)
11  Fab:  d'accord↓euh:m: ben écoute on va venir la voir: <est-ce
          all right uhm well listen we/someone will come see her
12        qu'elle a déjà r'çu que'qu'chose pour la douleur.
          has she already received something for the pain

(...)
22  May:  euh:: j'y ai donné 'y a: une demi-heure
          uhm I gave her half an hour ago
23        (0.4)
24  Fab:  o↓ké ↓euhm: c'que j'te propose c'est d'lui donner cinq
          okay uhm what I propose (to you) it's to give her five
25        cen:t milligrammes de: minalgine ↑gouttes,
          hundred milligrams of Minalgin drops
26  May:  ↑d'acco:rd h
          all right
27        (0.5)
28  Fab:  pour autant qu'(elle n'ait) pas d'allergi:e et puis euh: on va
          as long as she has no allergy and then uh we/someone will
29        v'nir la ↑voir.
          come see her
30        (0.3)
31  May:  £oké ça marche:£=
          okay that works
32  Fab:  =à tout à l'heure
          see you later
```

At the beginning of excerpt (2), the doctor produces a greeting and a recognitional token addressed to his interlocutor (l. 1). At this point, the nurse initiates the transition between the opening and the central part of the call, introducing the reason for it.

Following a pre-beginning hesitation mark ("uh"), the nurse produces a formulation—namely "saying-in-so-many-words-what-she-is-doing" (Garfinkel and Sacks 1970; Heritage and Watson 1979)—of her ongoing telephone action. She presents herself as the agent and the doctor as a recipient (she is calling him) and provides the name of the patient to whom the call will refer ("I I am calling you about Ms. Carlot", l. 2). This utterance functions as a preface for the actual reason for the call, which is presented in the next turn-at-talk (Potter and Hepburn 2003). The production of such prefaces is in fact a recurrent feature of nurse-to-doctor calls, in which doctors need to achieve recognition of the patient before a request with regard to this patient is issued. They allow the doctor to retrieve any previous information about the patient (Sterie 2016).

The nurse's preface has a conclusive intonation signaling turn completion (l. 2). It is followed by an inter-turn gap that lasts less than two-tenths of a second, and is thus not marked in the transcript, and a heavy inbreath which, although displaying the nurse's readiness to retake the floor, also delays the actual moment that she does it. The nurse thus provides an opportunity for the doctor to produce a go-ahead token displaying his recognition of the patient, the relevance of a call to him about "Ms. Carlot" and his availability for it. The doctor produces this multi-purpose display when uttering a "yes" (l. 4) in overlap with the nurse's launching of the reason for the call in a new turn-at-talk (l. 3).

From lines 3–8, the nurse produces a multi-unit turn enacting a report of a problematic situation concerning the previously mentioned patient. The report serves as a vehicle for the nurse to produce a request for the doctor's intervention—namely, him telling her how to address the problematic situation. The report is linked to the preface with the frame "because she complains that" (l. 3). The report is thus designed to convey the patient's complaints on her state. The frame indexes the subjective aspect of the claims about to be reported, as well as the nurse's own stance toward them (Holt and Clift 2007)—in particular, that she is reporting a patient's words instead of her own observations. The nurse continues by packaging the patient's claims in her turn. She first conveys the discomfort that the patient has been experiencing with her scar, which she then proceeds to detail (l. 3–5). Second ("and then"), she conveys the patient's issue with her left leg and also subsequently details that (l. 5–8). The fact that she is reporting on the patient's complaints and subjective experience is also conveyed, not only by the frame in line 3, but also by numerous clauses referring to the patient ("her scar", "it hurts her", "she has quite a lot of pain", "she has trouble moving it by herself"), used instead of itemized symptoms disengaged from the affected subject (e.g., "acute pain" or "mobility difficulties"). Another resource is the use of the colloquial expression "hard as concrete" (l. 5), which is more common for a layperson. This extreme case formulation (Pomerantz 1986) adds to the series of claims of discomfort to convey that the situation is problematic and justifies the nurse requesting the doctor's intervention, in the sense of asking him to tell her how to address the situation. Moreover, the report also projects a specific type of response in terms of what to do. What is projected is not a dismissal of the patient's complaints, but some type of remedial action (that remains unspecified) that could take into consideration the alleged importance of the reported symptoms.

The doctor deals with the request and grants it in the sense that he intervenes by telling the nurse how to deal with the reported problematic situation. Moreover, his response goes in the direction of taking action at the patient's side, thus orienting to something projected by the request. It is unclear, due to the overlap, whether the doctor registers the report as early as line 9, but he clearly does so following a silence in line 11 ("all right"). The receipt is followed by an elongated low-pitch hesitation mark plus another pre-beginning token ("well"). This series of components, starting with the silence in line 10, creates an effect of cautious consideration of the nurse's report. The doctor then produces an attention-grabbing device ("listen"), marking a shift in the exchange that was until this point led by the nurse and is now to be carried on by the doctor. The doctor next announces a visit to the patient (l. 11), a future remedial action, yet without articulating who exactly will do it (use of the French impersonal third-person singular pronoun *on* which can mean either "we" or "someone"). This initial response component is rapidly followed by a question, addressed to the nurse, that turns out to be the first of an interrogative series partially reproduced in the transcript (l. 11–24). Studies on requests in institutional encounters have recurrently identified interrogative series between the request and its response, functioning as pre-second inserted expansions (Zimmerman 1984; Wakin and Zimmerman 1999; Drew 2006). In Call 2, the doctor produces the first question of the interrogative series following an initial response component (announcing the visit). The response is suspended while the doctor asks for and collects information about the patient's prescribed and administered analgesic medication. The interrogative series displays that a full response to the nurse's request for the doctor's intervention is contingent on him obtaining additional information on the case, such as regarding the treatment, whereas the report concentrated on the patient's claims about her problematic state. The interrogative series also displays the inquiry work involved in reaching a medical decision that the doctor co-constructs and shares with the nurse. We can observe a striking contrast between this and the organization of the request sequence in Call 1, in which the nurse's request was followed by the porter's response to it in the next turn-at-talk.

In line 24, the doctor receives the nurse's response to the last question of the interrogative series ("okay"). He then resumes his response to the nurse's report in lines 3–8 by designating another remedial action. The doctor presents it as a proposal ("what I propose (to you)", l. 24), submitted to the nurse, thus conveying that both interlocutors share agency in deciding how to address the problematic situation (Houtkoop 1987) but also that they will both be agents and beneficiaries of the projected action (Couper-Kuhlen 2014).[10] In line 11, the doctor has given a first response component, committing to a visit to the patient. He now adds a second component to this (a verbal order for pain medication) that results from the interrogative series. He thus keeps granting the nurse's request for his intervention, as he is still engaged in telling her how to address the reported problematic situation. He also remains oriented to designating some type of rapid remedial action by the patient's side as projected by the request. Although the first response component, in line 11, designates a future remedial action (the doctor's visit), the second component, in lines 24–28, is in itself a remedial action (a verbal order for medication) whose site and time is the call itself.

Following the nurse's acknowledgment (l. 26), the doctor supplements the verbal order with a reference to contraindications, such as the patient potentially being allergic to the prescribed medicine (l. 28). In passing, this alerts the nurse to check the patient's file before administering it. The doctor then restates his prior commitment regarding the patient receiving a medical visit ("we/someone will come see her", l. 28–29) using an identical word choice as in line 11 when this part of his response was first issued. The nurse regards the designated remedial action as one that can easily be accommodated (l. 31) and the doctor moves to closing the call (l. 32). All in all, the doctor's response displays an orientation to the importance of the situation conveyed by the nurse's report. The doctor lays down a step-by-step and coordinated response to the situation that commits both the medical and the nursing team: The nurse will administer the medicine, once having checked for contraindications, while waiting for a doctor to come visit the patient.

To sum up, in Call 2, the nurse produces a report that serves as a vehicle for a request. She reports a problematic situation with a patient without specifically mentioning what could be done to address it or who should do it. The nurse remits the situation to the doctor, having herself already reached the limit of her own agency. As the report is delivered to the doctor and relates a situation that is medically problematic and actionable, it renders relevant the doctor's intervention, which consists of telling the nurse how to address the situation. Moreover, in her report, the nurse packages the patient's complains regarding her symptoms, displaying that they are in themselves worrisome enough to warrant some type of remedial action at the patient's side. In Call 2, the doctor grants the request not *ad minima*, by just telling the nurse what is to be done, but fully, by referring to remedial action to be taken rapidly, thus orienting to something projected by the report. Moreover, he designates specific remedial actions to be taken—a visit to the patient as well as the administering of a drug—which the report itself did not mention or project. The designation of these actions comes out as the doctor's contribution to dealing with the problematic situation; the nurse agrees with him on the actions to be taken even though she did not beforehand go on record as requesting them.

Discussion and Conclusion

The newcomer nurse faces daily work situations, which are furthermore shaped by the way the nurse reacts to them and presents them to interlocutors. The vehicle that the nurse uses when producing a request is part of the shaping of the situation at the basis of the request. By inquiring as to the interlocutor's ability of carrying out a specific action, the nurse responds to and produces an ordinary situation. The situation has less familiar contours when the nurse reports the situation as being problematic and without mentioning either what could be done to address it or by whom this could be done.

In Call 1, the nurse inquires as to the ability of her interlocutor to carry out a specific future action. This is a vehicle for a request that comes into play time and again when nurses ask porters to transport patients and objects to/from the care unit to other places in the hospital. Nurses also use it with doctors, though very rarely and almost exclusively in relation to routine medical tasks, such as having them come to the care unit to sign medication orders or for a scheduled patient visit. The inquiry displays the nurse's knowledge in regard to what needs to be done and by whom, her entitlement to ask for it, and a limited orientation to contingencies associated with the recipient's ability to grant the request. As previously explained, the porter picking up the phone implies that he is available for transportation action; otherwise, he would let the call pass on to another colleague's cellphone. This is something to which the nurse orients when moving straight from her self-identification to a request that she delivers in one go, with all the necessary information for the porter to satisfy it as soon as the call ends.

According to our data, the format employed for producing requests consisting of inquiring as to the ability of the doctor to carry out a specific future action is employed by nurses only when it is obvious that the doctor, and no one else, should be the one doing what is requested. However, in other calls to doctors, nurses may select reporting a problematic situation as a vehicle for requesting their intervention; such a format is only employed when contacting doctors and never, for example, when contacting porters. The report enacts a request for the doctor's intervention even without a specific action for him or her to take being mentioned. In Call 2, the nurse conveys that the patient's complaints are worrisome and refers to symptoms that are medically actionable. The nurse calling the doctor displays her understanding that the situation should be submitted to an authority competent to deal with it. The report makes relevant a doctor's intervention to state what (if anything) should be done to address the problematic situation. Moreover, the nurse shapes the report to make relevant rapid action at the patient's side, but leaves the details up to the recipient, such as what exactly should be done and by whom. By not referring to a specific action to be taken to remedy the problematic situation, the nurse avoids going on record with what this could be.

Call 1 and Call 2 are profoundly different in terms of display of knowledge relative to the action to take to address the two care-related situations that are the reason for the calls. In Call 1, the nurse handles a practical, very concrete and frequently encountered issue: a patient in need of being transported, which is related to patient care but nevertheless tangential to his medical situation. As previously discussed, the nurse and the porter refer to the patient only as the object of the transportation. The nurse displays her knowledge of how to handle the situation by calling the porter, making a request that tells him what to do and providing him with all the necessary information to act on the situation that is the reason for the call.

In contrast, in Call 2 the nurse makes no reference to what action to take on the reported problematic situation. The nurse does not display knowledge of what is to be done, except that something should be done, though this does not necessarily index a lack of more specific knowledge. While the nurse is trained to face medical problems, there is not just one way to address the one reported in Call 2, except maybe calling the doctor. In Call 1, the nurse acts as a coordination agent of a previously decided routine and practical undertaking, whereas in Call 2 she acts more as a care provider in a developing medical situation. Executing is the matter of Call 1. In contrast, the situation reported in Call 2 solicits clinical appraisal to address the patient's complaints about her condition and medical decision-making. Studies show that nurses usually stream medical knowledge difficultly and indirectly when talking to doctors (Apker et al. 2005). To deliver in Call 2 a request similar to the one to the porter would require the nurse to know what action to take to remedy the reported situation and to be able and entitled to display this knowledge. When producing a turn-at-talk restricted to a report of a problematic situation, the nurse avoids going on record with a view on a medical decision. Moreover, she displays that she calls the doctor not because she cannot cope with her own work but because the situation goes beyond her domain of expertise and right to take action. The deployment of a report thus exhibits the nurse's own access to knowledge as well as the relative legitimacy of her request.

Both the porter and the doctor engage in action to respond to the situation that is the reason for the call and involve the nurse in how to move forward in it; they nevertheless do it in ways that differ substantially. In Call 1, the porter instructs the nurse to prepare the patient for the transportation, something that facilitates his own work, displaying it as unproblematic but necessary to remind the nurse of. He does not make relevant the nurse's uptake of the instruction as he immediately proceeds to announce his immediate arrival in the unit. He thus displays entitlement to instruct the nurse and to expect her to do as told. Contrasting with the porter's expeditious response, in Call 2, the doctor delivers his own response in several steps moving from the first one to the second on the condition of an interrogative series. Several of his response turns feature pre-beginnings including elongated low-pitch hesitation marks that contribute to an effect of cautious consideration of the actions to be taken. Furthermore, he gives the verbal medication order in the form of a proposal submitted to the nurse, but without assigning the task of administering the medicine explicitly to her. He also provides several opportunities for the nurse to agree with the remedial action that he lays out, which the nurse promptly seizes. Interestingly enough, the interlocutor to whom the nurse addresses a request more cautiously is also the one who responds in the same vein. In fact, in both cases the response to the request mirrors the portrayal of the situation it is based on, as conveyed by the nurse. The porter's expeditious response confirms that the requested transport corresponds to an ordinary situation. The doctor's cautious and multi-staged response confirms that the situation is indeed complex and requires him to step in. This is not because of any insufficiency of knowledge on the nurse's part but because of the specific medical expertise and the rights to action needed to address the situation. As a result, the doctor and the nurse emerge as equally competent professionals, albeit with different domains of expertise and action.

The multifold concept of interactional competence (Pekarek Doehler 2006) includes the command of a practice, the ability to discernibly deploy it and the socially regulated legitimacy to do so. In this discussion, we have fixed on differentials of knowledge and displays of knowledge as grounds for a differential use of request practices. In terms of the present volume, the knowledge that each participant interactively ascribes to him and herself as well as to his or her interlocutor functions as a basis for the legitimacy of whatever the participants are doing. That is to say, the nurse's entitlement to make the request is shaped by the interlocutors' displays and ascriptions of knowledge. Forcefully conveyed when addressing the porter in Call 1, the nurse's entitlement to make the request is subtly tempered by the porter instructing her to prepare the patient in advance. In contrast, when displaying that deciding upon the remedial action is not self-evident, the doctor elevates the initially understated legitimacy of the nurse's request in Call 2. Moreover, access to knowledge and the right to display it constitute a resource not only for shaping the legitimacy of the request but more fundamentally for establishing the social identities and relationships of interlocutors (Raymond and Heritage 2006). The vehicles that the nurse deploys when addressing a request to the porter or the doctor display not only contrasting access and rights to knowledge and entitlement to make the request, but also who the speakers are, relative to one another. Instead of taking asymmetrical social identities and professional relationships as givens, we have shown ways in which these can be talked into being (Heritage 1984).

Notes

1. "New on the job. Relevance-making and assessment practices of interactional competencies in young nurses' hospital telephone calls," a study in the framework of the Sinergia IC-You project (SNSF grant no. 136291), conducted at the University of Fribourg in partnership with the *Haute école de Santé Arc* and the *Hôpital Neuchâtelois*. We thank Dr. Vassiliki Markaki for her contribution to the study and careful reading of the chapter, as well as the two anonymous reviewers for their insightful comments, and Elisabeth Lyman for her editing work. All remaining errors are our own.
2. In this chapter, we reserve the term "format" to refer to a grammatical form (an interrogative, for instance) and use the term "vehicle" to refer to an action (inquiring, for instance) that implements a second one (requesting, for instance), instead of using both terms indiscriminately as in Schegloff (2007).
3. For all purposes, we consider the three nurses as a group without making individual differences. The examined conversational practices are common

to the three newcomer nurses, but the collected data does not allow us to say if they are typical/atypical of newcomer nurses or experienced nurses in general.

4. Out of 56 telephone numbers, 20 correspond to doctors of the Surgery Department—cumulating 34% of the calls—and 1 to the main number of Porter Services—cumulating 14% of the calls. The remaining 52% of the calls are distributed between 35 telephone numbers corresponding to 17 interlocutors. None of these interlocutors cumulate individually more calls than the doctors or the porters.
5. Concomitantly, ensuing analysis in this chapter shows that dealing with, and making relevant, time constraints is a central dimension of the calls' organization. On calls to porters, see also: González-Martínez and Markaki 2013 and González-Martínez et al. 2014.
6. A main activity corresponds to what interlocutors shape as the business of the call or the reason for it. Besides requests, the identified main activities are informings, instructions and call transfers. The identification of the calls' main activities relies on our common sense and conversation analytic informed knowledge of how they are accountably accomplished at the hospital as well as in everyday life.
7. Following Schegloff (2007, 41–44), we indeed consider "telling" as a generic type of action taking a variety of forms including reporting, noticing, announcing and storytelling, among others.
8. González-Martínez et al. (2016), Sterie (2015) and Sterie (2016) demonstrate the recurrence in our corpus of the practices presented in the two excerpts of this chapter.
9. We have replaced the original names of persons and care units with fictional ones. The numbers in parentheses refer to the lines of the excerpt. See Appendix for a list of the transcription conventions following Jefferson (2004).
10. We are aware that "suggest" may be a more natural translation, in this particular context, of the original French-language expression *j'te propose* (l. 24) than "propose." We have nevertheless opted for a translation that preserves the distinction between "proposal" and "suggestion" advanced by Couper-Kuhlen (2014): Both the speaker and the recipient are agents and beneficiaries of the future action projected by a proposal, whereas only the recipient is the agent and beneficiary of the future action projected by a suggestion.

Appendix: Transcription Conventions

[ ]	overlapping talk
=	continuous talk
(0.2)	silence in tenths of a second
(.)	micro-pause
.	final intonation
,	continuing intonation
?	rising intonation
:	prolongation of the preceding sound
speci-	cut-off
<u>you</u>	emphasis
°all right	talk starts markedly soft
°yes°	softer talk
↑	rise in pitch
↓	fall in pitch
>yes<	talk is compressed
<because	hurried start
·h	inhalation
h	exhalation
( )	unachievable, likely or alternative hearing
£ciao£	smiling voice

References

Apker, J., Propp, K. M., & Zabava Ford, W. (2005). Negotiating status and identity tensions in healthcare team interactions: An exploration of nurse role dialectics. *Journal of Applied Communication Research, 33*(2), 93–115.

Asmuß, B. (2007). What do people expect from public services? Requests in public service encounters. *Hermes—Journal of Language and Communication Studies, 38*, 65–83.

Atkinson, P. (1995). *Medical talk and medical work: The liturgy of the clinic.* London: Sage.

Barenfanger, J., Sautter, R. L., Lang, D. L., Collins, S. M., Hacek, D. M., & Peterson, L. R. (2004). Improving patient safety by repeating (read-back) telephone reports of critical information. *American Journal of Clinical Pathology, 121*(6), 801–803.

Couper-Kuhlen, E. (2014). What does grammar tell us about action? *Pragmatics, 24*(3), 623–647.

Craven, A., & Potter, J. (2010). Directives: Entitlement and contingency in action. *Discourse Studies, 12*(4), 419–442.

Curl, T. (2006). Offers of assistance: Constraints on syntactic design. *Journal of Pragmatics, 38*(8), 1257–1280.

Curl, T., & Drew, P. (2008). Contingency and action: A comparison of two forms of requesting. *Research on Language and Social Interaction, 41*(2), 129–153.

Drew, P. (2006). Misalignments in "after-hours" calls to a British GP's practice: A study in telephone medicine. In J. Heritage & D. W. Maynard (Eds.), *Communication in medical care: Interaction between primary care physicians and patients* (pp. 416–444). Cambridge: Cambridge University Press.

Drew, P., & Couper-Kuhlen, E. (2014). Requesting: From speech act to recruitment. In P. Drew & E. Couper-Kuhlen (Eds.), *Requesting in social interaction* (pp. 1–34). Amsterdam: John Benjamins.

Garfinkel, H., & Sacks, H. (1970). On formal structures of practical actions. In J. C. McKinney & E. A. Tiryakian (Eds.), *Theoretical sociology: Perspectives and developments* (pp. 337–366). New York: Appleton-Century-Crofts.

González-Martínez, E., & Markaki, V. (2013). Dealing with time in nurses' phone requests to hospital porters. In *International conference on Conversation Analysis and Clinical Encounters*, University of York, 5 July 2013.

González-Martínez, E., Markaki, V., & Bovey, F. (2016). "Demandes régime dernière minute" lors de conversations téléphoniques infirmière-diététicienne. In K. Stroumza & H. Messmer (Eds.), *Langage et savoir-faire: des pratiques professionnelles du travail social et de la santé passées à la loupe* (pp. 85–110). Genève: Editions IES.

González-Martínez, E., Markaki, V., & Sterie, A.-C. (2014). Conversational and organizational temporal work in nurse-porter hospital calls. In *International conference on Conversation Analysis*, University of California, Los Angeles, 26 June 2014.

González-Martínez, E., & Sterie, A.-C. (2014). Request formats in nurses' hospital telephone calls. In *International conference on Applied Linguistics and Professional Practice*, University of Geneva, 11 September 2014.

Heinemann, T. (2006). "Will you or can't you?" Displaying entitlement in interrogative requests. *Journal of Pragmatics, 38*(7), 1081–1104.

Heritage, J. (1984). *Garfinkel and ethnomethodology*. Cambridge: Polity press.

Heritage, J. (2012). Epistemics in action: Action formation and territories of knowledge. *Research on Language and Social Interaction, 45*(1), 1–29.

Heritage, J., & Raymond, G. (2005). The terms of agreement: Indexing epistemic authority and subordination in talk-in-interaction. *Social Psychology Quarterly, 68*(1), 15–38.

Heritage, J. C., & Watson, D. R. (1979). Formulations as conversational objects. In G. Psathas (Ed.), *Everyday language: Studies in ethnomethodology* (pp. 123–162). New York: Irvington.

Holt, E., & Clift, R. (Eds.). (2007). *Reporting talk: Reported speech in interaction.* Cambridge: Cambridge University Press.

Houtkoop, H. (1987). *Establishing agreement: An analysis of proposal-acceptance sequences.* Dordrecht: Foris.

Jefferson, G. (2004). Glossary of transcript symbols with an introduction. In G. H. Lerner (Ed.), *Conversation analysis: Studies from the first generation* (pp. 13–31). Amsterdam: John Benjamins.

Kendrick, K. H., & Drew, P. (2014). The putative preference for offers over requests. In P. Drew & E. Couper-Kuhlen (Eds.), *Requesting in social interaction* (pp. 87–113). Amsterdam: John Benjamins.

Levinson, S. C. (2013). Action formation and ascription. In J. Sidnell & T. Stivers (Eds.), *The handbook of conversation analysis* (pp. 103–130). Malden, MA: Wiley Blackwell.

Lindström, A. (1999). *Language as social action. Grammar, prosody, and interaction in Swedish conversation. Grammatik, prosodi och interaktion i svenska samtal.* PhD, University of Uppsala.

Lindström, A. (2005). Language as social action: A study of how senior citizens request assistance with practical tasks in the Swedish home help service. In A. Hakulinen & M. Selting (Eds.), *Syntax and lexis in conversation: Studies on the use of linguistic resources in talk-in-interaction* (pp. 209–230). Amsterdam: John Benjamins.

Pekarek Doehler, S. (2006). Compétence et langage en action. *Bulletin suisse de linguistique appliquée, 84*, 4–45.

Pomerantz, A. (1986). Extreme case formulations: A way of legitimizing claims. *Human Studies, 9*(2), 219–229.

Potter, J., & Hepburn, A. (2003). "I'm a bit concerned": Early actions and psychological constructions in a child protection helpline. *Research on Language and Social Interaction, 36*(3), 197–240.

Raymond, G., & Heritage, J. (2006). The epistemics of social relations. Owning grandchildren. *Language in Society, 35*(5), 677–705.
Robinson, J. D. (2001). Asymmetry in action: Sequential resources in the negotiation of a prescription request. *Text, 21*(1–2), 19–54.
Sacks, H., Schegloff, E. A., & Jefferson, G. (1974). A simplest systematics for the organization of turn-taking for conversation. *Language, 50*(4), 696–735.
Schegloff, E. A. (2007). *Sequence organization in interaction: A primer in conversation analysis I.* Cambridge: Cambridge University Press.
Searle, J. (1975). Indirect speech acts. In P. Cole & J. L. Morgan (Eds.), *Syntax and semantics III: Speech acts* (pp. 59–82). New York: Academic Press.
Steensig, J., & Heinemann, T. (2014). The social and moral work of modal constructions in granting remote requests. In P. Drew & E. Couper-Kuhlen (Eds.), *Requesting in social interaction* (pp. 145–170). Amsterdam: John Benjamins.
Sterie, A.-C. (2015). Recalling the doctor to action: Two requesting formats employed by a nurse for making relevant the doctor's intervention. *Novitas Royal—Research on Youth and Language, 9*(2), 118–137.
Sterie, A.-C. (2016). *Nurses reporting problems in hospital telephone interaction. A practice for requesting doctors' intervention.* PhD, University of Fribourg.
Stevanovic, M. (2011). Participants' deontic rights and action formation: The case of declarative requests for action. *InLiSt—Interaction and Linguistic Structures, 52*, 1–37.
Stevanovic, M., & Peräkylä, A. (2012). Deontic authority in interaction: The right to announce, propose, and decide. *Research on Language and Social Interaction, 45*(3), 297–321.
Strauss, A. (1988). The articulation of project work: An organizational process. *The Sociological Quarterly, 29*(2), 163–178.
Thompson, S. A., Fox, B. A., & Couper-Kuhlen, E. (Eds.). (2015). *Grammar in everyday talk: Building responsive actions.* Cambridge: Cambridge University Press.
Vinkhuyzen, E., & Szymanski, M. (2005). "Would you like to do it yourself?": Service requests and their non-granting responses. In K. Richards & P. Seedhouse (Eds.), *Applying conversation analysis* (pp. 91–106). New York: Palgrave Macmillan.
Wakin, M., & Zimmerman, D. H. (1999). Reduction and specialization in emergency and directory assistance calls. *Research on Language and Social Interaction, 32*(4), 409–437.

Zimmerman, D. H. (1984). Talk and its occasion: The case of calling the police. In D. Schiffrin (Ed.), *Meaning, form, and use in context: Linguistic applications* (pp. 210–228). Washington, DC: Georgetown University Press.

Zimmerman, D. H. (1992). The interactional organization of calls for emergency assistance. In P. Drew & J. Heritage (Eds.), *Talk at work: Interaction in institutional settings* (pp. 418–469). Cambridge: Cambridge University Press.

Part II

Transitioning into Work

7

Becoming a "Good Nurse": Social Norms of Conduct and the Management of Interpersonal Relations

Helen Melander

This chapter concerns the notion of interactional competence in institutional practices with an interest in how interactional competence is related to socialization into socially and morally appropriate ways of acting in a professional practice. Interactional competence is discussed within an ethnomethodological and conversation analytic (henceforth EMCA) framework (e.g., Goodwin 2000), in which the aim lies in elaborating detailed descriptions of ordinary and professional practices, that include linguistic conduct integrated with the range of semiotic resources participants use to collaboratively accomplish social actions. The data that are used as a point of departure for the discussion consist of audio-video recordings of a training session, in which nursing students at a Swedish university hospital's clinical training center learn to insert peripheral venous catheters (PVC). At the center, the students practice their performance of particular professional skills. However, as I will show, the participants are also making relevant

H. Melander (✉)
Department of Education, Uppsala University, Uppsala, Sweden

S. Pekarek Doehler et al. (eds.), *Interactional Competences in Institutional Settings*, DOI 10.1007/978-3-319-46867-9_7

social skills and the management of interpersonal relations (see Nguyen 2006). In this chapter, I will explore how these latter are oriented to as an intrinsic aspect of interactional competence and "doing being" a competent nurse, and how questions of cultural and social norms are made relevant in interaction between a teacher and her students (see Bergmann 1998; Jacoby and Ochs 1995).

Interactional Competence and Participation in Situated Practices

Put simply, the notion of interactional competence involves knowing "when to speak, when not, and as to what to talk about with whom, when, where, in what manner" (Hymes 1972, 277). Interactional competence refers to the ability to use language accurately and appropriately in a social and cultural context, implying the capacity to coordinate actions with others (Hall and Pekarek Doehler 2011). The ability to communicate competently is not an individual achievement but is co-constructed by all participants in an interaction (Young 2013), and interactional competence encompasses knowledge of context-specific practices in which participant roles and role relationships are accomplished. Moreover, it includes the ability to deploy and to recognize patterns of interaction (e.g., turn-taking, recipient-design, joint attention and repair patterns), by which participants establish and maintain shared understanding of the interactional work that they are accomplishing together (Hall and Pekarek Doehler 2011, 2).

The concept of participation theoretically and analytically frames how human bodies interact in a socio-cultural environment and build action in concert with each other (Goodwin 2000). Participation involves not only social interaction but also interaction with artifacts and the material environment, in which "[p]articipants build actions by performing systematic operations on a public substrate which provides many different kinds of resources that can be reused, decomposed, and transformed" (Goodwin 2013, 8). Moreover, participants in face-to-face interaction put different multi-layered contextual configurations into play. From this perspective, actions are laminated, meaning that they consist of layers of modalities such as language, body (e.g., gaze, gestures) and the material world (Goodwin 2000). The notion of epistemic ecologies encompasses the public distribution and organization of knowledge and the dynamic relationships between different participant positions (Goodwin 2013). Within epistemic ecologies, actions are organized in ways that help to create and sustain socially organized ways of knowing, seeing and acting upon the world. Through apprenticeship within diverse epistemic ecologies, "communities invest their members with the resources required to understand each other in just the ways that make possible the accomplishment of ongoing, situated action" (Goodwin 2013, 9). In other words, members develop the interactional competence required to participate in professional practices.

Interactional Competence in Professional Practices

Within the rich body of EMCA research on the organizational features and interactional processes of medical encounters (for an overview, e.g., see Pilnick et al. 2010), there have been a number of studies focusing on medical training and socialization. What has been explored is, for example, the artful organization of instructions and demonstrations in authentic surgery, where novices are performing the surgery under the supervision of an expert surgeon (Koschmann et al. 2007; Hindmarsh and Pilnick 2007), or where they are watching while the expert is working (Sanchez Svensson et al. 2010; see also Mondada 2014a). Hindmarsh et al. (2011) have undertaken work within dental training where student dentists are treating real patients, focusing on how the instructors use not only talk but also bodily conduct to determine whether the students have reached a sufficient level of understanding. Within the context of a simulated environment, Hindmarsh et al. (2014) explored how tutors and student dentists attend to matters of realism in the course of instructional sequences, highlighting how tutors routinely invoke "real life" in instructional corrections. These sequences reveal the work that tutors undertake to compensate for the insufficiency of the simulator, linking actions performed on the mock-ups to what one needs to think about when performing the same actions on a live patient.

In those studies, the focus is primarily on the development of professional skills, whereas the primary interest in the current chapter is the notion of interactional competence and the management of interpersonal relations. With a similar interest, Nguyen (e.g., 2006, 2008, 2011), in the context of patient consultations in pharmaceutics, studied how novice pharmacists develop interactional competence in the workplace, focusing on epistemic and interpersonal skills in patient consultations. With a longitudinal perspective, Nguyen (2012) analyzed how the novices change their professional performance, exploring how a number of aspects of interactional competence develop over time: the sequencing of actions, the management of topics, the employment of specific linguistic resources in formulation and the co-construction of roles in interaction. She has, for example, shown how a novice pharmacist adapted his counseling over time so that it responded more effectively to the patients' displayed perspectives and needs, thus successfully managing the transactional and interpersonal functions of the consultations (Nguyen 2006, 2011). Nguyen (2011, 176) argues that "[i]t is the ability to utilize interactional resources to apply field-specific knowledge and skills appropriately in specific moments of interaction that marks one's performance as that of a competent professional." Given that interactional competence involves the ability to act in relevant ways in particular social and material contexts, norms of conduct and appropriateness are intrinsic to the concept (see Hymes 1972), that is, the aspect of interactional competence that is the focus of this chapter.

Social Norms and Interactional Competence

An EMCA approach to morality takes an interest in moral issues as they are coped with in discourse and explores "the situated, contingent nature of moral life" (Cromdal and Tholander 2014, 156), focusing on morality-in-interaction, that is, morality as it evolves in unfolding courses of action. Morality is omnipresent in everyday life and is constructed in and through social interaction. Morality and interaction are intertwined, and virtually any kind of utterance may take on a moral meaning. Bergmann (1998) writes that participants draw upon a multitude of resources in conveying moral meanings either explicitly or implicitly. A primary resource is vocabulary and the use of words with an evaluative tone in constructing an utterance. Para-verbal means, such as laughter, are used to signal moral issues and represent indirect modes of moralizing. Another powerful means by which participants evaluate each other's actions is through stance-taking, for example, when reporting what others have said. Moral work is also done through references to membership categories, by which participants convey cultural and moral knowledge about social life. In such a way, members constitute themselves as moral agents in and through dialogue, and it is through an analysis of everyday interactions that the workings of morality can be revealed (Linell and Rommetveit 1998).

In a slightly different but related tradition, language socialization studies examine routine mundane language activities for their socializing import. Although focusing mainly on children and families, these studies relate the conversational work of participants to the co-construction of socio-cultural competence across the life span. In such a perspective, novices at any age are seen as simultaneously appropriating and transforming both language activities and the socio-cultural structures they index (Jacoby and Ochs 1995, 175). According to this perspective, children or novices are socialized to "think and feel in ways that resonate with notions of morality that relate to social situations, specifically to expected and preferred modes of participation in these situations" (Ochs and Kremer-Sadlik 2007, 5).

In a similar vein, by examining what sense of morality is being practiced and accomplished in the training sessions as situated activities, the aim of this chapter is to explore how student nurses are socialized to act in accordance with cultural and social norms of the professional practice of nursing. What do the participants consider as the social norms and moral expectations of their future profession? Which interactional resources do they draw upon when making relevant cultural and social norms of conduct?

Research Setting and Analytic Approach

The interactions analyzed in this chapter are drawn from an audio-video recording (five hours in total) of one training session in which nursing students at a Swedish university hospital's clinical training center practice how to insert PVC. A PVC is a small, flexible tube (a catheter) that is placed into a peripheral vein in order to administer medication or fluids. The PVC is introduced into the vein by a needle that is subsequently removed while the catheter remains in place. Six students and one teacher were participating in the training session. The students first practiced the insertion on paper tissue and then on two different mock-ups: (1) a small device imitating a part of skin and vessels referred to as a "pillow" and (2) a plastic full-size arm. As a last stage, they inserted the PVC on a fellow student. This last part was not compulsory, and the students could choose whether they wanted to participate or not.[1]

Within medical training, it is common to work in simulated environments (Rooney et al. 2015), such as clinical training centers, in order for the students to develop professional skills and competences without the constraints that work on patients' entail. However, the fact that the students in the current case also practice doing the insertions on each other, that is, on a human body, implies that what they are practicing here-and-now closely resembles future work on a live patient. The training session is designed to provide the students with opportunities to practice professional skills, but as will be shown, they also develop interactional competences as ways of managing interpersonal relations.

The participants were found to mobilize the category term "patient" (Schegloff 2007) as a resource when actualizing preferred or expected modes of participation. The excerpts selected for analysis all contain references to the category and show a variety of ways in which the students and their teacher orient to cultural and social norms of conduct in this setting, and how these can be understood as constituting intrinsic aspects of interactional competence and socialization into a professional practice.

The analysis addresses the emergent properties of objects and bodies, and pays specific attention to the ways in which verbal as well as bodily conduct is reflexively produced in a material environment (Goodwin

2000). It explores how participants in social interaction mobilize a set of resources for the local situated, intersubjective and methodic organization of action (Mondada 2014b), focusing on issues of social conduct and interpersonal relations. The excerpts have been transcribed following conventions developed within conversation analysis (e.g., Jefferson 2004; see Appendix for symbols used here). Drawings made from video frames are integrated within the transcripts in order to highlight analytically relevant embodied actions and the participants' orientations to the social and material environment. The participants are speaking Swedish, and the English translations are done with the aim of staying as close as possible to the Swedish word order and ways of expression.

Analysis

In the remainder of the chapter I will analyze the interactional resources that the participants draw upon to embody what they consider as the social norms and moral expectations of their future profession as nurses. The analysis is divided into three sections. The first section (exx. 7.1, 7.2) contains an analysis in which the category term "patient" is mobilized to call the students' attention to the fact that they in the future will be working on patients that have cognitive and emotional capacities. In the second section (Ex. 7.3), the participants use quoted speech and enactments to invoke a hypothetical scenario involving a nurse and a patient, in order to teasingly criticize problematic student conduct. In the third and last section (Ex. 7.4), two of the students co-construct a hypothetical narrative, an *atrocity story* (Dingwall 1977) staging a nurse with questionable morals, thus playfully exploring social norms of proper nurse conduct.

The Patient as a Cognitive and Feeling Subject

In excerpt 7.1, the category term "patient" is invoked by the teacher to remind the students that when performing the insertion of the PVC, they will need to consider the patient not only as an object of a medical intervention but also as a "living person" (l. 8). The teacher and two of the students, Amir and Gustav, are sitting at a table. The students have finished practicing on the mock-ups and are getting ready to do the insertion on each other. In preparation, the participants are talking through the procedures (Excerpt 7.1).

Ex. (7.1): Not an arm, a living person
K1-040108-2 08.27-08.48

```
 1 AMI: hands- de va tvätta händerna, h[andskar]na,
        glove- it was wash your hands, gloves,
 2 TEA:                                  [m       ]
 3 TEA: m:¿
 4 AMI: e: sprita orden:tligt,
        uh: put alcohol pro:perly,
 5      (1.9)
 6 GUS: >plockar ja fram-<
        >I take out-<
 7 TEA: *innan #1 de: (.) nu har ni en *patient*, inte en
         before   tha:t (.) now you have a patient, not an
        *hand stop signal                *beat*
 8      #2 *arm, en  #3   *le:vande* (.) person¿ va gör ni då?
            arm, a          li:ving (.) person¿ what do you do then?
          *indicating arm *beat*
```

```
 9 GUS: informe:rar.
        info:rm.
10 TEA: >m< om va:d¿
        >m< about wha:t¿
11      (1.1)
12 GUS: va vi ska göra för nåt.
        what we're going to do.
13      (0.7)
14 TEA: °m::¿° (0.6) <och> (0.5) varför va.
        °m::¿° (0.6) <and> (0.5) why right.
15 GUS: °°ja,°°
        °°yes,°°
16 TEA: +m¿+
17 ami  +nods+
```

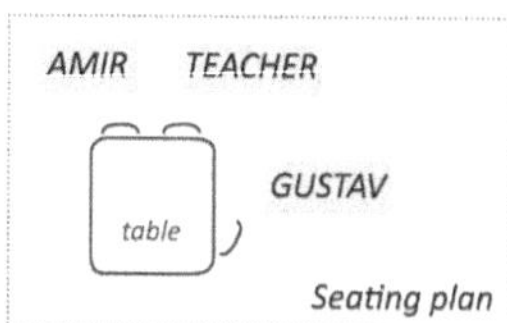

Amir has enumerated some of the required preparative actions when Gustav in line 6 initiates a list of items that they need to take out. The teacher interrupts and a correction sequence is initiated (McHoul 1990) in which the category "patient" is invoked: *nu har ni en patient, inte en arm, en le:v&e (.) person¿* "now you have a patient, not an arm, a li:ving (.) person¿," describing the patient as a living person and not a plastic arm. This is highlighted by embodied actions that build a contrast between the material object (the arm) that they have in front of them on the table and the imagined patient, by switching position of the hand from the shape of a stop sign, to indicate the mock-up arm, and then back up again (see fig. 1–3 in Ex. 7.1). Gustav's answer *informe:rar* "info:rm" in line 9 aligns with this change in footing and is oriented toward having a patient that they can talk to in front of them. The teacher responds with a brief >*m*< that acknowledges that it is the question of information that she was looking for, however, that she is in search of a more elaborate answer is displayed by the addition of an open repair initiator *om va:d¿* "about wha:t¿" that leaves a clue about the domain of the answer, but leaves an opportunity for the student to self-correct (McHoul 1990, 357). The silence in line 11 indicates that Gustav has problems answering the question, but he then adds the format tied *va vi ska göra för nåt* "what we're going to do." The lack of uptake in line 13, the minimal acknowledgement token that is followed by a suitable answer gap (McHoul 1990), a drawn-out *<och>* "<and>" that explicitly requests additional information and one more answer gap indicate (1) that the students are having problems coming up with more answers, and (2) that the teacher is not content with the answer. When no answer is forthcoming, the teacher herself adds the correct one: *varför va*, "why right".

The students are having difficulties answering the teacher's question. They are oriented toward the (technical) performance of the procedure itself, whereas the teacher emphasizes that the patient needs to be informed about the medical procedure. In particular the question of why can be understood as related to the management of interpersonal relations and is making relevant a treatment of the patient as a cognitive subject. In other words, the students are orienting toward the patient as an object (if indeed orienting to the patient at all), whereas the teacher is invoking the patient as a subject with cognitive and rational capacities.

In excerpt 7.2, another aspect of the management of interpersonal relations is made relevant that is related to being able to understand what the patient is experiencing and thereby show empathy. The category "patient" is invoked in order to encourage one of the students to use her own experiences of pain as a resource when talking to a future patient (l. 7–8). The procedure that they are performing should not be very painful (although some pain can be accepted) as this indicates that something is wrong. Inflicting pain on someone is a moral theme (Bergmann 1998; Heritage and Lindström 1998), even within a medical context where the patient can be expected to tolerate some pain (see Heath 1989). Hedda's first attempt was a failure as the needle was not placed correctly and went through the vessel. Malin expressed audible pain that was however not ratified by either Hedda or the teacher, who instead focused on withdrawing the PVC. The second attempt is successful, and when excerpt (7.2) begins, the PVC is in place and Hedda is fixing it by taping it to Malin's skin. All through the excerpt, Hedda is working on the dressing under supervision of the teacher, who switches her focus between the two students (Excerpt 7.2).

Ex. (7.2): Tell the patient how it feel
K1-040108-3 09.42-09.53

1 HED: *gör de ont nu Malin.
does it hurt now Malin.
2 *tea* **gazes at Hedda ->**
3 MAL: >nä< a: svider li:te li:te grann fast asså verklien-
>no< uh: burns a li:ttle li:ttle bit but you know really-
4 TEA: *insticksstället sv-svider lite.
the place of insertion bu-burns a little.
gazes at Malin ->
5 MAL: *ja? men de va ve:rklien b[ra asså.]
yes? but that was rea:lly good you know.
6 *tea* **gazes at Hedda ->**
7 TEA: [då kan du-] då kan du
then you can- then you can

8 berätta för pati↑enten också hur de känns va.=
tell the ↑patient too how it feels right.
gazes at Malin ->
9 MAL: =m:?=
10 TEA: =å då förstå:r du att de gör ont.
and then you understa:nd that it hurts.
11 °att då kanske du inte-°
°that then maybe you don't-°
12 *(.) visst e den ↑där bra? ((referring to the dressing))
(.) isn't ↑that one good?
**gazes at Hedda ->*

At the beginning of excerpt (7.2), Hedda asks Malin if it hurts now, which is oriented to the fact that the previous try was painful. Malin initially responds with a no, but then confirms that it does hurt, providing more information about the pain: *svider li:te li:te grann fast asså verklien-* "burns a li:ttle li:ttle bit but you know really-." By adding "a little little bit" she is minimizing the possible damage, and downplays the importance of her pain. Malin goes on to initiate an assessment of Hedda's action that is abandoned as she is interrupted by the teacher, who intervenes and claims to know where Malin feels the pain (the assessment is fully delivered in line 5, in a slightly reformulated shape). This requires the student to be more precise in locating where it is hurting, and she acknowledges that it is at the insertion site that she is experiencing a burning sensation.

The teacher uses the pain as a point of departure for a pedagogical point about how the student, based on the fact that she now understands that the insertion can hurt, can use this experience when telling the patient how it feels (l. 7–10). Heritage and Lindström (1998) demonstrate how a British community nurse (a health visitor) uses her own experiences to encourage and advice a mother who does not feel appropriate affection for her newborn child. They show how the participants, as they gradually move into this moral realm, abandon the discourse of technical and medical advice-giving in favor of an autobiographical and experiential approach in which the health visitor addresses the mother's experience (see also Linell and Bredmar 1996). When the teacher tells Malin how she can use her experience of how it feels to have a PVC inserted into the body, it is this move into another domain that the student is socialized into. Referrals to one's own experiences add compassion, empathy and authenticity to the interaction, a moral stance in the midst of neutral institutional discourse (Linell and Rommetveit 1998). The student is instructed on how she, in her future role as a nurse, can act as a moral member of this community of practice, and by drawing on her own experiences can show "documented empathy" (Heritage and Lindström 1998, 419).

By invoking the category term "patient," the teacher is making relevant a hypothetical future situation, and she broadens the scope of what it is that they are going to do; practicing on a fellow student is a preparation for future situations in which they will be working on a patient. In excerpts 7.1 and 7.2, the category "patient" is occasioned as a resource to call the student nurses' attention to the fact that they will work on and with live persons with cognitive and emotive capacities, and that it is important to treat the patients as such when performing different procedures.

Attending to Misconduct

In excerpt 7.3, the category term "patient" is invoked within the context of quoted speech and enactments that make relevant what is expected of a "good nurse." The teacher notices something that one of the students says (l. 2–3) and orients to the utterance as a breach of proper conduct. She highlights the utterance as potentially problematic by the use of quoted speech. Malin has been practicing on a mock-up arm for a while; however, the arm that she has been working on is stiff, and she has problems inserting the needle into a vessel (Excerpt 7.3).

When having failed again, Malin turns to Gustav, asking him if she can try his arm. She adds an account for why she makes this request, saying that the mock-up arm *e så himla hå:rd* "is so terribly ha:rd." Gustav orients to the reference to "your arm" in line 2 as his own arm, and rather than to answer in a serious manner, he turns to Malin and offers his arm, playfully pretending to pull up his sweater. Malin engages in the non-serious activity, and turns toward Gustav, pointing the needle at his arm.

Overhearing the students, the teacher intervenes and, in a serious voice, asks Malin *ska du säga så till patienten.* "are you going to say that to the patient," thus orienting to the complaining aspect of Malin's request. The category "patient" is being occasioned as a resource in constructing a tease: The teacher somewhat mocks the student, quoting her and presenting what she has just said, *den här e så himla hå:rd* "this one is so terribly ha:rd" (l. 3), as inappropriate in a future situation (l. 6–8). Drew (1987) has shown how a tease can follow upon a complaint that is oriented to as

Ex. (7.3): You were so difficult to inject
K1-040108-1 26.15-26.37

1 mal ((attempts to insert a PVC into a plastic arm))
2 MAL: Gustav kan inte ja få prova på din ↓arm
Gustav can't I try on your ↓arm
3 för *den här e så himla hå:rd.*
because this one is so terribly ha:rd.
feeling the hand of the mock-up arm with her hand
4 GUS: +ja kan dra upp.+
I can pull up.
+stretches his arm toward Malin+
5 MAL: a, *shoot.*
yeah, shoot.
points with the PVC to Gustav's arm

6 TEA: *‡ska du säga så till patienten. nä nu tar ja en
are you going to say that to the patient. no now I'm going to take
‡walks toward Malin ->
7 mal *gazes at teacher ->
8 annan patient. de e så himla £hå:(h)rt ‡här.£ #1
another patient. it's so terribly £ha:(h)rd here.£
->‡grabs Malin's arm ->
9 MAL: a precis.*‡ #2((moderate laughter 0.9))
yeah right.
->*looks away from teacher toward mock-up arm->*
10 tea ->‡turns away, smiling ->‡

11 MAL: *du va så svårstucken. ‡kan ja ta din sängk(h)a(h)mrat(h).
you were so difficult to inject. can I take your bedf(h)e(h)llow(h).
*gazes at teacher and keeps her body oriented toward her->>
12 tea ‡gazes at Malin ->>
13 MAL: hh.hh
14 ALL: ((laughing 1.2))
15 MAL: men ja tror den här- (.) den e liksom asså *hela plasten
but I think this- (.) it's like really the whole plastic
*points at the problematic part of the PVC->
16 bara (.) korv↑ar sej* för att den e så (.) trö:g. (.)
just (.) s↑ags because it's so (.) sti:ff. (.)
->*
17 °ja vet inte riktigt.°
°I don't really know.°

exaggerated, and where the tease puts the complaint back in proportion by, for example, treating it as overdone. The teacher is aware of the problems that the students claim to be experiencing, and immediately preceding excerpt 7.3 she has encouraged them to make sure that they switch between the "pillows" and the mock-up arms so that everyone gets to try the different models. The fact that the students keep complaining could be understood as providing grounds for the teacher to orient to the complaint as exaggerated. However, the critique is softened, as the reported speech is delivered with a smile voice and a slight hint of laughter: *de e så himla £hå:(h)rt här.£* "it's so terribly £ha:(h)rd here.£." The teacher also leans toward Malin, grasping her arm as if to feel how hard it is as she smiles (fig. 1–2 in Ex. 7.3). The quote "parasitically exploits" (Drew 1987, 243) what the student has said as a resource for the construction of the tease and as a way of displaying some skepticism about her claims. The teacher introduces a hypothetical scenario suggesting something that could happen, but—as shown by the hint of laughter and smiling—is not a serious proposal (see Holt 2007, 62). At the same time as the teacher's criticism is defused, the delivery of the critique can be understood as oriented toward building rapport with the student. As Nguyen (2007, 293) has shown, such a playful shift in footing can serve to maintain a close relationship between the teacher and the student. By formulating her critique of the student's utterance within the participation framework of the student as a future nurse with patients, the teacher displays that the students will have to cope with difficulties in the future, and that the alternative of switching arms—or patients—will not be available.

The student initially responds to the non-serious aspect of the utterance, aligning with the teacher's hypothetical scenario with an *a precis.* "yeah right." and laughter, displaying that she recognizes that the teacher is teasing her. An enactment follows placing the student in a hypothetical scenario of talking to a patient, rephrasing and developing what the teacher just said: *du va så svårstucken. kan ja ta din sängk(h)a(h)mrat(h).* "you were so difficult to inject. can I take your bedf(h)e(h)llow(h)." She plays along with the tease and laughingly agrees with it (cf. Drew 1987, 225). The other students join in laughing, displaying their interpretation of the exchange as playful, and the usual sequential implications of the prior turn (l. 6–8) are momentarily suspended (Holt 2013). In her enactment, Malin uses more precise terminology than the teacher about the problems that they may encounter and that are well known, namely that a patient can be difficult to perform the insertion on due to the difficulty of finding a vessel (rather than due to having a stiff arm similar to the mock-ups). In other words, she reformulates the critique by referring to a recurrent problem and displays her understanding of the joke and her willingness to go along with it by contributing further with an enactment (Holt 2007, 65).

As has been shown, the student initially aligns with the tease. However, following the enactment of a future situation, the student instead rejects the tease and develops the account about the problems that she has encountered. In rejecting the suggestion in a tease, participants have been shown to hold on to the validity of their original claims and to display that their prior claims were not overdone, but instead represent real versions (Drew 1987, 243). In such a vein, Malin reformulates and elaborates her complaint. The second complaint is introduced by the contradicting conjunction "but" and a serious reception, as Malin shifts to talk about how the plastic on the PVC sags because of the stiffness of the plastic arm. Linking back to her initial account in line 3, the student now develops what the problem is. Looking at the PVC, she describes how it sags because of the stiffness of the plastic arm: *för att den e så (.) trö:g* "because it is so (.) sti:ff" (l. 16). This works as an account for why she proposed the change of arms in the first place and rejects the relevance of the teacher's criticism.

In sum, the format of quoted speech is used to enact a future situation and to target problematic conduct at the same time as it is used to soften aspects of the teacher's criticism of the student. The non-serious aspects of the interaction allow the participants to focus on the problematic aspects of what the student has said, by referring to the inappropriateness of complaining about the mock-up arm and—although cast within a playful frame—the fact that in the future the students will not be able to switch patients when they encounter problems. Simultaneously, the playfulness and non-seriousness of the situation permit the student to reject the teacher's criticism by insisting on her complaint and to pursue the switch of mock-up arm.

A Nurse Without Moral Stature

In the analysis of the last excerpt, I will show how the categories "patient" and "nurse" are enacted as protagonists in a narrative actualizing social norms of conduct. As Rooney et al. (2015) point out, it is central to the pedagogy of simulation that the participants are *not* in a hospital, working on live patients, but that they are in a classroom. This allows the participants to do things that would otherwise not be possible. When working on the models, the students take the opportunity of talking more casually with each other. Forms of humor are recurrent and the students often joke and laugh together. In excerpt 7.4, the students construct an *atrocity story* (Dingwall 1977) about nurses and patients, in which they depict a nurse without moral stature that challenges social norms of proper nurse conduct. The term "atrocity story" was introduced to characterize stories that retell dramatic events staged between groups of friends or acquaintances that draw on shared understandings about the way of the world (Dingwall 1977). The stories are, for example, told by patients to retrospectively interpret their encounters with the medical profession and to negotiate norms for the behavior of doctors and patients by voicing complaints. As Dingwall (1977) remarks, these stories can however be expected to be told in any profession as well as by patients about doctors and vice versa, with the teller cast as hero, in the right where others were wrong. The story told by Hedda and Malin differs in important respects from the stories analyzed by Dingwall, for example, by not staging the nurse as a hero, being able to solve an extraordinary situation, but instead quite the opposite: the nurse as an anti-hero, causing trouble. The story is animated by enactments (Holt 2007).

Malin and Hedda are sitting beside each other practicing on the mock-ups and talking. At the beginning of the excerpt Malin picks up a PVC and looking at it produces an initial "response cry" (Goffman 1981), then comments ironically that the needle is not "so used" (l. 1). A needle should only be used once. This is maintained in the training situation where it is only when the students are practicing on paper tissue that they are allowed to use the same PVC more than once. Malin's observation is the start of a collaborative construction of a hypothetical narrative (Excerpt 7.4).

Ex. (7.4): This needle wasn't so used
K2-040108-1 31.54-32.42

1 MAL: ↑oj. den där va in- inte så använd den här nålen.
↑oops. that one wasn'- not so used this needle.

2 (1.1)

3 MAL: £pfh b(h)ättre begagnad.£
£pfh h(h)ardly used.£

4 (1.2)

5 HED: bättre begagnad.
hardly used.

6 (1.2)

7 MAL: (så) kan man säga till en patient också. då tror ja den
(that) one can say to a patient too. then I think it

8 blir <jätte (.) ↑glad,>
will be <really (.) ↑happy,>

9 (1.2)

10 HED: °nu: e de fullt.°
°no:w it's full.°
((referring to salt-solution that she has drawn into a syringe))

11 MAL: den här nålen e inte så: an:vän:d. (.) säger man innan man
this needle is not so: us:ed. (.) one says before one

12 sticker.
does the insertion.

13 (1.2)

14 HED: bara använt den på han som ligger bredvid. men ni
only used it on him who lies beside. but you

15 känner ju varann¿
already know each other¿

16 MAL: han e ju- han har inte va ja vet nån blo:d↑smitta.
he is [PRT]- he doesn't have contaminated ↑bloo:d as far as I know.

17 HED: °nej.° (.) vi kollade väl inte de ↑nu: men-
°no.° (.) we didn't (like) check that right ↑no:w but-

18 MAL: men han e ju- han e [ju- han ser ju-]
but he is [PRT]- he is [PRT]- he looks [PRT]-

19 HED: [han va ju på sån här] ba:rn
he was [PRT] at this chi:ld

20 MAL: [<preci::s,>]
<exa::ctly,>

21 HED: [när han va li:ten] va han ju på (.) fyraårskontroll
when he was li:ttle he [PRT] was at (.) a fourth-year check up

22 å sånt å då hade han ju inte de,
and like and then he [PRT] didn't have it,

23 (2.1)

24 MAL: å sen ser han ju [*ro- £>sen ser han ju< ros- han ser ju ro-£]
and then he looks [PRT] ro- £then he [PRT] looks ros- he looks [PRT] ro-£
**looks up at Hedda, smiling ->*

25 HED: [de skulle vara nån sexuellt överför]d
it would be some kind of sexually transmitted

26 sjukdom i så fall.
disease in that case.

27 MAL: #1 £han ser ju rosig och frisk ut.*£
£he looks [PRT] rosy and healthy.£
->*

28 HED: +du har v‡äl inte lega‡t me nån som e sjuk.
you haven't slept with someone who is ill.
+gazes at Malin ->
‡touches Malin's arm‡

29 kan man frå+ga patienten.
one can ask the patient.
->+

Looking at the PVC, Malin describes it as *pfh b(h)ä̲ttre begagnad.* "pfh h(h)a̲rdly used." The utterance is delivered in a smile voice with embedded particles of aspiration that together indicate the utterance as non-serious (see Holt 2007; Ex. 7.3). Hedda, who is fully concentrated on drawing salt-solution into a syringe, repeats the utterance, displaying that she has noticed the utterance as worthy of attention; however, she does not align with Malin's smile voice but instead answers in a serious manner. Malin pursues the joke by retrospectively constructing the utterance produced in lines 1–3 as an enactment: *(så) kan man säga till en patient också.* "(that) one can say to a patient too." Hedda, who is focused on her task, does not immediately respond and instead comments that the syringe is now full (l. 10). The lack of uptake on the non-serious aspects of Malin's utterance may account for the repetition and further elaboration of the joke done by Malin in lines 11–12, where she recycles her initial noticing in line 1, this time retrospectively framing the enactment with a prefatory framing component: speech verb-plus-pronoun (Holt 2007) quoting a hypothetical nurse, *den hä̲r nålen är inte så̲ : an:vän:d. (.) säger man innan man sticker.* "thi̲s needle is not so̲: us:ed (.) one says before one does the insertion." The structure of the narrative corresponds with the pattern described by Holt (2007, 68) where a joke initiation, that involves one of the participants suggesting something that could happen but is not a serious proposal, is followed by one or more enactments. This time Hedda responds and the two students collaboratively construct a scenario in which two nurses are talking about and to a patient. Hedda enacts talking to a hypothetical patient, imagining a scenario with two patients that lie beside each other and that the nurses are using the same needle on the two of them (l. 14–15).

In their hypothetical narrative, the students refer to blood infections and how they are transmitted: by sharing needles and by sexually transmitted diseases. At the same time they are depicting an ignorant nurse, who suggests that the fact that the patients know each other (l. 14–15) would be a reason to use the same needle on the two patients. When Malin supports this statement adding that the patient to their knowledge does not have contaminated blood, Hedda agrees, however, she adds that they have not checked this now, but that the patient as a child went to a fourth-year checkup and that his blood was all right at that time. There is a heightened intensity in the telling at this time, where Hedda and Malin add elements to the story, attempting to surpass each other with more incredible grounds for judging that it would be all right to use the same needle on two patients (i.e., that the patients know each other, that the first patient went to a fourth-year checkup, that he looks healthy). The participants display their understanding of the activity they are engaged in through a shift of footing to contribute to the hypothetical dialogue. They show their willingness to go along with the joking initiation by contributing with enactments. The enactments extend and elaborate the joke (Holt 2007).

Hedda, in line 25, adds some doubt in that she enacts a realization that the patient might have a sexually transmitted disease, that is, something that might have happened between childhood and the present. Sexuality is a classic target of moralization. Bergmann (1998, 298) writes that people take precautions in order to protect each other's face and talk about issues of sexuality in an indirect, vague and allusive manner. Hedda instead suggests that one can ask the patient: *du har väl inte legat me nån som e sjuk.* "you haven't slept with someone who is ill." (l. 28). The enacted nurse approaches the patient with an overt moralizing statement. This can also be contrasted with the findings reported by Linell and Bredmar (1996) in which midwives treat morally sensitive topics in indirect ways, gradually approaching and quickly retreating from them, so as to distance themselves from morally loaded aspects. Although morality is frequently backgrounded in institutional and professional contexts, in medical contexts, patients are often held responsible for their lifestyles and hence for their health (Bergmann 1998). In such a vein, Hedda and Malin work to escalate the impropriety of the story by evincing what they take to be appropriate contributions to the ongoing sequence.

The students revel in the atrocious nurse, at the same time as they are distancing themselves from the characters in the story. This can, for example, be seen in the use of pronouns, where the students overwhelmingly talk about the patient in third person (referring to a "patient" or "he"). In lines 7–8, Malin refers to the patient using a third-person personal pronoun that is used to refer to objects and animals—*då tror ja den blir <jätte (.) ↑glad,>* "then I think it will be <really (.) ↑happy,>"—thus objectifying the patient. Moreover, when they enact what they could say to a patient, the quotes are presented with the indefinite generic third-person pronoun *man* "one" (l. 7, 11, 29). By shifting footing and putting the enacted utterances into the imagined voice of someone other than the speaker, that is, ventriloquizing, the students figure as animators rather than principals of the utterances (Defibaugh 2014; Goffman 1981). This enables them to stand in a reduced responsibility for their enacted comments (Holt 2007, 78). At the same time as they are enacting a narrative, they distance themselves from the characters, thus avoiding moral responsibility. Dingwall (1977, 377) has shown how atrocity stories cover a variety of bizarre or extraordinary events and that they may "serve as demonstrations by the students to each other of their ability to monitor the social world as competent nurses." In a similar way, the story told by Hedda and Malin displays their knowledge of cultural and social norms as they simultaneously appropriate and transform the social and moral institutional order relevant for members of this professional practice (see Jacoby and Ochs 1995).

Concluding Discussion

In this chapter, I have examined how a group of student nurses, together with their teacher, make relevant what they consider as the social norms and moral expectations of the professional practice of nursing. I have shown how the students explore norms of proper nurse conduct, thus negotiating preferred modes of participation in future interactions with patients.

I set out to explore what is the sense of morality that is being practiced in the training sessions, and how the students are socialized to think and feel in ways that relate to social situations and the management of interpersonal relations. The participants were found to draw upon a variety of resources in conveying these moral meanings. An important condition of the training sessions is that they take place at a clinical training center, in an environment of simulation. Some parts of the training session are more firmly set in an educational context (working on the different models and mock-ups), whereas others are more similar to the workplace (performing the insertions on a fellow student). The results of the analyses indicate that the participants deal with problems that they encounter in different ways depending on whether they are working on the mock-ups or on a live body. For example, problems with the stiff plastic arms and the PVC occasion the telling of an atrocity story and enactments, whereas a student feeling pain during the insertion of a PVC is instructed in how to use this experience in future encounters with patients. When doing the insertions on live bodies, a situation is invoked that to a higher degree resembles an authentic situation with a patient, something that can account for the seriousness the participants display as the students are preparing to perform the insertion on each other (Ex. 7.1) or have just finished it (Ex. 7.2). When working on the mock-ups, the participants instead often create a playful frame for the activities, providing opportunities for non-serious talk, jokes and laughter, in the midst of serious business. In such a way, the teacher uses humor and teasing to soften aspects of a critical comment. The students construct an atrocity story in which they are rather outspoken, simultaneously displaying knowledge of cultural and social norms and the moral order of the institutional context.

When analyzing how the participants orient to a patient as a resource in making relevant the management of interpersonal relations, an image of the "good nurse" appears. The "good nurse" that emerges in interaction between the participants is a nurse who talks to the patient about what is going to happen and why, who treats the patient as a living and thinking being (Ex. 7.1), who anticipates what the patient might experience and who is able to use not only medical terminology but refer to his/her own experiences and autobiographical references as resources when encountering a patient (Ex. 7.2). A "good nurse" should keep trying and not blame the patient when something does not work (Ex. 7.3). Quoted speech and enactments have been shown to be powerful means by which the participants can stage improper conduct, at the same time as they distance themselves from the enacted utterances, thus portraying something that they should not say or do. In excerpt (7.3), this is made explicit when the enactments are framed by the teacher's questioning stance and criticism of something that the student has said. The student's enactment is produced in response to this framing, as something that she would not say and that is delivered as something to be laughed at. By playing with the student's complaint, the participants display its incongruous and unexpected nature, thus shedding light on what is institutionally expected of a student and a nurse. When constructing the atrocity story (Ex. 7.4), the students in a similar way add enactments that allow them to say the impossible. By delivering these utterances as quotes, the students can simultaneously distance themselves from the moral implications of the told narrative. The students explore norms of proper nurse conduct by playing on normative ideals and creating a narrative about a nurse who is incompetent, who acts in inappropriate ways and who moralizes over the patient. The construction of the narrative represents a playful way of exploring what it means to be a competent and professional nurse. The narrative is not explicitly treated as a breach of the moral order; however, that it is a breach lurks under the surface and becomes visible in the ways in which the students distance themselves from the "bad nurse."

The examination of how the students appropriate and transform cultural and social norms of proper nurse conduct also shows how the nursing students make relevant the transition from educational setting to workplace context. References to a patient are occasioned by contingencies in the here-and-now, but they provide us with a lens through which we can observe how the student nurses are preparing themselves for future work by bringing in the notion of a patient into the educational setting, and placing the participants in a future (hypothetical) scenario. Thus light is shed on how, in the midst of an activity designed to train professional skills, the student nurses develop interactional competences as ways of managing interpersonal relations with (future) patients.

Note

1. The recordings, that were part of a pilot study, were made in January 2004. As of the writing of this chapter, the students are no longer allowed to practice the insertions on a peer.

Appendix: Transcription Conventions
(Adapted from Jefferson 2004; Mondada 2009)

[ ]	Overlapping talk.
=	Equal signs indicate no break or gap between the lines.
(0.8) (.)	Numbers in parentheses indicate length of silence in seconds. A dot in parentheses indicates a micropause.
. , ¿ ?	The punctuation marks indicate intonation. The period indicates falling intonation; the comma, continuing intonation; the inverted question mark, slightly rising intonation; and the question mark indicates a rising intonation.
: :	Colons are used to indicate prolongation or stretching of the immediately prior sound.
-	A hyphen after a word indicates a cut-off or self-interruption.
word WOrd	Underlining indicates some form of stress or emphasis. The more the underlining, the greater the emphasis. Especially loud talk is indicated by upper case.
° °	The degree signs indicate that the talk between them was quieter than its surrounding talk.
£word£	The pound signs indicate a smile voice.
↑	The up arrow marks a sharp rise in pitch.
< >	Left/right carats indicate that the talk between them is slowed down.
.h .hh	Audible inbreath is shown with a ".h"—the more h's the more inbreath.
wo(h)rd	Laugh particles.
(( ))	Double parentheses are used to mark transcriber's descriptions of events.
( )	Empty parentheses indicate that something is being said, but it is incomprehensible.
* *	Gestures and action descriptions are delimited between two identical symbols and are synchronized with corresponding stretches of talk.
->	Gesture or action described continues after excerpt's end.
*->	Gesture or action described continues across subsequent lines
->*	until the same symbol is reached.
ami	Participant doing the gesture is identified when (s)he is not the speaker.

References

Bergmann, J. (1998). Introduction: Morality in discourse. *Research on Language & Social Interaction, 31*(3–4), 279–294.

Cromdal, J., & Tholander, M. (2014). Morality in professional practice. *Journal of Applied Linguistics & Professional Practice, 9*(2), 155–164.

Defibaugh, S. (2014). Management of care or management of face: Indirectness in nurse practitioner/patient interactions. *Journal of Pragmatics, 67*, 61–71.

Dingwall, R. (1977). "Atrocity stories" and professional relationships. *Sociology of Work & Occupations, 4*(4), 371–396.

Drew, P. (1987). Po-faced receipts of teases. *Linguistics, 25*, 219–253.

Goffman, E. (1981). *Forms of talk*. Philadelphia: University of Philadelphia Press.

Goodwin, C. (2000). Action and embodiment within situated human interaction. *Journal of Pragmatics, 32*(10), 1489–1522.

Goodwin, C. (2013). The co-operative, transformative organization of human action and knowledge. *Journal of Pragmatics, 46*, 8–23.

Hall, J. K., & Pekarek Doehler, S. (2011). L2 interactional competence and development. In J. K. Hall, J. Hellermann, & S. Pekarek Doehler (Eds.), *L2 interactional competence & development* (pp. 1–15). Bristol: Multilingual Matters.

Heath, C. (1989). Pain talk: The expression of suffering in the medical consultation. *Social Psychology Quarterly, 52*(2), 113–125.

Heritage, J., & Lindström, A. (1998). Motherhood, medicine, and morality: Scenes from a medical encounter. *Research on Language & Social interaction, 31*(3–4), 397–438.

Hindmarsh, J., Hyland, L., & Bannerjee, A. (2014). Work to make simulation work: 'Realism', instructional correction and the body in training. *Discourse Studies, 16*(2), 247–269.

Hindmarsh, J., & Pilnick, A. (2007). Knowing bodies at work: Embodiment and ephemeral teamwork in anaesthesia. *Organization Studies, 28*(9), 1395–1416.

Hindmarsh, J., Reynolds, P., & Dunne, S. (2011). Exhibiting understanding: The body in apprenticeship. *Journal of Pragmatics, 43*, 489–503.

Holt, E. 2007. "I'm eyeing your chop up mind": Reporting and enacting. In E. Holt & R. Clift (Eds.), *Reporting talk. Reported speech in interaction* (pp. 47–80). Cambridge: Cambridge University Press.

Holt, E. (2013). "There's many a true word said in jest": Seriousness and nonseriousness in interaction. In P. Glenn & E. Holt (Eds.), *Studies of laughter in interaction* (pp. 69–89). London: Bloomsbury.

Hymes, D. H. (1972). On communicative competence. In J. B. Pride & J. Holmes (Eds.), *Sociolinguistics: Selected readings* (pp. 269–293). Harmondsworth: Penguin Books.

Jacoby, S., & Ochs, E. (1995). Co-construction: An introduction. *Research on Language & Social Interaction, 28*(3), 171–183.

Jefferson, G. (2004). Glossary of transcript symbols with an introduction. In G. H. Lerner (Ed.), *Conversation analysis. Studies from the first generation* (pp. 13–31). Amsterdam: John Benjamins.

Koschmann, T., LeBaron, C., Goodwin, C., Zemel, A., & Dunnington, G. (2007). Formulating the triangle of doom. *Gesture, 7*(1), 97–118.

Linell, P., & Bredmar, M. (1996). Reconstructing topical sensitivity: Aspects of face-work in talks between midwives and expectant mothers. *Research on Language & Social Interaction, 29*(4), 347–379.

Linell, P., & Rommetveit, R. (1998). The many forms and facets of morality in dialogue: Epilogue for the special issue. *Research on Language & Social Interaction, 31*(3–4), 465–473.

McHoul, A. W. (1990). The organization of repair in classroom talk. *Language in Society, 19*(3), 349–377.

Mondada, L. (2009). The embodied and negotiated production of assessments in instructed actions. *Research on Language & Social Interaction, 42*(4), 329–361.

Mondada, L. (2014a). Instructions in the operating room: How the surgeon directs their assistant's hands. *Discourse Studies, 16*(2), 131–161.

Mondada, L. (2014b). The local constitution of multimodal resources for social interaction. *Journal of Pragmatics, 65*, 137–156.

Nguyen, H. T. (2006). Constructing 'expertness': A novice pharmacist's development of interactional competence in patient consultations. *Communication & Medicine, 3*(2), 147–160.

Nguyen, H. T. (2007). Rapport building in language instruction: A microanalysis of the multiple resources in teacher talk. *Linguistics & Education, 21*(4), 284–303.

Nguyen, H. T. (2008). Sequence organization as local and longitudinal achievement. *Text & Talk, 28*(4), 501–528.

Nguyen, H. T. (2011). Achieving recipient design longitudinally: Evidence from a pharmacy intern in patient consultations. In J. K. Hall, J. Hellermann, & S. Pekarek Doehler (Eds.), *L2 interactional competence & development* (pp. 173–205). Bristol: Multilingual Matters.

Nguyen, H. T. (2012). *Developing interactional competence. A conversation-analytic study of patient consultations in pharmacy*. Houndmills: Palgrave Macmillan.

Ochs, E., & Kremer-Sadlik, T. (2007). Introduction: Morality as family practice. *Discourse & Society, 18*(1), 5–10.

Pilnick, A., Hindmarsh, J., & Gill, V. T. (2010). Beyond 'doctor and patient': Developments in the study of healthcare interactions. In A. Pilnick, J. Hindmarsh, & V. T. Gill (Eds.), *Communication in health care settings. Policy, participation & new technologies* (pp. 1–16). Malden, MA: Wiley Blackwell.

Rooney, D., Hopwood, N., Boud, D., & Kelly, M. (2015). The role of simulation in pedagogies of higher education for the health professions: Through a practice-based lens. *Vocations & Learning, 8*, 269–285.

Sanchez Svensson, M., Luff, P., & Heath, C. (2010). Embedding instruction in practice: Contingency and collaboration during surgical training. In A. Pilnick, J. Hindmarsh, & V. T. Gill (Eds.), *Communication in health care settings. Policy, participation & new technologies* (pp. 99–116). Malden, MA: Wiley Blackwell.

Schegloff, E. A. (2007). Categories in action: Person-reference and membership categorization. *Discourse Studies, 9*(4), 433–461.

Young, R. F. (2013). Learning to talk the talk and walk the walk: Interactional competence in academic spoken English. *Ibérica, 25*, 15–38.

8

Toward a Conversation Analytic Framework for Tracking Interactional Competence Development from School to Work

Hanh Thi Nguyen

Introduction

Professional communication training aims to prepare learners with the interactional competencies needed for handling workplace tasks. However, participants in training setting and workplace setting orient to institutional goals and contextual constraints that do not map exactly onto each other. What is the relationship between the interactional competencies developed in the training setting and the interactional competencies mobilized in workplace communication? While there has been some research on novices' development of interactional competence at the workplace (e.g., Li 2000; Hosoda and Aline 2010; Rine and Hall 2011; 2012a), and the contrast between the training setting and the workplace with respect to communication practices and learning affordances (e.g., Parks 2001; Lingard et al. 2003; Filliettaz et al. 2013), there has been

H.T. Nguyen (✉)
Hawaii Pacific University, Honolulu, HI, USA

S. Pekarek Doehler et al. (eds.), *Interactional Competences in Institutional Settings*, DOI 10.1007/978-3-319-46867-9_8

little discourse-based research on the linkage between communication skills developed in educational settings and those employed at the workplace.[1] What is needed is data-driven and fine-grained analysis of the range of procedures, trajectories and dynamics in which novices develop the competence to handle work-related tasks in instructional settings, and the extent to which this competence is performed and modified to handle these tasks at the workplace. The answer to this question can help us understand the kind of adaptations that individuals make as they "staff" different but related social arenas. It can also provide useful implications for vocational training.

Such an endeavor can greatly benefit from ethnomethodology's (EM) and conversation analysis' (CA) conceptualization of and insightful findings on the nature of social interaction. In this chapter, I will first situate the notions of competence and competence development in EM and CA traditions. Then, informed by previous research, I discuss the challenges of tracking the development of interactional competence and attempt to outline a general procedure for analysis. I extend this discussion to the study of competence development at the workplace, followed by an example analysis of a pharmacy novice's transitioning from classroom role-plays to actual workplace interactions.

Competence and Competence Development in EM and CA

Interactional competence is the ability to utilize interactional practices contingently in context to achieve actions jointly with other participants in social interaction. In the last two decades or so, there have been substantial discussions on the nature of interactional competence (e.g., Hall 1993, 1995a, 1999; Young 1999, 2011; Sanders 2003; Mondada 2006; Pekarek Doehler 2006, 2010; Kasper 2009; Hall and Pekarek Doehler 2011; Nguyen 2012a; Pekarek Doehler et al. forthcoming). There has also been a growing number of empirical studies that operationalize the notion of interactional competence at the analytic level to examine interactional competence development (e.g., Markee 1994, 2000, 2008; Brouwer and Wagner 2004; Mondada and Pekarek Doehler 2004; Ishida 2006, 2009, 2011; Nguyen 2006, 2008, 2011a,b, 2012a,b; Cekaite 2007; Hellermann 2007, 2011; Melander and Sahlström 2009; Melander 2012; Lee and Hellermann 2014; Dings 2014; Pekarek Doehler and Pochon-Berger 2015). Drawing mainly from ethnomethodological conversation analysis (EMCA), this burgeoning body of research has elucidated how novices develop the competencies to participate in new social activities.

In taking up EMCA's conceptualization of interactional competence, however, a research agenda on development also departs in a crucial way from these theoretical traditions: a focus on *individuals*, and particularly *not-yet-competent members* (Schegloff's (1989) term). In the paragraphs below, I will attempt to examine the nature of this departure and discuss its implications for research on the development of interactional competence. I will argue that although a focus on the individual has not been central in EMCA, this focus does not violate EMCA's tenets and in fact can contribute to a less-explored area in this field.

Ethnomethodology holds the view that social orders exist *in* "enacted local practices" (Garfinkel 1996, 8). That is, EM considers social practices and procedures to be situation based, context bound and independent of the actual individuals who carry out these practices and procedures. Garfinkel gave the example of Los Angeles freeway traffic flow, where traffic patterns are still there despite different drivers. He referred to an *immortal* ordinary society, in which the production of a "witnessable" local setting is staffed by individuals but it does not matter which cohorts of individuals are staffing it, because the focus is on the structures and procedures of society and not on the specifics of the cohorts:

> *Immortal* is used to speak of human jobs as of which local members, being in the midst of organizational *things*, know, of just *these* organizational things they are in the midst of, that it preceded them and will be there after they leave it. Immortal is a great metaphor for the recurrencies of ordinary society, staffed, provided for, produced, observed, and observable, locally and naturally accountable in and as of an "assemblage of haecceities." (Garfinkel 1996, 10–11, emphasis original)

Further, in EM, it is the production of social interaction's procedures and structures that *makes* its participants into the population that staffs that interaction. In Garfinkel's example of freeway traffic flow, "it is the workings of the traffic that make its staff available as 'typical' drivers, 'bad' drivers, 'close in' drivers" and so on (p. 5).

This view in EM is continued in CA, expressed succinctly in Schegloff's (1999) discussion of speech-exchange systems (SESs) (Sacks et al. 1974). Speech-exchange systems are recurring, recognizable episodes of interaction with distinctive practices for turn-taking, sequence organization, repair, overall structural organization and so on—practices that are co-constructed and oriented to by participants and are constrained by functional needs and contextual factors (Schegloff 1999).[2] In line with EM's perspective, Schegloff asserted that these "recurrent structures of sociality … recruit constantly shifting cohorts of participants to staff the episodes of conversation and other forms of talk-in-interaction which they organize" (1999, 427), and CA's main concern is to describe the "procedural infrastructure of interaction and talk-in-interaction" rather than the individuals that come together in interactional arenas (p. 426).

While not focusing on individuals, both EM and CA take the notion of *competence* as central in the realization of social orders exhibited in the organization of interactional practices. Garfinkel noted that participants produce and reproduce immortal social orders locally in interaction according to their *vulgar competence* (1996, 7–10). Carrying this idea further, CA "is concerned with the analysis of *competence* which underlies ordinary social activities" and it does this by "describing and explicating the competences which ordinary speakers use and rely on when they engage in intelligible, conversational interaction" (Heritage 1984, 241, emphasis original). It is important to note that EM and CA consider competence to emerge from common courses of action in social interaction and is thus collective rather than individually based. In Garfinkel's words, participants "treat the organizational *thing* as of their doing, as of their own, but *not* of their very own, singular, distinctive authorship" (1996, 10, emphasis original). Similarly, Garfinkel and Sacks made it clear that the term "member" in "members' methods" does not refer to a person but "it refers instead to mastery of natural language" (1986, 163). Thus, EM and CA aim to study members' competence at work in social interaction, but more attention is paid to the *workings* of this competence rather than where it comes from and how it may emerge for individual participants.

The question of how individuals acquire the competence in order to be a member in the staff of a social activity has, however, been pondered upon in EM and CA literature. For example, Garfinkel speculated that Agnes, an individual born and raised a male then starting to live as a woman, must have secretly learned the "rules" of acting as a woman "only over the course of the actual interaction, as a function of actual participation, and by accepting the risks involved" (1967, 146). Sacks also raised the question about what it takes in social interaction for children to learn to participate in interaction as competent members (1995, 120–121). And Schegloff noted that "it [conversational interaction] surely appears to be the basic and primordial environment for the development, the use, and the *learning* of natural language" (1996b, 4, emphasis added; see also Schegloff 1989, 2006). Questions about learning in EM and CA, however, have often been asked in order to refocus the analysis on interaction's workings rather than taken up as analytical projects. Thus, Garfinkel discussed Agnes's case to demonstrate how her methodological practices teach us that it is through "actual witnessed displays of common talk and conduct" that members produce sexuality (1967, 181), and Schegloff mentioned learning to emphasize the importance of social interaction.

Indeed, Zimmerman pointed out the need for *vertical comparison* in CA, or developmental comparative research on "the process and stages by which interactive talk emerges" (1999, 198). To date, this need still remains. Conversation analysis studies involving longitudinal data with the same individuals may not involve vertical comparison (e.g., Beach (2001) analyzed consecutive phone calls among family members over a 13-month period in order to provide the temporal framework to illuminate understandings of episodic data). Further, vertical comparison in some longitudinal CA studies may not be about learning by individuals (e.g., Heritage and Clayman (2013) tracked changes in a question form in presidential news conferences from 1954 to 2000 to show how they became more adversarial over time). Finally, only longitudinal studies on learning as development of practices involve vertical comparison (in contrast to studies on how participants conduct learning and teaching as a social practice) (Kasper and Wagner 2011). Despite CA's robust contributions to a vast range of topics, how competencies are developed by individuals is still an under-studied area.

Although EM's and CA's core investigation has not been about describing the manners and procedures in which individuals develop the competence to participate in social interaction, EMCA provides the theoretical compass for such an inquiry. Garfinkel posited that interaction itself affords learning: "Phenomena of order are made *instructably* in formal analytic details of concertedly *recurrent achievements* of practical action ... as the work of a population that staffs its production" (1996, 92, emphasis added). Members' methods are described as "situatedly tutorial" and "instructably witnessable" (p. 101) in the sense that participants' displays of their competence in using interactional practices in talk can become the learning resources for newcomers who get to witness these displays repeatedly in social interaction (see also Kasper 2009). Further, Garfinkel emphasized that learning requires direct participation in interaction: Interactional practices "cannot be learned or taught by imagining them" and "can only be empirically found out" (1996, 111). More specifically, Schegloff suggested that not-yet-competent members "learn to deal with the moment-to-moment contingencies of life in interaction, and the details of language use and conduct, *in* the moment-to-moment contingencies of life in interaction, with their deployments of language and other conduct" (1989, 152, emphasis original). Thus, new members to an SES learn its structures and procedures in the very process of *using* these structures and procedures in recurrent interaction (see also Firth and Wagner 1997; Markee and Kasper 2004; Kasper 2009; Pekarek Doehler 2010; and especially Pekarek Doehler 2006, on *competence-in-action* as well as Firth and Wagner 2007, on *learning-in-action*).

It follows that EMCA-informed research on the development of competence by individual novices should focus on the practices and procedures that these novices and their co-participants employ in the contingencies of talk, with special attention to the novices' changes over time in the production of these practices and procedures. This also means that the novices' handling of tasks should be examined locally and contingently in talk rather than being compared with those by competent members as etic rubrics for evaluation.

While EM and CA provide a strong basis for the study of interactional competence development, they do not spell out a specific methodological procedure for tackling this question empirically (see also Kasper 2009; Pekarek Doehler 2010). The next section will discuss the methodological challenges faced by a research endeavor to study the development of interactional competence and, informed by previous studies, attempt to sketch a general methodological procedure.

Tracking the Development of Competence

Challenges

The study of interactional competence development as *changes over time* using an EMCA approach faces an important challenge. That is, on the one hand, for cross-episode comparison, the analysis must show that the interactional episodes being examined contain some regularities, and on the other, for demonstration of developmental changes, it must show that there are some differences in the learner's practices. Koschmann referred to this as "'same-but-different' analysis" (2013, 2). Further, once differences are identified, there is the question of attribution: Among the observable differences in interactional conducts by the same individual across episodes, which ones are adaptations to the local context and which ones are displays of the learner's modification of competence and thus can be counted as evidence for learning (see also Pekarek Doehler 2010, 121; Hall and Pekarek Doehler 2011, 7)? Analysis of competence development by not-yet-competent members differs from analysis of competent members in this differentiation task. In analysis of social interaction involving competent members, the analyst looks for regularities that pattern across cases amidst variations due to participants' adaptations to the local context, that is, doing "horizontal comparison" (Zimmerman 1999). Figure 8.1 attempts to illustrate this comparison process. In the analysis of competence development over time by not-yet-competent members, that is, doing "vertical comparison" (Zimmerman 1999), the analyst also establishes regularities across cases, but needs to further draw a distinction between variations that are adaptations to context and those that

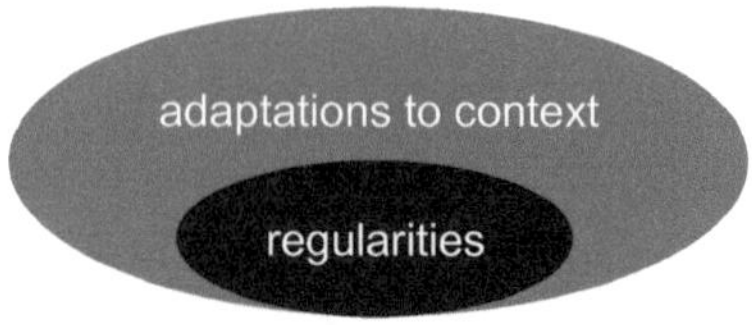

Fig. 8.1 Horizontal comparison in analysis of social interaction by competent members

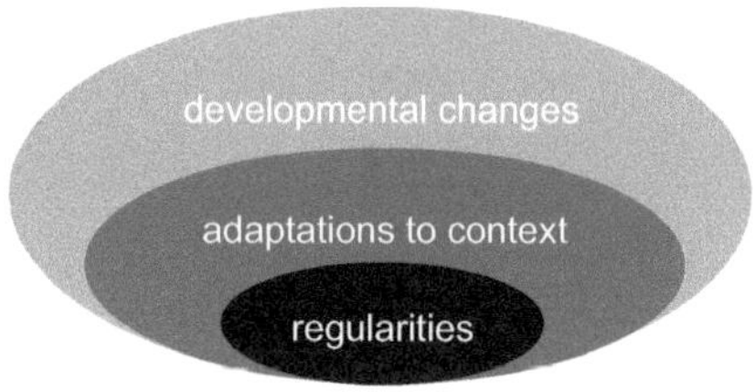

Fig. 8.2 Vertical comparison in analysis of social interaction by not-yet-competent members

are exhibitions of developmental changes (Fig. 8.2). This is a tricky task because there are no uniformed criteria to distinguish between these two types of differences. Like the process of doing EMCA itself, this differentiation has to be worked out hermeneutically, locally and contingently.

Several studies have taken up the challenge to document learning as changes over time. While their analytical targets varied, they all involve fine-grained analysis that pays full attention to contingent details of talk, followed by abstraction from local contingencies for cross-episode comparison in order to identify developmental changes. This abstraction often involves the analyst's interpretation of the learner's effective accomplishment of the most fundamental organizing force in talk-in-interaction: *actions*. Given that "[a] culture is an apparatus for generating recognizable actions" (Sacks 1995, 226, emphasis removed) and given CA's central concern with an empirical account of action (Schegloff 1996a), it makes sense to focus on how a newcomer to a culture utilizes interactional practices to accomplish actions. Indeed, in Hall and Pekarek Doehler's conceptualization of interactional competence, they highlighted the focus on actions: "IC [interactional competence] … implies the ability to mutually coordinate our *actions*" (2011, 2, emphasis added).[3] Also, in the process of abstraction for comparison, effectiveness is often assumed to mean either fewer interactional troubles or more economical and efficient accomplishment of the learner's goals, although this also depends on contextual factors (see below).

Toward a Methodological Procedure

Based on previous research on the development of interactional competence, I outline below a general procedure in CA-based studies on competence development. Throughout this procedure, the issues of regularities and differences—both those that display contextual adaptations and those that exhibit developmental changes—are of central concern.

First, the research project begins with *identifying an SES that the learner[4] participates in recurrently to collect data.* Some examples of SESs examined so far include business phone calls (Brouwer and Wagner 2004), patient consultations in pharmacy (Nguyen 2012a), university office hours (Young and Miller 2004; Nguyen 2011a,b), peer group interactions in classrooms (Pallotti 2002; Cekaite 2007; Melander 2012), conversations for language learning (Ishida 2006; Dings 2014), and teacher-student and student-student interactions in language classrooms (Mondada and Pekarek Doehler 2004; Hellermann 2008; Hosoda and Aline 2010). Researchers in this area strive to keep the collection of the target SES as uniform as possible to increase regularities across cases. For example, in my study of pharmacy novices' development of interactional competence in patient consultations (Nguyen 2012a), originally all patient consultations were collected. Upon examining the data, I found that consultations involving refills took a very different shape compared to those involving new prescriptions, and decided to exclude refill consultations in the data pool for analysis. Another important consideration in selecting an SES is whether the learner interacts over time with the same co-participant(s) (e.g., Markee 1994; Brouwer and Wagner 2004; Ishida 2009, 2011; Melander and Sahlström 2009; Melander 2012; Nguyen 2011a,b; Rine and Hall 2011) or different co-participants (e.g., Nguyen 2006, 2011b, 2012a; Hellermann 2007, 2008, 2011; Lee and Hellermann 2014). In the former scenario, changes in the learner's practices over time may indicate both increased efficiency in action accomplishment *and* adaptations to the evolving personal relationship with the co-participant(s); both have been considered integral parts of the learner's socialization (e.g., Ishida 2009). In the latter scenario, researchers can focus on action accomplishment that is not also embedded in relationship building; however, the consistency of the co-participants may become an issue. Researchers have attempted to overcome this by limiting the co-participants to the same membership category in a shared location and community, such as classmates in the same class (e.g., Hellermann 2011) or patients at the same pharmacy (e.g., Nguyen 2011a).

Within the selected SES, the analyst may choose to *identify an action or activity in which the learner engages recurrently.* Because SESs are recurrent social structures, it is likely that they also contain several recurrent actions and activities, thus leading to regularities across cases. Conversation analysis findings on interactional practices have often helped define the target of inquiry in this area. Examples of the actions or activities examined in previous research include telephone conversation opening in business (Brouwer and Wagner 2004), task opening in dyadic classroom interaction (Hellermann 2007, 2008), turn initiation in classroom interactions (Cekaite 2007), storytelling initiation in dyadic classroom interaction (Hellermann 2008; Lee and Hellermann 2014), responding to storytelling by host family members (Ishida 2011), word definition in classroom interaction (Markee 1994), giving assessments to students (Hosoda and Aline 2010) and advice-giving in patient consultations (Nguyen 2011b, 2012a), to name a few. Once a target action or activity has been identified, the analyst searches in the data corpus to build a collection of the episodes in which the learner engages in the identified action or activity.

It is sometimes necessary to *narrow down the collection to reduce contextual variations to the extent possible.* Given that CA data is naturally occurring, it is not possible to have two episodes that are exactly alike, but efforts are made to keep the action and co-participants (or category of co-participants) the same in order to maintain regularities across cases. One strategy employed in Markee's (1994) analysis of second language learners' competence development in the action of word definition is to first arrive at a prototypical structure of the definition sequences found in the data, then use this prototypical structure to delimit the data collection.

In my own work (Nguyen 2012a), I employed another strategy in which the uniformity of the data corpus was maintained by removing subsets that involved variations from the main corpus. For instance, one of the analytical foci was the pharmacy novice's change over time with respect to advice sequence organization (pp. 123–156). In order to concentrate on the novice's role in organizing advice, I excluded advice sequences initiated by a patient's request and those in which the novice referenced the doctor's prescription. The resulted corpus consisted of only pharmacist-generated advice.

Once a collection of same-type episodes has been established, typically, researchers perform *analysis of the learner's use of interactional practices in each episode, following CA protocol.* During this phase, the analyst suspends the research agenda and examines all details of talk to interpret what is going on from the participants' perspectives, that is, answering the CA question, "why this now?" In line with CA's protocol, the analysis pays attention to local contingencies as well as the achievement of actions.

The next step has a clear focus on tracking developmental changes. Here, the analyst begins to *make comparison across episodes over time regarding the manners and degree of effectiveness in which actions or activities are achieved.* This is when abstraction from local contingencies is made in order to draw a line between differences that are exhibitions of adaptations to context and those that are possible indicators of competence modifications. Unlike quantitative coding, where contextual variations that do not fall inside a coding scheme are ignored in order to fit particular tokens into the coding scheme, EMCA research on development centralizes cross-case variations. The task of teasing developmental changes apart from contextual adaptations is not a simple one, as it has to be done interpretatively in ways that are specific to the data at hand. A general guide seems to be that if a change cannot be witnessably attributed to contextual variations, it may be an indication of development. Developmental changes can be further confirmed by examining the individual's subsequent interactions. If a modified or newly developed practice occurs again to achieve a similar action in later interactions, it is plausible that that practice has become part of the individual's competence. It is important to note that more effective use of interactional practices may not always lead to more successful goal accomplishment, especially where the learner's participation is policed by central members and there exists an asymmetry in power relationship. For example, Karrebaek (2010) documented a kindergartener's entry negotiation in interactions with peers over time, and found that although the boy increased his repertoire of communicative resources, his integration to the peer group was only successful initially, followed by sanction and blocked participation.

Finally, research on competence development may also aim to *locate the possible triggers for the observed changes over time*. These triggers may be observable in talk: They may be the participants' (including the learner's) (a) displayed orientation to new understanding (e.g., Markee 2008; Pekarek Doehler 2010) or (b) modifications of conduct which result in the absence of an interactional trouble that occurred previously (e.g., Nguyen 2008; Ishida 2009) or a more economical and effective way to achieve the same action (e.g., Brouwer and Wagner 2004; Nguyen 2006; Ishida 2011; Lee and Hellermann 2014). In both cases, the use of CA can potentially enable the identification of interactional forces that may have shaped observable changes in the learner's interactional practices. If these observable triggers are not present, the analyst may at times go beyond CA and refer to ethnographic information to speculate on possible explanations for the changes. This extension clearly is not within CA's domain but can bring in a broader picture of the learning process.

Tracking the Development of Competence from School to Work

Garfinkel (2002) observed that interaction at the workplace, which he referred to as the Shop Floor Problem, are "staff-specific," "work-site specific" and "discipline-specific" rather than being generic descriptions (p. 113). Importantly, talk-at-work is simultaneously members' methods (competence)[5] *and* "instructed actions" (p. 110) (see also Zemel and Koschmann 2014). This means that novices at the workplace develop their competence as they work out the Shop Floor Problem *in interaction* while getting the job done.

Tracking competence development from school to work involves documenting the continuity, adaptation and emergence of interactional practices by comparing the learner's interactional conducts in the training setting and in actual workplace performance. In such a project, it is useful to select an activity that is taught in school and is later performed at the workplace. In my view, role-plays or mock activities serve as a fertile ground for this type of investigation, because (a) they are prevalent in education and (b) they aim to simulate the activity at work as much as possible, including tasks, participant frameworks and often times also the content of talk. It is important to note that since a mock-up is oriented to and treated as "a guide to practical actions in the actual situation" (Garfinkel and Sacks 1986, 184), it both provides for "an accurate representation of features in the actual situation" and makes "specifically and deliberately false provision for some of the *essential* features of that situation" (p. 184, emphasis original). Role-played interaction in instructional settings has been shown empirically to differ from actual workplace performance in activity frames (Seale et al. 2007; Hindmarsh et al. 2014) and goals (Félix-Brasdefer 2007; Stokoe 2011), which may lead to differences in the interactional practices used. Stokoe (2011), for example, found that officers in role-played police interviews tend to use more elaborate turns and turns that orient to the instructional model and assessment criteria compared to actual interviews.[6] A study on competence development from school to work may then analyze (a) a novice's development of *interactional practices* to handle work-related tasks (actions) over time in instructional role-plays and (b) the same novice's handling of these tasks (actions) at the workplace, with a focus on which interactional practices they employ and how these practices may relate back to those developed in training. In the next section, I will provide a brief illustration of what this analysis may look like and the challenges that it faces.

Illustrative Analysis: From Role-played to Actual Patient Consultations

The SES selected for analysis here is pharmacy patient consultation in the USA. Patient consultation is a required component of US pharmaceutical care; it is taught in most pharmacy schools and practiced at most pharmacies in one form or another. The novice in focus is a pharmacy student with the pseudonym Jim.

Data[7]

The data includes two sets. The first set consists of 10 videotaped consultation role-plays between Jim and a "standardized patient" (lay actors in the community acting as patients based on given profiles), recorded weekly over the course of one semester in a third-year communication course at a pharmacy school. Of these 10 role-plays, only the 1st, 2nd, 3rd and 10th involved new prescriptions and therefore only these 4 role-plays will be included in the analysis. The role-plays took place in individual cubicles with a desk and two facing chairs. Jim had in front of him the written patient profile (similar to what pharmacists receive at pharmacies) and Jim's pre-lab notes. A camera, operated by Jim, was placed at one end of the table. After each role-play, the students watched the tape and received the instructor's feedback, which was based on the communication strategies taught in the course. One of these strategies is the use of an interactive approach, implemented via the use of "prime questions" (Gardner et al. 1991), that is, three questions designed to elicit the patient's existing knowledge about the drug therapy purpose ("What did the doctor tell you this medication is for?"), the drug administration methods ("How did the doctor tell you to take this medication?") and expectations regarding side-effects and outcomes ("What did the doctor tell you to expect from this medication?").

The second dataset consists of 40 videotaped consultations with real patients at a pharmacy where Jim interned for two months. Of these consultations, only 25 involved new prescriptions and these were included for analysis. In the six months between the communication course and this clerkship, Jim completed the last semester at the school and one clerkship involving intensive home care, while working part-time (once every two weeks) at a chain pharmacy. The recorded clerkship was the first time for Jim to work at a local pharmacy. The videos were recorded in Jim's second, fifth and eighth weeks during the clerkship. A preceptor was present and occasionally joined the consultations, but for the most part, Jim was solo in interactions with the patients. At the time of the data collection, the "prime questions" model was not used by the senior pharmacists at Jim's clerkship site. Jim's consultation videotapes were not reviewed and evaluated by the instructor or the preceptor.

A patient consultation consists of several actions (see Nguyen 2012a), but for illustration purpose, I will focus only on the *orientation* to consultation, which takes place near the consultation's beginning. An orientation consists of these actions: *Inquiry* about the patient's medical history (familiarity with the prescribed drug and known drug allergies), and *drug identification and exposition*, which can range from mentioning of the drug's name, category and purpose to a more elaborate description of the drug's ingredients and how it works. The analysis concentrates on changes in Jim's interactional practices to achieve *drug identification and exposition* in the role-plays and how this action was accomplished later at the pharmacy.

Role-played Patient Consultations

Overall, Jim seemed to change his practices to better fit the instructed model of patient consultation rather than to resolve any interactional troubles that arose in the interaction itself. (In the role-play excerpts, Jim is referred to as "Ph/S" and the standardized patient as "SP".)

Excerpt (1a) is from Jim's very first role-play in the communication course, prior to the introduction of any consultation model.

Ex. (1a): Role-Play 1 (Antibiotic)

```
→ Ph/S: the prescription for you today is the amoxicillin?
        (0.2)
  Ph/S: a new one?
        (0.3) ((SP nods))
    SP: °ri[ght°.
→ Ph/S:    [antibiotic?
        (1.0) ((SP nods))
  Ph/S: doctor have you taken that before?
    SP: ↑no. °I haven't°=
  Ph/S: ='kay. you don't get any allergies to medicines:?
        (0.2)
    SP: u:::h. (0.2) no. I don't. [not that I know of.
  Ph/S:                           [okay.
  Ph/S: okay.
        (0.2)
→ Ph/S: ((louder)) the Amoxicillin °like I said° is an antibiotic,
        =the doctor wants you to have it <↑three times a da:y.>
```

Jim identifies the medicine by its name, "Amoxicillin" (l. 1), and category ("antibiotic") (l. 6). These turns are produced as statements of knowledge that Jim already has. The patient orients to these statements by providing receipt tokens and non-verbal acknowledgments (l. 4, 5, 7). Before Jim launches the first advice (l. 17), he refocuses on the medicine by reiterating the brief drug exposition in a slightly louder voice (l. 16). Neither participant seems to treat this interaction as problematic, suggesting that Jim has accomplished the tasks effectively.

Jim's drug identification and exposition in the second role-play (Ex. 1b) was achieved by several similar practices, but with a noticeable shift. It is relevant to note that this role-play took place after the introduction of the "prime questions" in the course.

Ex. (1b): Role-Play 2 (Eye-drop)

```
   Ph/S: you've got ↑new medicines today:,
     SP: ↓m↑hm,
         (1.0) ((Ph/S looks down at papers))
→  Ph/S: one is called cosopt. it's an eye drop.
         have you ever used (0.2) an eye drop before:, or:
     SP: u:h I've used other eye drops. yeah:.
   Ph/S: okay.
     SP: °but° not this one. ((SP points to bottles))
         (0.8) ((Ph/S looks down at paper))
→  Ph/S: what did the doctor tell you this one's for,
         (0.2)
     SP: glaucoma?=
   Ph/S: =yeah.
         (1.0) ((Ph/S looks down at paper))
   Ph/S: ((creaky)) °so°.
         (0.7) ((Ph/S looks down at paper))
   Ph/S: >he wants you to put< ↑one ↓dro:p, er
         (0.2) ↑both ↓eyes. twice a day.
```

In this second role-play, Jim also announces the drug's name and category (l. 4). Unlike in the first role-play, however, Jim produces an inquiry about the drug's purpose (l. 10). After a brief pause, the patient provides a response (l. 12), which Jim acknowledges with a minimal token (l. 13). The drug exposition is thus jointly accomplished rather than by only Jim. After some pauses (l. 14, 16) and a minimal token (l.

15), Jim launches the first advice. Here again, neither party seems to treat the interaction as problematic.

The inquiry about the therapy purpose is clearly a new practice compared to the first role-play. Given that students were trained to ask the "prime questions"—one of which involves the therapy purpose—it is plausible that Jim's change in this case was influenced by the instructions and assessment scheme rather than some troubles that arose endogenously from the interaction.

Jim's third role-play shows a recurrence of the same practices of inquiring about the therapy purpose (Ex. 1c).

Ex. (1c): Role-Play 3 (Antidepressant)

```
1     Ph/S:  so we've got (0.2) two new ones to fill out?
2            (0.3)
3       SP:  ye[ap,
4→    Ph/S:    [we've got (0.2) paxil, and iburprofene.
5       SP:  ↓m↑hm,
6→    Ph/S:  did the doctor tell you anything about the medicine:, the paxil:?
7            (0.4)
8       SP:  WELL, (0.2) he actually told me it's an antidepressant.
9     Ph/S:  okay,
10           (0.2)
11    Ph/S:  yeah.
12           (0.9)
13→   Ph/S:  and yuh- (0.2) you're using it for depression:,
14      SP:  well, (0.2) yeah. (0.2) evidently.=
15    Ph/S:  =okay.
16           (0.3)
17    Ph/S:  it could be used for (several) different things, too:,
18      SP:  ye[ah.
19    Ph/S:    [so.
20           (1.6) ((Ph/S shifts body in chair))
21    Ph/S:  so everything's cool:. uhm. did he go over with you
22           anything like directions:, (as far as) just (0.2) taking it?
```

Jim states the medicines' names (l. 4) as before, but there is no drug exposition. Instead, he quickly initiates a broad inquiry about the medicine (l. 6), which opens up a slot for the patient to provide his knowledge about the medicine's category (l. 8). At the same time, Jim maintains the same practice of using an inquiry to establish the drug therapy purpose with the patient (l. 13): Jim's formulation of the inquiry as a statement about the patient strongly projects a confirmation from the patient

(Labov and Fanshel 1977; Heritage and Roth 1995). However, given the fact that the medicine's category (anti-depression) implies its main purpose, this inquiry could be heard as redundant in this particular consultation. Indeed, the patient implies the redundancy of Jim's inquiry by prefacing his turn with a nonconforming "well" (Schiffrin 1987) and saying "evidently" (l. 14). Jim's orientation to the patient's challenge to his inquiry's relevance can be seen in the account given in line 17.

While Jim's inquiry is treated as having low local relevancy, it does fit the prescribed model for patient counseling, namely, to include a question about the therapy purpose. I submit that Jim's continuation of this practice despite local redundancy is again influenced by the course instructions.

The 10th role-play was aimed to integrate all skills learned in the course (Ex. 1d). To gauge the students' progress, the instructor designed this role-play to involve the same medicine as in the first role-play.

Ex. (1d): Role-Play 10 (Antibiotic)

```
   Ph/S: we have the new one for you the amoxicillin antibiotic,
         (0.2)
     SP: mhm,
   Ph/S: that you dropped off earlier today,=
     SP: =mhm,
         (0.7) ((Ph/S looks to the side at bottles))
→  Ph/S: uh ↑what are you gonna be using that one for:.
     SP: I've got ↓bronchitis.
   Ph/S: okay.
         (0.2)
   Ph/S: did the doctor tell you anything to expect (0.2)
         while you're on that one?
```

As before, Jim states the drug's name and category in the beginning (l. 1). He also maintains the practice of issuing an inquiry about the drug therapy's purpose (l. 7), as was found since the second role-play.

Thus, over the course of the semester, to provide the drug identification and exposition as part of the orientation to consultation, Jim shifted from *stating* to *inquiring* about the drug therapy's purpose. He then maintained these practices consistently after the first role-play.

Next, I will examine Jim's interactional practices to accomplish the action of drug identification and exposition at the pharmacy, about six months later. This part of the analysis focuses on the question: How did Jim employ the practice that developed in the role-plays, namely, using inquiries to establish drug therapy purpose, in the consultations at the pharmacy?

Workplace Patient Consultations

Jim performed drug identification and exposition in every consultation at the pharmacy, but how he employed the inquiry about the therapy purpose was different compared to the role-plays. Whereas Jim became more routinized in producing inquiries about the therapy purpose in the role-plays, this practice appeared only occasionally in the consultation orientations at the pharmacy (7 times out of 25 consultations). This suggests that a developed practice from the role-plays was not performed consistently at the workplace. Further, this practice seemed to be employed for different functions compared to the role-plays.

First, all of the seven cases when Jim inquired about the therapy purpose before advice-giving involved a medicine that could be used for different purposes (e.g., swelling vs. blood pressure, smoking cessation vs. anti-depression). This posed a problem for counseling regarding which drug effect was the desired outcome and which was the side-effect. The pharmacist's inquiry about the therapy's purpose could resolve this problem and thus bore consequences for the organization and content of the upcoming advice sequences. For example, the medicine in excerpt (2a) draws fluid out from the blood stream and therefore can be used to reduce either blood pressure or swelling. The inquiry sequence starts in line 7.

Ex. (2a): Clerkship 5-12 (Diuretic)

7→ Ph: what do they want you to use this one <u>for</u>:,
8 (1.2)
9 Pt: it's like a diuretic?
10 (0.2)
11 Pt: [°isn't it°?

Ph: [okay. just- to: (0.2) for swelling?
(0.4)
Pt: [U::HM
Ph: [or for blood pressure.
(0.2)
Pt: no. no. (0.2) f' swelling.=
Ph: =swelling? okay.
Pt: °swelling°.
((lines omitted))
Ph: so like you said it's a diuretic it's (gonna) make you
lose that fluid so it's really best to take it in the morning,
Pt: okay,
Ph: early in the morning so you're not up all night
going to the bathroom.
(0.2)
Pt: °I have problems getting sleep anyway°,
[so. heh heh heh
Ph: [yeah.
(0.2)
Ph: it will have some effects on your blood pressure,
it will lower your blood pressure a little so be
careful first thing in the morning or after you've
been sitting down for a while you might be
[a little light headed or dizzy,

A detailed analysis of this episode can be found in Nguyen (2013). Here, I will mention that Jim pursues a response through several turns, until line 19. This suggests that Jim genuinely depends on the information from the patient to proceed. Indeed, the outcome of the inquiry shapes the upcoming advice sequences (l. 82–96). This is a different function compared to the role-plays.

Notably, the practice of inquiring about the therapy purpose was also employed once during *pre-closing* and served to build rapport with the patient. Excerpt (2b) takes place near the end, after several advice sequences have closed.

Ex. (2b): Clerkship 2-1 (Pain)

Pt: with that, and actually:: (0.2) was able to take
ah ibuprofen last night, so at least I could have
a couple hours sleep, so=
Ph: =yea:h.
(0.2)
→ Ph: ↑what kind of pain was it fo:r,
Pt: ↑a:h. (0.2) knee.
Ph: knees.
(0.2)

```
119   Ph:  yeah. the ibuprofen would probably definitely help you.
120        (0.2)
121   Ph:  <withthis>.
122   Pt:  °oh yeah. (I don't like to keep playing with this°) ((smiles))
124   Pt:  ((creaky)) °I don't want a chiropractor, ((smiles, signs paper))
126        I know it's not gonna work, (for this thing°).
127        (0.4) ((Ph smiles, looking at client))
```

Right before this excerpt starts, Jim began to put the medicine into its bag and write on the insurance form as pre-closing actions. The inquiry about the therapy purpose (l. 115) thus is not placed to shape advice-giving. Further, after this inquiry, Jim provides an optimistic projection (l. 119), another pre-closing move (Jefferson 1988). The fact that the patient responds with a light comment while smiling (l. 122–126) and Jim also smiles (l. 127) suggests that the inquiry in line 115 is for rapport building. Thus, the practice of inquiring about the therapy's purpose, which emerged in the role-plays to co-construct drug exposition with the patient, is now used to achieve a goal that is more relevant to workplace patient consultation: maintaining relationship with a client.

Conclusion

This chapter has attempted to locate the concept of competence development in EM and CA and outline a methodological procedure for tracking development over time. The illustrative analysis of a novice's journey from the classroom to the workplace shows that a practice developed in training may be repurposed to achieve relevant local tasks at the workplace. Competence development in this case involves contingent utilization of interactional practices, which selectively draw on trained procedures.

A core challenge in this analysis was how to determine "sameness" in the midst of situational differences, especially when going from one setting (classroom) to another (workplace). I have attempted to maintain "sameness" by anchoring the analysis to the same action and practices, but given each setting's goals and constraints, changes in how the novice utilized these practices may be adaptations to each context for more effective goal achievement. The development of interactional competence from school to work may very well lie in this contextualized and dynamic adaptation. Further research is needed to better understand the dynamics and complexity of this development.

Notes

1. A rare study by Riddiford and Joe (2010) shows that the socio-pragmatic awareness in requests by an immigrant learner of English was successfully transferred from role-plays in an ESL class to the workplace.
2. Related to CA's notion of SES are "language game" (Wittgenstein 1967), "speech event" (Hymes 1964), "oral practice" (Hall 1993), "discursive practice" (Young 2008) and "interactive practice" (Hall 1995b; Nguyen 2012a).
3. Along the same veins, Hellermann (2008) put the spotlight on actions in his book's title, "Social *actions* for classroom language learning" (emphasis added).
4. This procedure applies to a single case. When more than one learner is studied, each learner's developmental trajectory needs to be analyzed before attempts are made to draw similarities and differences among the cases (e.g., Nguyen 2012a).
5. Garfinkel referred to studies of workplace interaction as "hybrid studies" and noted that "'hybrids' properties are about competence" (2002, 101).
6. Stokoe (2011) did not track the same police officers from role-plays to actual interviews.
7. Transcriptions notation is based on the Jefferson (2004) system. Non-verbal actions during silent periods and speech are described in double parentheses after the silence or speech.

References

Beach, W. A. (2001). Stability and ambiguity: Managing uncertain moments when updating news about mom's cancer. *Text, 21*, 221–250.

Brouwer, C. E., & Wagner, J. (2004). Developmental issues in second language conversation. *Journal of Applied Linguistics, 1*, 29–47.

Cekaite, A. (2007). A child's development of interactional competence in a Swedish L2 classroom. *The Modern Language Journal, 91*, 45–62.

Dings, A. (2014). Interactional competence and the development of alignment activity. *Modern Language Journal, 98*(3), 742–756.

Félix-Brasdefer, J. C. (2007). Natural speech vs. elicited data: A comparison of natural and role play requests in Mexican Spanish. *Spanish in Context, 42*(2), 159–185.

Filliettaz, L., Losa, S., & Duc, B. (2013). Power, miscommunication, and cultural diversity: Applying a discourse analytic lens to vocational education practices. In I. de Saint-Georges & J. J. Weber (Eds.), *Multilingualism and multimodality: Current challenges for educational studies* (pp. 153–181). Rotterdam, Netherlands: Sense Publishers.

Firth, A., & Wagner, J. (1997). On discourse, communication, and (some) fundamental concepts in SLA research. *The Modern Language Journal, 81*(3), 285–300.

Firth, A., & Wagner, J. (2007). Second/foreign language learning as a social accomplishment: Elaborations on a reconceptualized SLA. *The Modern Language Journal, 91*, 800–819.

Gardner, M., Boyce, R., & Herrier, R. (1991). *Pharmacist-patient consultation program: An interactive approach to verify patient understanding*. Rockville, MD: U.S. Public Health Service, Indian Health Service/Roerig Division of Pfizer Pharmaceuticals.

Garfinkel, H. (1967). *Studies in ethnomethodology*. Englewood Cliffs, NJ: Prentice Hall.

Garfinkel, H. (1996). Ethnomethodology's program. *Social Psychology Quarterly 59*(1), 5–21.

Garfinkel, H. (2002). *Ethnomethodology's programs: Working out Durkheim's aphorism*. New York: Rowman & Littlefield Publishers.

Garfinkel, H., & Sacks, H. (1986). On formal structures of practical actions. In H. Garfinkel (Ed.), *Ethnomethodological studies of work* (pp. 157–191). London: Routledge (originally 1970).

Hall, J. K. (1993). The role of oral practices in the accomplishment of our everyday lives: The sociocultural dimension of interaction with implications for the learning of another language. *Applied Linguistics, 14*(2), 145–167.

Hall, J. K. (1995a). "Aw, man, where you goin'?": Classroom interaction and the development of L2 interactional competence. *Issues in Applied Linguistics, 6*(2), 37–62.

Hall, J. K. (1995b). (Re)creating our worlds with words: A sociohistorical perspective of face-to-face interaction. *Applied Linguistics, 16*(2), 206–232.

Hall, J. K. (1999). A prosaics of interaction: The development of interactional competence in another language. In E. Hinkel (Ed.), *Culture in second language teaching and learning* (pp. 137–151). Cambridge: Cambridge University Press.

Hall, J. K., & Pekarek Doehler, S. (2011). L2 interactional competence and development. In J. K. Hall, J. Hellermann, & S. Pekarek Doehler (Eds.), *L2 interactional competence and development* (pp. 1–15). Bristol, UK: Multilingual Matters.

Hellermann, J. (2007). The development of practices for action in classroom dyadic interaction: Focus on task openings. *Modern Language Journal, 91*(1), 83–96.

Hellermann, J. (2008). *Social actions for classroom language learning*. Clevedon, UK: Multilingual Matters.

Hellermann, J. (2011). Members' methods, members competencies: Looking for evidence of language learning in longitudinal investigation of other-initiated repair. In J. K. Hall, J. Hellermann, & S. Pekarek Doehler (Eds.), *L2 interactional competence and development* (pp. 147–172). Clevedon, UK: Multilingual Matters.

Heritage, J. (1984). *Garfinkel and ethnomethodology*. Cambridge and New York: Polity Press.

Heritage, J., & Clayman, S. (2013). The changing tenor of questioning over time: Tracking a question form across us presidential news conferences, 1953–2000. *Journalism Practice, 7*(4), 481–501.

Heritage, J., & Roth, A. (1995). Grammar and institution: Questions and questioning in the broadcast news interview. *Research on Language and Social Interaction, 28*(1), 1–60.

Hindmarsh, J., Hyland, L., & Banerjee, A. (2014). Work to make simulation work: "Realism", instructional correction and the body in training. *Discouse Studies, 16*(2), 247–269.

Hosoda, Y., & Aline, D. (2010). Learning to be a teacher: Development of EFL teacher trainee interactional practices. *JALT Journal, 32*(2), 119–147.

Hymes, D. (1964). Toward ethnographies of communication: The analysis of communicative events. In P. P. Giglioli (Ed.), *Language and social context: Selected readings* (pp. 21–44). Harmondsworth, UK: Penguin.

Ishida, M. (2006). Interactional competence and the use of modal expressions in decision making activities: CA for understanding microgenesis of pragmatic competence. In K. Bardovi-Harlig, C. Félix-Brasdefer, & A. Omar (Eds.), *Pragmatics and language learning* (Vol. 11, pp. 1–28). Honolulu, HI: National Foreign Language Resource Center, University of Hawai'i.
Ishida, M. (2009). Development of interactional competence: Changes in the use of "ne" in L2 Japanese during study abroad. In H. T. Nguyen & G. Kasper (Eds.), *Talk-in-interaction: Multilingual perspectives* (pp. 351–385). Honolulu, HI: National Foreign Language Resource Center, University of Hawaii.
Ishida, M. (2011). Engaging in another person's telling as a recipient in L2 Japanese: Development of interactional competence during one-year study abroad. In G. Pallotti & J. Wagner (Eds.), *L2 learning as social practice: Conversation-analytic perspectives* (pp. 45–85). Honolulu, HI: National Foreign Language Resource Center, University of Hawaii at Manoa.
Jefferson, G. (1988). On the sequential organization of troubles-talk in ordinary conversation. *Social Problems, 35*(4), 418–441.
Jefferson, G. (2004). Glossary of transcript symbols with an introduction. In G. H. Lerner (Ed.), *Conversation analysis: Studies from the first generation* (pp. 13–31). Amsterdam and Philadelphia: John Benjamins.
Karrebaek, M. S. (2010). I can be with! A novice kindergartener's successes and challenges in play participation and the development of communicative skills. In G. Kasper, H. T. Nguyen, D. Yoshimi, & J. Yoshioka (Eds.), *Pragmatics and language learning* (Vol. 12, pp. 327–359). Honolulu, HI: National Foreign Language Resource Center, University of Hawaii at Manoa.
Kasper, G. & Wagner, J. (2011). A conversation-analytic approach to second language acquisition. In D. Atkinson (Ed.) *Alternative approaches to second language acquisition* (pp. 117–142). London & New York: Routledge
Kasper, G. (2009). Locating cognition in second language interaction and learning: Inside the skull or in public view? *IRAL, 47*, 11–36.
Koschmann, T. (2013). Conversation analysis and learning in interaction. In C. A. Chapelle (Ed.), *The encyclopedia of applied linguistics*. Chichester, UK: Blackwell Publishing. doi:10.1002/9781405198431.wbeal0208.
Labov, W., & Fanshel, D. (1977). *Therapeutic discourse: Psychotherapy as conversation*. New York: Academic Press.
Lee, Y.-A., & Hellermann, J. (2014). Tracing developmental changes through conversation analysis: Cross-sectional and longitudinal analysis. *TESOL Quarterly, 48*(4), 763–788.

Li, D. (2000). The pragmatics of making requests in the L2 workplace: A case study of language socialization. *Canadian Modern Language Review, 57*(1), 58–87.

Lingard, C., Schryer, C., Garwood, K., & Spafford, M. (2003). "Talking the talk": School and workplace genre tension in clerkship case presentations. *Medical Education, 37*, 612–620.

Markee, N. (1994). Toward an ethnomethodological respecification of second-language acquisition studies. In E. Tarone, S. Gass, & A. Cohen (Eds.), *Research methodology in second language acquisition* (pp. 89–118). Hillsdale, NJ and Hove, UK: Lawrence Erlbaum Associates Publishers.

Markee, N. (2000). *Conversation analysis*. Mahwah, NJ and London: Lawrence Erlbaum Associates Publishers.

Markee, N. (2008). Toward a learning behavior tracking methodology for CA-for-SLA. *Applied Linguistics, 29*(3), 404–427.

Markee, N., & Kasper, G. (2004). Classroom talks: An introduction. *The Modern Language Journal, 88*(4), 491–500.

Melander, H. (2012). Transformations of knowledge within a peer group. Knowing and learning in interaction. *Learning, Culture and Social Interaction, 1*(3–4), 232–248.

Melander, H., & Sahlström, F. (2009). Learning to fly—The progressive development of situation awareness. *Scandinavian Journal of Educational Research, 53*(2), 151–166.

Mondada, L. (2006). La compétence comme dimension située et contingente, localement évaluée par les participants. *Bulletin Suisse de Linguistique Appliquée, 84*, 83–119.

Mondada, L., & Pekarek Doehler, S. (2004). Second language acquisition as situated practice: Task accomplishment in the French second language classroom. *The Modern Language Journal, 88*(4), 501–518.

Nguyen, H. t. (2006). Constructing "expertness": A novice pharmacist's development of interactional competence in patient consultations. *Communication and Medicine, 3*(2), 147–160.

Nguyen, H. t. (2008). Sequence organization as local and longitudinal achievement. *Text and Talk, 28*(4), 501–528.

Nguyen, H. t. (2011a). A longitudinal microanalysis of a second language learner's participation. In G. Pallotti & J. Wagner (Eds.), *L2 learning as social practice: Conversation-analytic perspectives* (pp. 17–44). Honolulu, HI: National Foreign Language Resource Center, University of Hawaii at Manoa.

Nguyen, H. t. (2011b). Achieving recipient design longitudinally: Evidence from a pharmacy intern in patient consultations. In J. K. Hall, J. Hellermann, & S. Pekarek Doehler (Eds.), *L2 interactional competence and development* (pp. 173–205). Bristol, UK: Multilingual Matters.

Nguyen, H. t. (2012a). *Developing interactional competence: A conversation analytic study of patient consultations in pharmacy.* Basingstoke, UK: Palgrave Macmillan.

Nguyen, H. t. (2012b). Social interaction and competence development: Learning the sequential organization of a communicative practice. *Learning, Culture and Social Interaction, 1*(2), 127–142.

Nguyen, H. t. (2013). The prime questions in authentic patient consultations: A call for additional research on current and new paradigms. *Research in Social and Administrative Pharmacy, 9*, 339–352.

Pallotti, G. (2002). Borrowing words: Appropriations in child second-language discourse. In J. Leather & J. van Dam (Eds.), *Ecology of language acquisition* (pp. 183–202). Dordrecht: Kluwer Academic Publishers.

Parks, S. (2001). Moving from school to the workplace: Disciplinary innovation, border crossings, and the reshaping of a written genre. *Applied Linguistics, 22*(4), 405–438.

Pekarek Doehler, S. (2006). Compétence et langage en action. *Bulletin Suisse de Linguistique Appliquée, 84*, 9–45.

Pekarek Doehler, S. (2010). Conceptual changes and methodological challenges: On language and learning from a conversation analytic perspective on SLA. In C. Jenks & S. Walsh (Eds.), *Conceptualizing learning in applied linguistics* (pp. 105–126). Basingstoke, UK: Palgrave Macmillan.

Pekarek Doehler, S., González-Martínez, E., & Wagner, J. (forthcoming). *Longitudinal studies in conversation analysis.* Basingstoke, UK: Palgrave Macmillan.

Pekarek Doehler, S., & Pochon-Berger, E. (2015). The development of L2 interactional competence: Evidence from turn-taking organization, sequence organization, repair organization and preference organization. In T. Cadierno & S. Eskildsen (Eds.), *Usage-based perspectives on second language learning* (pp. 233–267). Berlin, Germany: Mouton de Gruyter.

Riddiford, N. & Joe, A. (2010). Tracking the development of sociopragmatic skills. *TESOL Quarterly, 44*(1), 195–205.

Rine, E. F., & Hall, J. K. (2011). Becoming the teacher: Changing participant frameworks in international teaching assistant discourse. In J. K. Hall,

J. Hellermann, & S. Pekarek Doehler (Eds.), *L2 interactional competence and development* (pp. 244–274). Bristol, UK: Multilingual Matters.

Sacks, H. (1995). *Lectures on conversation, Vol. I and II*. Oxford, UK: Blackwell Publishers.

Sacks, H., Schegloff, E. A., & Jefferson, G. (1974). A simplest systematics for the organization of turn taking for conversation. *Language, 50*(4), 696–735.

Sanders, R. E. (2003). Applying the skills concept to discourse and conversation: The remediation of performance defects in talk-in-interaction. In J. Greene & B. Burleson (Eds.), *The handbook of communication and social interaction skills* (pp. 221–256). Mahwah, NJ: Erlbaum.

Schegloff, E. A. (1989). Reflections on language, development, and the interactional character of talk-in-interaction. In M. H. Bornstein & J. S. Brunner (Eds.), *Interaction in human development* (pp. 139–153). Hillsdale, NJ: Lawrence Erlbaum.

Schegloff, E. A. (1996a). Confirming allusions: Towards an empirical account of action. *American Journal of Sociology, 104*, 161–216.

Schegloff, E. A. (1996b). Issues of relevance for discourse analysis: Contingency in action, interaction and co-participant context. In E. H. Hovy & D. Scott (Eds.), *Computational and conversational discourse: Burning issues—An interdisciplinary account* (pp. 3–38). Heidelberg: Springer Verlag.

Schegloff, E. A. (1999). Discourse, pragmatics, conversation, analysts. *Discourse Studies, 1*(4), 405–435.

Schegloff, E. A. (2006). Interaction: The infrastructure for social institutions, the natural ecological niche for language, and the arena in which culture is enacted. In N. J. Enfield & S. C. Levinson (Eds.), *Roots of human sociality: Culture, cognition and interaction* (pp. 70–96). London, UK: Berg.

Schiffrin, D. (1987). *Discourse markers*. Cambridge: Cambridge University Press.

Seale, C., Butler, C. C., Hutchby, I., Kinnersly, P., & Rollnick, S. (2007). Negotiating frame ambiguity: A study of simulated encounters in medical education. *Communication and Medicine, 4*(2), 177–187.

Stokoe, E. (2011). Simulated interaction and communication skills training: The "conversation analytic role-play method". In C. Antaki (Ed.), *Applied conversation analysis: Changing institutional practices* (pp. 119–139). Basingstoke, UK: Palgrave Macmillan.

Wittgenstein, L. 1967. *Philosophical investigations* (G. E. M. Anscombe, Trans.) (3rd ed.). Oxford: Basil Blackwell.

Young, R. F. (1999). Sociolinguistic approaches to SLA. *Annual Review of Applied Linguistics, 19*, 105–132.

Young, R. F. (2008). *Language and interaction: An advanced resources book*. London and New York: Routledge.

Young, R. F. (2011). Interactional competence in language learning, teaching, and testing. In E. Hinkel (Ed.), *Handbook of research in second language teaching and learning* (pp. 426–443). New York, NY: Routledge.

Young, R. F., & Miller, E. (2004). Learning as changing participation: Discourse roles in ESL writing conferences. *The Modern Language Journal, 88*(4), 519–535.

Zemel, A., & Koschmann, T. (2014). "Put your finger right in here": Learnability and instructed experience. *Discourse Studies, 16*(2), 163–183.

Zimmerman, D. (1999). Horizontal and vertical comparative research in language and social interaction. *Research on Language and Social Interaction 32*(1, 2), 195–203.

9

Transitions and Interactional Competence: Negotiating Boundaries Through Talk

Meredith Marra, Janet Holmes, and Keely Kidner

Transitions at Work

Transitions are complex activity systems whereby social actors move from one environment to another. In the workplace context specifically the boundary crossing inherent to these transitions may involve a move from country to country, subsidiary to subsidiary, workplace to workplace, profession to profession, department to department, language to language, or activity type to activity type. Surprisingly these transitions, which are so common in our everyday lives, have received relatively little attention within the field of workplace discourse (the field within which the authors locate themselves). Instead, and perhaps reflecting the relative youth of the field, workplace discourse scholars have focused on a range of discrete workplace activities: meetings (e.g., Chan 2005; Marra and Angouri 2011), giving directives (Vine 2001; Takano 2005), decision-making (Marra 2003; Angouri and Angelidou 2012), small talk

M. Marra (✉) • J. Holmes • K. Kidner
Victoria University of Wellington, Wellington, New Zealand

S. Pekarek Doehler et al. (eds.), *Interactional Competences in Institutional Settings*, DOI 10.1007/978-3-319-46867-9_9

(Holmes 2000; Chan 2005; Kuiper and Flindall 2000) and humor (Schnurr 2009; Plester 2016). In this chapter, we build on the knowledge gained through these research foci and consider how participants move between these activities.

In the past five years, there has been growing interest in how newcomers negotiate their membership of workplace communities (see, e.g., chapters in Angouri et al. 2017). Joining the workforce, joining a new team or joining a new society are all examples of different kinds of transitional activity. At a societal level, the boundary crossing occurs at a macro level of abstraction entailing negotiation of ideologies and societal values. In the case of joining new groups and engaging in new discourse types, the transition occurs at the meso and micro levels involving negotiation of new interactional norms with colleagues and other employees. Is there a case to be made about the similarities? How can we embrace the wide range of boundary-crossing activities in which we naturally engage in our working lives?

Although omnipresent, transitions remain an underrepresented research agenda. In this chapter, we argue the case for transitions as a distinct category of talk for analysis purposes, a category bound by a range of relevant constraints, from wider societal ideologies through industry and organizational-specific norms to micro-discursive patterns. We thus aim to extend workplace discourse beyond discrete genres and to test a sociolinguistic assumption about the directness of the relationship between micro and macro levels of interaction (Ainsworth-Vaughn 1992; Drew 2002; Messer et al. 2012; West and Garcia 1988).

In order to illustrate these claims, we draw on interactional data collected on two different building sites in New Zealand. Our specific interest is the discourse used to socialize apprentices into the building industry. The apprenticeship model represents an explicit, mentored trajectory from student to professional. Learning how to be a builder involves not only acquiring the jargon, and how to do the required jobs, but also how to participate "appropriately" in the transactional and relational talk, whether this appropriacy is related to one's society, one's industry, one's team or one's status as a professional. As such, it provides a rich context in which to explore transitions of many kinds.

Transitions as a Category of Workplace Talk

While not a regular focus of workplace discourse analysts, transitions have been investigated in a range of disciplines, notably education, sociology and management. In education, researchers have explored factors (such as identity and status) involved in school leavers' shift into work, and the role that workplace preparation and apprenticeships play in this transition (e.g., Bennert 2002; Blau 2000; Filliettaz et al. 2010). The sociological literature emphasizes the role of life phases (e.g., school–work–retirement), highlighting the mechanisms that shape these transitions and noting the potential non-linear progression of phases (Bradley and Devadason 2008; George 1993). Literature emanating from the field of management has typically taken a macro perspective on transitions amid organizational change, recognizing the crucial role of communication for managers and employees in this process (Ashforth et al. 2000; Ebberwein et al. 2004; Halford and Leonard 2006; Ibarra and Barbulescu 2010; Nicholson 1984).

By contrast, and despite its obvious relevance in examining the process of workplace identity construction, the concept of transition has been greatly underinvestigated in sociolinguistic approaches. Historically, sociolinguistic research has considered micro-level transitions in talk, often with reference only to the immediate context (e.g., Ainsworth-Vaughn 1992; Drew 2002; West and Garcia 1988), and country-level or organizational transitions, mainly in relation to macro issues such as power and ideology (Angouri 2011; Messer et al. 2012). The relationship between the two has not been explored. Our experience in interpreting recorded workplace interactions has identified the importance of contextual constraints as newcomers learn to construct an acceptable professional identity within their workplace teams. Constructing a professional identity in any employment context generally involves representing oneself as competent in relevant professional areas, including the pertinent discourse norms. Learning how to manage the discourse involved in negotiating expected competencies, rights and obligations, and power relationships in the process of professional identity construction can be problematic for newcomers. Managing the transitions between different types of discourse activity analyzable in terms of different layers of social constraint (macro, meso, micro) presents further challenges. To elaborate this theoretical position, we have developed a social realist model of interaction (see Holmes et al. 2011).

A Social Realist Model of Workplace Discourse

A number of theorists have pointed out that while people tend to assume their behavior (including verbal behavior) in different contexts is relatively unconstrained, the reality is very different (Coupland 2001; Ehrlich 2008; Cameron 2009). The complex relationship between individual agency and more abstract social structures needs to be recognized. Social realism, in particular, provides a useful theoretical account of this relationship, proposing that individual behavior (including language) is influenced by outside "reality" (Bourdieu 1979; Bhaskar 2008; Collier 1994; Coupland and Jaworski 2009, 17). Our 20 years of workplace discourse analysis provides convincing support for this theoretical position. We argue that layers of normative constraints shape the way we negotiate our identities in interaction with others in the workplace. These constraints work together in a kind of "layered simultaneity" (Blommaert 2005) to form the contextual environment in which language is used.

The most macro layer of our model is conceptualized as incorporating societal ideologies, or the Discourses (Gee 1990) which underpin social norms. For the data analyzed in this chapter, this entails the values and norms of the imagined community of New Zealand (Anderson 1983), Western ideologies more generally, and high-level concepts such as the gender order (Connell 1987; Eckert and McConnell-Ginet 2014). Moving to meso levels of abstraction we recognize the constraints of a particular industry or organization, loosely labeled as the occupational or workplace culture in lay terms, and often understood as a social network, team or Community of Practice by discourse analysts. At a more micro level, we identify the norms of a particular discourse activity (talking like a professional, enacting a specialist activity such as participating in an industry inspection). Taking account of these constraints, individuals then negotiate their workplace identities using indexical stances (e.g., Eckert 2008; Silverstein 2003) and locating themselves in conversation by adopting particular dynamic "positions" (Davies and Harré 1990) which are salient to their community membership and are interpretable by their interactants. Identity negotiation is the activity in which we find discursive evidence of the balance between individual agency and the many layers of constraint. The concept of identity is thus the core focus for analysis.

To provide a more concrete understanding of these constraints in the context of the building apprentices that we use for illustration below, these layers include (among a potentially infinite number of "forgotten contexts" Blommaert 2005):

1. The (Western) gender order: Building sites are regularly understood as normatively masculine environments (see Baxter and Wallace 2009).
2. New Zealand norms: In previous research, we have argued the relevance of egalitarianism, indirectness, implicitness and so on (see Holmes et al. 2012, forthcoming).
3. The unwritten "rules" of the building industry: Not only do builders share specialist knowledge and terminology, but there are also shared communicative practices about how to treat colleagues and other tradespeople, and of course clients.
4. The established norms of the team in which the builders are working: Shared practices are jointly developed over time and reinforced in ongoing practices (see the Community of Practice framework developed by Wenger 1998).
5. The specific activity in which the builders are engaged: In the case of the apprentices, their training and enactment of their training seems a fruitful focus when considering transitions.

People negotiate their identity positions through language and (re)produce the norms that influence their ongoing contexts (Davies and Harré 1990). To demonstrate the influence of these constraints in practice, we use an admittedly complex, but usefully illustrative example collected on one of our building sites. The team is working alongside the client, Darren, on this building project (perhaps an unusual situation in other settings but reflecting an egalitarian approach which, as noted above, is prevalent in New Zealand society). Darren and Rodney, the company owner, are long-term friends, a fact which has no doubt contributed to

Darren's choice of builder and also to the level of informality apparent in this excerpt. This humorous example sheds light on shared understandings of gender and sexuality, and stereotypes of builders in New Zealand society. In the first example, Rodney (the foreman) teases Darren (the client and his friend) about his pink shirt. (See Appendix for transcription conventions).

1.	Rodney:	might take my t shirt off er at least my shirt off + Darren
2.	Darren:	mhm
3.	Rodney:	got that pink shirt on again //bloody me\
4.	Darren:	/I think\\ this is the same one actually
5.	Rodney:	no (it isn't) nah
6.	Darren:	I think the pink I think the sh- original pink shirt
7.		is out there
8.	Rodney:	really? still going? +++ I've got a very pink one at home [Darren goes to get the shirt][…]
9.	Darren:	that's the original shirt
10.	Rodney:	[mocking tone]: oh tres pink tres tres pink mon ami: [laughs]

In a quip as he sheds his own shirt (an action which arguably masculinizes him while simultaneously signaling the effort he is devoting to his work), Rodney teases Darren about his "pink shirt" (l. 3) punctuated with his choice of the expletive "bloody me." The focus on pink has two possible meanings: Either this refers to Darren's washing skills which have rendered pale shirts pink when mixed by error with red washing items, or it indexes an association with femininity and by extension homosexuality. This second interpretation becomes more relevant in the context of line 10 where Rodney (using a highly Anglicized[1] and mocking tone which indexes a somewhat pretentious or camp meaning for his utterance) chooses French to comment on the shirt. The "play" frame is clearly indicated by the tone and by the dynamic positioning of the participants as oxymoronic faux feminine builders. The humor here relies on the informality of the New Zealand context where a builder can tease the client, a shared understanding of building as a hyper-masculinized environment (to which they are contrasting themselves, especially as Darren does not exhibit any discomfort in acknowledging that he has multiple pink shirts and Rodney talks about his own pink shirt), and a shared understanding of this particular building team as highly educated and able to call on other languages in the teasing activity.

For a newcomer, understanding these layers is a challenge. The norms of the particular building team and the norms of the discourse activity (i.e., teasing) each present their own difficulties. But there is a point of commonality, namely a transition between communities and activities that is actualized through talk.

One further concept that proves valuable in the analysis of transitions is the notion of "frame." Expanding on the concept of "frame," introduced by Bateson (1972) and Goffman (1974), Tannen and Wallat (1993) argue for its usefulness in analyzing interaction in context. They define an interactive frame as "a sense of what activity is being engaged in" (1993, 60) or "what is going on," and illustrate how people identify frames in interaction using linguistic and paralinguistic cues (such as the mocking tone in Ex. 1). Like Blommaert (2005), they argue that social life is layered as experience is recast and transformed through language (cited in Gordon 2015, 327), exploring Goffman's insight that "within one alignment another can be fully enclosed" (Goffman 1981, 155). This insight is especially relevant in the analysis of transitions.

Transition Talk

Whether the transition is between topics and discourse activities (micro), between networks and communities (meso) and or moving from one country to another (macro), workers must manage the layered constraints we refer to above. While previous researchers have tended to focus on one layer (Ainsworth-Vaughn 1992; Drew 2002; Messer et al. 2012; West and Garcia 1988), or possibly two of the levels we describe (Angouri 2010; Angouri and Miglbauer 2013; Filliettaz 2009; Filliettaz et al. 2010; Kerekes 2007; Kerekes et al. 2013), to date there has not been much focus on what we can learn by examining multiple layers and the ways they interact. We argue here for the relevance of an analytical category of talk comprising these boundary-crossing activities and these levels of abstraction.

A strong and relevant commonality is that transitions generally involve either a *break in frame* (Sarangi and Roberts 1999) or a "lamination" (Goffman 1974) or "blending" (Gordon 2008) of components from different frames, as in excerpt (1) above, where the serious professional builder frame encountered the "play" or teasing frame. In particular, there is typically some mismatch in expectations, notably in terms of the norms associated with each context. Here the layers of constraint in our model offer a lens through which to view these frames. While experienced participants skillfully laminate or blend different frames, newcomers often break frame. The breaks expose potential for "interactional trouble" (Trinch and Berk-Seligson 2002), identifying the challenges that newcomers need to navigate as they engage with others in a new workplace context. Whether participants expertly blend frames or face problems in their attempts to do so, in these instances they engage in a distinct type of discursive behavior: transition talk. Transition talk is therefore defined by contrasting expectations, the relevance of potentially competing norms, and the process of negotiation in which interactants are involved when engaged in boundary crossing.

Illustrating Transition Talk

Our argument is, as is standard practice for the Language in the Workplace team, data driven. To explain the relevance of transitions, we draw on naturally occurring data collected on building sites. A core activity is "apprenticing" whereby senior builders facilitate an apprentice's transition from school-leaver to builder through both explicit and implicit training.

Data and Method

The data analyzed below was recorded on two building sites in the greater Wellington region of New Zealand. Interestingly, while the two teams shared underlying industry knowledge and practices and are both recognized as having high status in their field (which justified the team's appreciative inquiry approach as discussed in Holmes and Stubbe 2015), there were also some quite distinct communicative behaviors which reflected the very different communities of practice that had developed over the lifetime of the teams.

The first team aligned most closely with a New Zealand stereotype of builders as operating in a hyper-masculinized context where hard work and physical dexterity is prized. The stated values of the team (gathered in informal interviews and during observations) were to produce work of the highest quality and to engage in their tasks with professionalism and high levels of commitment. The interactional style captured by our recordings included regular occurrences of topics such as rugby, personal relationships, weekend activities, and interactions in the local community, and the language use was characterized by swearing, informality and a discourse of "mateship" (Phillips 1996).

The second team seemed to be engaged in an active challenge to this stereotype, perhaps reflecting the white-collar professions in which key team members had previously worked. A highly educated team, the owner had switched professions and brought other educated friends into the team. Unsurprisingly, their stated and enacted values involved education (including the education of the apprentice), family life and client relationships. The topics most often discussed included the daily collaborative completion of a "5 minute quiz" from the newspaper, and music, from the classical tunes they whistled, to the soft-rock ballads that played on their onsite radio. The interaction was notably more formal, articulate and urban compared with the interactions of team one. Notwithstanding these social differences, both teams were engaged in high-quality building work and were committed to socializing their apprentices as efficient and productive members of the building profession.

Data was collected by male research assistants trained in the standard, but flexible, data collection methodology which has been adopted by the Language in the Workplace team over the last 20 years (Holmes and Stubbe 2015; Marra 2008). Viewing all participants as active co-researchers, we negotiated mutually beneficial goals and after a period of (participant) observation to understand the contextual environment, we handed over control of the recording process to the builders themselves.

On each site, two key team members (the foreman and the apprentice) wore a small digital recorder on their non-dominant arm over a period of about two weeks. Early trialing of this technique indicated that keeping the recorder off the arm that was involved most in hammering, lifting and so on improved the quality of the sound, and wearing the recorder on the arm captured speech while not disrupting work activities. Participants were free to turn the recorder on and off as they pleased in order to increase their comfort in sharing their talk with us. Wellington is known for its high winds, so to further improve the quality of the recordings, tracks from both recorders were synchronized and wherever possible the noise of the wind was reduced digitally. The following example illustrates the cooperative participation of the builders, and the relationship with us as co-researchers. Here our research assistant, Andy, has just finished briefing Alex, apprentice on team two, about the recording process.

1.	Alex:	so we're just to go about our daily jobs
2.		and talk the talk and all that
3.	Andy:	yeah //just\ as normal as you can [laughs] +
4.	Alex:	/okay\\
5.	Andy:	despite the distraction
6.	Alex:	fair enough that's all good

Alex reiterates his understanding of the process (l. 1 - 2), Andy makes light of the somewhat unusual situation of recording your everyday talk (l. 5), and Alex's casual response provides support for his willingness to participate (l. 6). The result was around 25 hours of useable audio recordings from each of the two sites.

The analysis below examines examples from both teams to illustrate transition talk at macro, meso and micro levels.

Macro Transitions

In our separation of macro, meso and micro, we conceptualize the boundary between nations as the highest level of transition. Moving across national boundaries typically results in experiencing relatively large differences in worldviews. To illustrate the relevance of the national context, we focus in excerpts (3) and (4) on the influence of New Zealand societal norms on the talk captured on site. While our recordings included only New Zealanders, since no non-New Zealanders volunteered to carry a recorder while engaged in building work, we are aware of the salience of the national (imagined community) norms. These shared understandings create challenges for those from other countries, including the influx of Irish builders we have seen in New Zealand as the demand for skilled workers has dramatically increased for the "rebuild" required in Christchurch following two major earthquakes.

Excerpt (3), an instance of the relational talk that regularly occurs on both sites as the builders go about their tasks, demonstrates the topics and discourse strategies associated with masculinity in New Zealand (Daly et al. 2004; Holmes 2000, 2006). Max, the apprentice from team one is talking to another tradesman on site.

1.	Max:	[clears throat] did you get did you watch any of the league
2.		or the highlights or anything
3.	B1:	oh I've seen saw a few games eh
4.	Max:	fuck man there are some pretty decent hits man
5.	B1:	yeah

The short extract includes many stereotypical features of New Zealand males in interaction: the topic of sport in the form of rugby league (notably also a choice which reflects the social groups from which the builders come in contrast to the more educated team from site two), the expletive use (l. 4), "man" as an address term for his colleague (twice in l. 4) and the tradesman use of the discourse particle "eh"[2] in line 3 (Meyerhoff 1994; Vine and Marsden 2016). These features instantiate masculine gender positioning within a social rather than a professional builder frame. In other words, this is solidarity construction in interaction and these professional builders manage the transitions from transactional talk to social talk involving macro-level values enacted in micro-level interaction without any trouble. However, such transitions often represent a challenge for those from other cultures where such talk is not the norm while on the job (Holmes and Stubbe 2015).

The same point is illustrated with an even more pithy exchange in excerpt (4) from team two. The senior builder, Brian, and the apprentice Alex make use of the same features indexing a masculine orientation. This time, however, a play frame is implicitly invoked since there is an element of mockery involved, signaled by intonation and tone of voice. Brian (the senior builder) rips/breaks something with his hands in front of Alex. Ex. (4)

1.	Alex:	guns buddy [...] ripped it
2.	Brian:	ripped it to shreds man

In line 1, Alex teases his senior by referring to his muscles with the exaggerated metaphor ("guns buddy"). Elsewhere in the data, Brian and the owner, Rodney, are referred to as "boss" by Alex. For humorous effect in excerpt (4), however, Alex uses an incongruent address term "buddy" which positions him temporarily as an equal and mate. Brian, accepting the play frame, positions himself as a cooperative interactant and reciprocates in kind, using an equally exaggerated metaphor, saying that he "ripped it to shreds," and using the same stereotypically masculine address term as Max in excerpt (3): "man." Interestingly, our ethnographic analysis indicated that these discourse strategies are standard for team one, but humorous for team two. In both cases there is an orientation to societal gender norms, but in team two the community norms come to the fore. In both contexts the orientation to New Zealand societal values such as egalitarianism (here expressed through humor, informal address terms and temporary suspension of status differences), and masculinity (expressed through address terms, swear words, rugby topic and the exaggerated "strength" metaphor) present potential challenges to newcomers from different countries with different societal values.

Meso Transitions

To capture the relevance of these community norms in interaction, we make use of a meso class of transitions. This refers to the network, community of practice or team within which the interaction takes place. The first example in this section has been taken from team one. The tradesmen are discussing Rick, the work experience builder who is only just beginning his transition from student to professional. Rick has left work early, contrasting with the expectation of hard work and dedication which is so important to the team norms. Ex. (5[3])

1.	Tom:	oh is he gone
2.	Max:	yeah ++ when we were inside he said oh tell Tom I'm
3.	Tom:	oh young Rick
4.	Max:	yeah young Rick
5.	Tom:	//fuck he doesn't have many days where he stays here all
6.		day does he\
7.	M2:	[mocking tone]: /he's got a hairdressing appointment\\:
8.	Max:	eh?
9.	M2:	[mocking tone]: //he's got a hairdressing appointment\:
10.	Tom:	/doesn't often get through a full\\ day

Rick's behavior in leaving early for a "hairdressing appointment" elicits a despairing comment prefaced by a typical expletive from the foreman Tom: "fuck he doesn't have many days where he stays here all day does he" (l. 5 - 6), and mockery from another builder on the site (l. 7, 9). Tom then repeats his complaint "doesn't often get through a full day" (l. 10) clearly indicating that Rick fails to measure up on the work ethic of the building site team. Their professional values entail working a full day and Rick has failed to register this important information. His casual behavior can be considered an instance of a break in frame in that it indicates he does not treat the building site work seriously and is oblivious to the professional standards of the experienced builders which result in very different attitudes and behavior.

In an example from team two, we again see the effect of the community as a constraint. The extract involves Alex (the apprentice) in interaction with a tradesman from outside his community. While Alex has learnt and actively contributes to the norms of his particular team, it is also apparent that he has control over norms of tradesmen more generally, norms which align more obviously with those of team one. In excerpt (6), he is assisting Nate, a visiting tradesman, to complete a specialist task. Ex. (6)

1.	Nate:	could you pass me those pieces of iron out of there please [...]
2.	Alex:	[teasing tone]: cos your legs are fucked and
3.	Nate:	yep293
4.	Alex:	they don't bend anymore as well as they used to:
5.		do you want them all
6.	Nate:	yes please (6)
7.	Alex:	what about this
8.	Nate:	could you (put) that back to where you were
9.		no give me those ( )
10.	Alex:	you don't want this one?
11.	Nate:	no
12.	Alex:	[sarcastic tone]: shee you've done all that today:
13.	Nate:	don't be a wanker [laughs]

This interaction neatly laminates or blends two frames, a transactional frame oriented to the building task being undertaken, and a play frame expressed in Alex's teasing of Nate, his senior. At a surface level it appears that Alex is being very irreverent in the context of the hierarchy of tradesmen—he is after all a junior builder and tasked with learning from his seniors, both within and outside his team, in his quest to become a professional. However, Nate's chiding (expressed in a humorous insult in line 13) gives a more accurate indication of the warm, friendly tone of this interaction. Nate, as the senior, gives Alex a directive (l. 1) and then responds to Alex's requests for clarification (l. 5, 7, 10). Within this transactional frame expressed through the task-based talk, Alex playfully teases Nate as the older and slower worker. He accuses him of being lazy and decrepit (l. 2) and challenges him for taking excessive time to complete the job (l. 12). When the playful ribbing goes too far, or perhaps to reciprocate in tone, Nate responds in what can also be seen as a humorous albeit superficially "non-professional" manner: "don't be a wanker" (l. 13), with the paralinguistic feature "laugh" signaling its non-serious import.

This close laminating or blending of transactional and social frames in workplace talk is an important aspect of workplace interaction, and one which the newcomers with whom we have worked in recent years find particularly challenging (Holmes and Woodhams 2013; Holmes and Riddiford 2010). Our final class of transitions addresses these micro activity types more directly.

Micro Transitions

The first example in this section shows just how thoroughly laminated or blended transactional and social frames can be by those who share knowledge schemas (Tannen and Wallat 1993), or expectations and experience. As Tom and Max (the foreman and apprentice from team one) talk through their task, they also share a story about a parachuting accident[4]. Ex. (7)

1.	Tom:	oh right yeah ++ um (10)
2.	Max:	someone broke their leg + hey you got a bottom
3.		corrugation
4.	Tom:	bottom second down bottom of the corrugation
5.		yeah like bottom of that board
6.	Max:	thirty nine
7.	Tom:	yeah thirty nine + what's someone broke their leg where
8.	Max:	oh they were doing like a half time display
9.		of people like parachuting in //+\ or like hang-gliding in
10.	Tom:	//[laughs]\\ at the super fourteen game
11.	Max:	nah what he was saying ( ) //+\
12.		and then some dude like broke his leg
13.	Tom:	[laughs]: oh yeah: (9)
14.	Max:	do you want to go cut another one
15.		I can keep doing this

16. Tom: yeah do you think
17. Max: I'll just do one now or //I mean\

The men are working closely together at this point and they drop and pick up the social topic of what happened at the Super-14 rugby game as their work allows. The transactional frame and the social frame are neatly blended as the interaction shifts seamlessly between the work talk and the relational narrative: [relational] "someone broke their leg" + [transactional] "hey you got a bottom corrugation" (l. 2 - 3), and [transactional] "yeah thirty nine" + [relational] "what's someone broke their leg where" (l. 7). This integration presents no problem to either participant. Managing these swift and minimally marked transitions between social and transactional frames on the job is clearly an important aspect of constructing a plausible workplace identity, and can be challenging for newcomers (see Holmes and Woodhams 2013).

The following example is probably the most explicit teaching moment in our selected data and one which illustrates a break in frame by a newcomer who has not yet developed the relevant knowledge schema or experience to recognize the features of the technical frame invoked by the professional builder. Tom, the foreman on site one, is teaching Rick how to enact a particular technique. He is also implicitly demonstrating how builders train each other. We have also selected this example because it very clearly illustrates a discrete activity as indicated by particular discourse features, most relevantly utterance initial discourse markers. Ex. (8)

1. Tom: right +now just get your um your rule
2. and just slide it in underneath that
3. just one just one thickness of it +
4. slide it in on that flashing
5. Rick: to stop sitting on one
6. Tom: yeah well just one well
7. you haven't got it you've unfolded it eh
8. Rick: yep
9. Tom: yeah oh yeah you can have two bits in there that's alright +
10. now just slide this back hard into the timber +
11. that's it

12.	Rick:	and then just chuck a nail in it
13.	Tom:	er nah I'll just do this end
14.		I just want to check it for level off that as well
15.	Rick:	yep

The linguistic and paralinguistic features in this excerpt signal a professional work frame. This is transactional talk illustrating the explicit and detailed guidance provided to Rick, the work experience student, as Tom teaches him how to move from one very specific aspect of building activity to another. At the micro level of interaction, Tom explicitly marks the transitions from one step to the next in the activity with a series of discourse markers: "right" plus a pause (l. 1), "now" (l. 1), "now" (l. 10), and Rick contributes "and then" (l. 12). Tom also provides feedback to mark the satisfactory completion of steps: "that's alright" (l. 9) and "that's it" (l. 11).

It is noticeable that Rick does not really tune in to the professional frame characterized by the level of technical detail and precision that Tom presents in this teaching frame. Tom signals early that Rick is not following instructions carefully enough: "you haven't got it you've unfolded it eh" (l. 7). Perhaps Tom's encouraging use of the friendly discourse particle "eh" misleads Rick so that he misses the cues that this is technical discourse. Rick's informal and colloquial response "and then just chuck a nail in it" (l. 12) breaks frame contrasting markedly with Tom's precise instructions: for example, "just one thickness of it" (l. 3), "just slide this back hard into the timber" (l. 10). Tom's reaction to Rick's casual and rather imprecise suggestion is to take over control "nah I'll just do this end" (l. 13), and to follow up with an indication of the precision required "I just want to check it for level off that" (l. 14), both responses supporting the suggestion that Rick has broken frame in moving from technical to non-technical discourse. At both the micro and the meso levels (as seen above in Ex. 5), Rick has missed the discourse signals that this is professional talk which characterizes this community of practice, and has responded as if Tom is an equal rather than an experienced builder introducing him to technical skills and jargon.

Transitions and Interactional Competence

We have argued in this chapter that workplace transitions constitute a category of talk that merits close attention and that their relative neglect has led researchers to overlook important aspects of workplace learning. Examining transitions at macro, meso and micro levels has enabled us to identify a number of ways in which different values and norms become relevant in different workplace contexts. These transitions impact on the identity work in which individuals engage in negotiation with others. In the extracts described here, our focus has been the identity negotiation of newcomers to the building industry in particular. In this enterprise the concept of frame has proved particularly valuable since many transitions involve developing awareness of new norms, the evidence for which can be analyzed in terms of blended or laminated frames, or even of breaking frame.

At the macro level, societal values constitute a very real set of constraints which influence behavior at the meso level of teams and communities of practice, as well as the micro level of face-to-face interaction. In New Zealand, egalitarianism and the gender order are prime examples of such values, illustrated in their manifestations in the workplace interactions exemplified in excerpts (3) and (4) where the builders construct their identity as professionals despite their fledgling status. These examples involve the lamination of a social or a play frame with a transactional frame since they introduce non-technical topics such as sport (Ex. 3) or involve humor (Ex. 4), a type of interaction that is classically regarded as challenging or subverting expectations (e.g., Plester 2016).

Excerpts (6) and (7) illustrate quite explicitly how two frames may be blended in instances of workplace interaction in which transactional talk is interspersed with humorous or social talk. In excerpt (6), Alex, an apprentice, teases an experienced builder, effectively invoking a ludic frame through his light playful tone to sanction his apparent impertinence. His success in this attempt signals an appropriate professional identity construction within the contextual setting. Excerpt (7) provides another example of the topic of sport, here introduced in the form of a narrative about a rugby game. The narrative components of this social frame are neatly blended with work or transactional talk in a seamless construction which presents no problems to the participants, though a newcomer without interactional competence would undoubtedly find following and interpreting the interaction extremely challenging.

Finally, excerpts (5) (representing the meso level) and (8) (the micro) illustrate that learning to behave and interact like a professional builder includes absorbing the relevant societal and professional values. This can be very challenging since the contextual cues are often inexplicit and require careful attention to the micro-level discourse. These examples provide evidence that Rick's behavior breaks frame by treating the serious transactional business of the building site too casually. He has perhaps been misled by their friendly social talk and camaraderie and missed the discourse signals that these men orient to highly valued professional standards and respect each other's technical skills. Unsuccessful identity negotiation as seen in these examples helps us identify the interactional competence required for engaging appropriately in transition talk.

Developing interactional competence in a new work environment entails developing awareness of relevant societal values and the related constraints (macro level), navigating the unfamiliar norms of a specific workplace team or community of practice (meso level) and learning how to move smoothly between activities and between different frames within workplace activities (micro level). Modern working lives are characterized by change. Effective workplace communication involves interacting across numerous boundaries, whether negotiating the ubiquitous transitions between topics and (discourse) activities, the competing interactional norms of distinct groups, or the communication demands inherent in crossing international borders. It is at these junctures that transition talk can prove a helpful analytical concept. By becoming aware of and developing navigational skills for such talk, newcomers also develop their interactional competence. The often implicit and taken-for-granted norms that become apparent through the analysis of transition talk are indeed subtle, but necessary to recognize and understand in order to become a full-fledged member of a new community. This chapter has indicated some of the challenges which this process may involve for workplace newcomers.

Acknowledgment We would like to express our gratitude to all those who have worked with us as workplace collaborators and who have allowed us to record their interactions. We also thank other members of the Language in the Workplace team including the research assistants who provided valuable help with data collection (especially Jay Woodhams and Andy Gibson) and transcription.

Notes

1. Pronounced with an English phonological accent, that is, /trez/.
2. *Eh* is commonly used to indicate informality and solidarity, especially among New Zealand men (see Meyerhoff 1994; Vine and Marsden in press).
3. This example is also discussed in Holmes and Woodhams (2013) although analyzed from a different perspective.
4. This example is also discussed in Holmes and Woodhams (2013).

Appendix: Transcription Conventions

[laughs]::	Paralinguistic features and other information in square brackets, colons indicate start/finish
[...]	Section omitted
+	Pause of up to one second
(6)	Timed pause in seconds
... //......\ ...	Simultaneous speech
.../.......\\...	Simultaneous speech
( ), (hello)	Unclear utterance, transcriber's best guess at an unclear utterance
B1, B2 etc	Unidentified tradesman on site
-	Cut off utterance
?	Questioning intonation
All names are pseudonyms	

References

Ainsworth-Vaughn, N. (1992). Topic transitions in physician-patient interviews. *Language in Society, 21*(3), 409–426.

Anderson, B. (1983). *Imagined communities: Reflections on the origin & spread of nationalism*. London: Verso.

Angouri, J. (2010). 'If we know about culture it will be easier to work with one another': Developing skills for handling corporate meetings with multinational participation. *Language & Intercultural Communication, 10*(3), 206–224.

Angouri, J. (2011). 'We are in a masculine profession…': Constructing gender identities in a consortium of two multinational engineering companies. *Gender & Language, 5*(2), 373–404.

Angouri, J., & Angelidou, E. (2012). Managing the director's views: Decision making in a small firm context. In S. Măda & R. Săftoiu (Eds.), *Professional communication across languages & cultures* (pp. 61–82). Amsterdam and New York: John Benjamins.

Angouri, J., Marra, M., & Holmes, J. (2017). *Negotiating boundaries at work*. Edinburgh: Edinburgh University Press.

Angouri, J., & Miglbauer, M. (2013). Local languages and communication challenges in the multinational workplace. In F. Sharifian & M. Jamarani (Eds.), *Intercultural communication in the new era* (pp. 225–245). Amsterdam and New York: John Benjamins.

Ashforth, B. E., Kreiner, G. E., & Fugate, M. (2000). All in a day's work: Boundaries and micro role transitions. *Academy of Management Review, 25*(3), 472–491.

Bateson, G. (1972). A theory of play and fantasy. In G. Bateson (Ed.), *Steps to an ecology of mind* (pp. 177–193). New York: Ballantine.

Baxter, J., & Wallace, K. (2009). Outside in-group and out-group identities? Constructing male solidarity and female exclusion in UK builders' talk. *Discourse & Society, 20*(4), 411–429.

Bennert, K. (2002). Formulations of participation and nonparticipation in trainees' narratives of school-to-work transitions. *Text, 22*(3), 369–392.

Bhaskar, R. A. (2008). *Fathoming the depths of reality*. London: Routledge.

Blau, G. (2000). Job, organizational, and professional context antecedents as predictors of intent for interrole work transitions. *Journal of Vocational Behavior, 56*(3), 330–345.

Blommaert, J. (2005). *Discourse: A critical introduction*. Cambridge: Cambridge University Press.

Bourdieu, P. 1979. *Outline of a theory of practice* (R. Nice, trans.). Cambridge: Cambridge University Press.

Bradley, H., & Devadason, R. (2008). Fractured transitions: Young adults' pathways into contemporary labour markets. *Sociology, 42*(1), 119–136.
Cameron, D. (2009). Theoretical issues for the study of gender and spoken interaction. In P. Pichler & E. M. Eppler (Eds.), *Gender & spoken interaction* (pp. 1–17). London: Palgrave Macmillan.
Chan, A. (2005). *Small talk in business meetings in Hong Kong & New Zealand.* Ph.D., Victoria University of Wellington.
Collier, A. (1994). *Critical realism: An introduction to Roy Bhaskar's philosophy.* London: Verso.
Connell, R. W. (1987). *Gender & power: Society, the person & sexual politics.* Stanford, CA: Stanford University Press.
Coupland, N. (2001). Introduction: Sociolinguistic theory and social theory. In N. Coupland, S. Sarangi, & C. N. Candlin (Eds.), *Sociolinguistics & social theory* (pp. 1–26). London: Longman.
Coupland, N., & Jaworski, A. (2009). Social worlds through language. In N. Coupland & A. Jaworski (Eds.), *The new sociolinguistics reader* (pp. 1–21). Basingstoke: Palgrave Macmillan.
Daly, N., Holmes, J., Newton, J., & Stubbe, M. (2004). Expletives as solidarity signals in FTAs on the factory floor. *Journal of Pragmatics, 36*, 945–964.
Davies, B., & Harré, R. (1990). Positioning: The discursive production of selves. *Journal for the Theory of Social Behaviour, 20*(1), 43–63.
Drew, P. (2002). Out of context: An intersection between domestic life and the workplace, as contexts for (business) talk. *Language & Communication, 22*(4), 477–494.
Ebberwein, C., Krieshok, T., Ulven, J., & Prosser, E. (2004). Voices in transition: Lessons on career adaptability. *The Career Development Quarterly, 52*(4), 292–308.
Eckert, P. (2008). Variation and the indexical field. *Journal of Sociolinguistics, 12*(4), 453–476.
Eckert, P., & McConnell-Ginet, S. (2014). *Language & gender.* Cambridge: Cambridge University Press.
Ehrlich, S. (2008). Sexual assault trials, discursive identities and institutional change. In R. Dolón & J. Todolí (Eds.), *Analysing identities in discourse* (pp. 159–177). Amsterdam: John Benjamins.
Filliettaz, L. (2009). Les discours de consignes en formation professionnelle initiale: une approche linguistique et interactionnelle. *Education & Didactique, 3*(1), 91–111.

Filliettaz, L., de Saint-Georges, I., & Duc, B. (2010). Skiing, cheese fondue and Swiss watches: Analogical discourse in vocational training interactions. *Vocations & Learning, 3*(2), 117–140.
Gee, J. P. (1990). *Social linguistics & literacies: Ideology in discourses.* London: Taylor and Francis.
George, L. (1993). Sociological perspectives on life transitions. *Annual Review of Sociology, 19,* 353–373.
Goffman, E. (1974). *Frame analysis.* New York: Harper and Row.
Goffman, E. (1981). Footing. In E. Goffman (Ed.), *Forms of talk* (pp. 124–159). Philadelphia: University of Pennsylvania Press.
Gordon, C. (2008). A(p)parent play: Blending frames and reframing in family talk. *Language in Society, 37,* 319–349.
Gordon, C. (2015). Framing and positioning. In D. Tannen, H. E. Hamilton, & D. Schiffrin (Eds.), *The handbook of discourse analysis* (2nd ed., pp. 324–345). Oxford: Wiley Blackwell.
Halford, S., & Leonard, P. (2006). Place, space and time: Contextualizing workplace subjectivities. *Organization Studies, 27*(5), 657–676.
Holmes, J. (2000). Doing collegiality and keeping control at work: Small talk in government departments. In J. Coupland (Ed.), *Small talk* (pp. 32–61). London: Longman.
Holmes, J. (2006). *Gendered talk at work: Constructing gender identity through workplace discourse.* New York and Oxford: Blackwell.
Holmes, J., Marra, M., & Kidner, K. (forthcoming). Managing transitions through discourse at work. *Journal of Applied Linguistics & Professional Practice.*
Holmes, J., Marra, M., & Vine, B. (2011). *Leadership, discourse & ethnicity.* Oxford: Oxford University Press.
Holmes, J., Marra, M., & Vine, B. (2012). Politeness and impoliteness in New Zealand English workplace discourse. *Journal of Pragmatics, 44,* 1063–1076.
Holmes, J., & Riddiford, N. (2010). Professional and personal identity at work: Achieving a synthesis through intercultural workplace talk. *Journal of Intercultural Communication, 22.* Retrieved July 1, 2016, from http://www.immi.se/intercultural/
Holmes, J., & Stubbe, M. (2015). *Power & politeness in the workplace: A sociolinguistic analysis of talk at work* (2nd ed.). Abingdon: Routledge.
Holmes, J., & Woodhams, J. (2013). Building interaction: The role of talk in joining a community of practice. *Discourse & Communication, 7*(3), 275–298.

Ibarra, H., & Barbulescu, R. (2010). Identity as narrative: Prevalence, effectiveness, and consequences of narrative identity work in macro work role transitions. *Academy of Management Review, 35*(1), 135–154.

Kerekes, J. A. (2007). The co-construction of a gatekeeping encounter: An inventory of verbal actions. *Journal of Pragmatics, 39*(11), 1942–1973.

Kerekes, J. A., Chow, J., Lemak, A., & Perhan, Z. (2013). Trust or betrayal: Immigrant engineers' employment-seeking experiences in Canada. In C. N. Candlin & J. Crichton (Eds.), *Discourses of trust* (pp. 269–284). Basingstoke: Palgrave Macmillan.

Kuiper, K., & Flindall, M. (2000). Social rituals, formulaic speech and small talk at the supermarket checkout. In J. Coupland (Ed.), *Small talk* (pp. 183–207). London: Longman.

Marra, M. (2003). *Decisions in New Zealand business meetings: A sociolinguistic analysis of power at work*. Ph.D., Victoria University of Wellington.

Marra, M. (2008). Recording and analyzing talk across cultures. In H. Spencer-Oatey (Ed.), *Culturally speaking: Managing rapport through talk across cultures* (2nd ed., pp. 304–321). London: Continuum.

Marra, M., & Angouri, J. (2011). Investigating the negotiation of identity: A view from the field of workplace discourse. In J. Angouri & M. Marra (Eds.), *Constructing identities at work* (pp. 1–16). Basingstoke: Palgrave Macmillan.

Messer, M., Schroeder, R., & Wodak, R. (Eds.). (2012). *Migrations: Interdisciplinary perspectives*. Vienna: Springer.

Meyerhoff, M. (1994). Sounds pretty ethnic, eh?: A pragmatic particle in New Zealand English. *Language in Society, 23*(3), 367–388.

Nicholson, N. (1984). A theory of work role transitions. *ASQ, 29*(2), 172–191.

Phillips, J. (1996). *A man's country?: The image of the Pakeha male: A history*. Auckland: Penguin Books.

Plester, B. (2016). *The complexity of workplace humour*. New York and Heidelberg: Springer.

Sarangi, S., & Roberts, C. (Eds.). (1999). *Talk, work & institutional order: Discourse in medical, mediation & management settings*. Berlin: Mouton de Gruyter.

Schnurr, S. (2009). Constructing leader identities through teasing at work. *Journal of Pragmatics, 41*(6), 1125–1138.

Silverstein, M. (2003). Indexical order and the dialectics of sociolinguistic life. *Language & Communication, 23*(3), 193–229.

Takano, S. (2005). Re-examining linguistic power: Strategic uses of directives by professional Japanese women in positions of authority and leadership. *Journal of Pragmatics, 37*(5), 633–666.

Tannen, D., & Wallat, C. (1993). Interactive frames and knowledge schemas in interaction. In D. Tannen (Ed.), *Framing in discourse* (pp. 57–76). Oxford: Oxford University Press.

Trinch, S. L., & Berk-Seligson, S. (2002). Narrating in protective order interviews: A source of interactional trouble. *Language in Society, 31*(3), 383–418.

Vine, B. (2001). *Workplace language & power: Directives, requests & advice.* Ph.D., Victoria University of Wellington.

Vine, B., & Marsden, S. (2016). *Eh* at work: The indexicality of a New Zealand English pragmatic marker. *Intercultural Pragmatics, 13*(3), 383–405.

Wenger, E. (1998). *Communities of practice: Learning, meaning & identity.* Cambridge: Cambridge University Press.

West, C., & Garcia, A. (1988). Conversational shift work: A study of topical transitions between women and men. *Social Problems, 35*(5), 551–575.

10

Transitioning to Effective Medical Practice: Junior Doctors' Learning Through Co-working with Pharmacists

Christy Noble and Stephen Billett

Co-working and Learning Through Practice Transitions

The transition from educational programs to effective occupational practice is often perceived as difficult and challenging for novices and as frustrating for colleagues (Perrone and Vickers 2003). Smooth transitioning of students from educational institutions to practice is a key priority for all stakeholders. However, sometimes overlooked by educators and employers is that students' experiences in educational institutions and the knowledge these institutions generate are quite different from the knowledge required to perform in practice (Billett 2001). Indeed, a key factor

C. Noble (✉)
Gold Coast Hospital and Health Service, Southport, QLD, Australia
School of Medicine, Griffith University, Gold Coast, QLD, Australia

S. Billett
School of Education and Professional Studies, Griffith University, Brisbane, QLD, Australia

S. Pekarek Doehler et al. (eds.), *Interactional Competences in Institutional Settings,* DOI 10.1007/978-3-319-46867-9_10

contributing to the difficulty of transitioning to practice is that effective occupational performance is premised not only on learning a body of occupational knowledge (i.e., concepts, procedures and dispositions) but also on how that knowledge needs to be applied to meet the requirements of specific work settings (Brown et al. 1989). These requirements are likely to differ according to the kinds of work undertaken, their pace and intensity, the interpersonal and interprofessional relationships, and the specific circumstances of practice. For instance, the practice of prescribing pharmaceuticals differs across hospital wards and specialties. So, given the differences between the requirements of these circumstances and those where professional preparation tends to occur (i.e., educational institutions), it is not surprising that medical graduates feel uncertain or hesitant and that they lack readiness in applying what they have learnt to practice (Brennan et al. 2010; Teunissen and Westerman 2011). The higher the degree of risk associated with decision-making and procedures comprising an occupation—such as medicine—the greater the prospects for dissonance for novices as they transition to occupational practice. This is one reason why work-based experiences are increasingly being included in programs that prepare graduates for specific occupations (Billett 2015).

Despite the inclusion of lengthy work-based experiences, junior doctors' readiness to engage effectively in clinical activities is not strong (Brennan et al. 2010; Teunissen and Westerman 2011). In a study by Cleland et al. (2014), junior doctors reported lacking abilities to engage effectively in clinical reasoning, to adapt to the particular requirements of clinical settings and to respond to challenges to enact complex clinical tasks effectively. Therefore, on its own, the inclusion of work-based experiences in professional preparation programs may not be sufficient, because junior doctors continue to struggle to make an effective transition to practice. These transitioning difficulties include lacking confidence about prescribing (Rothwell et al. 2012), with a UK study finding that almost one in ten prescriptions written by a junior doctor contained an error (Dornan et al. 2009).

One consideration for promoting effective transition into situated practices such as prescribing is enabling learning through co-working; that is, providing guidance by expert co-workers or more informed partners (Billett 2001; Ingold 2000; Rogoff 1990). This guidance is likely to be required when junior doctors engage in critical aspects of their work that they have not engaged in during their medical education, such as clinical decision-making or prescribing (Billett 2001). Hence, engaging in the thinking and acting associated with clinical reasoning and practices while being able to access guidance that is supportive in ways that are interdependent (i.e., mutually engaged and reliant) may promote learning ensuring patient safety.

Much work in health care settings tends to be interprofessional in nature, thus guidance can be provided by members of other health care professions. However, for effective and collaborative co-working to be enacted across professions, some level of intersubjectivity (i.e., shared understandings) is required (Billett 2014). In the context of prescribing, this means that professional groups have shared ways of understanding prescribing tasks and that they work toward achieving common goals (i.e., safe and effective use of medications).

Using a focus on prescribing, this chapter discusses and appraises the interdependent process of learning through co-working and how this kind of guidance can assist junior doctors to transition effectively to medical practice. Broadly, interdependent learning processes rely on mutual contributions between the individual, and others or objects (Billett 2006). Hence, instead of a focus on independent learning that characterizes much of the educational processes—or being directed without understanding what has to be done and why—the process of co-working focuses on an interdependence between individual learners and sources of guidance (Billett 2006, 2008). Moreover, the learners' engagement has to be active, and the learners need to be actively and selectively engaged with what has to be learnt (Billett 2001). The instance explored here is junior doctors' co-working with pharmacists, with attention given to how this can contribute to junior doctors developing their prescribing capacities. Moreover, as pharmacists sit outside of the medical team, part of the consideration here is how such a specialist can most effectively engage with junior doctors as part of their work practices. Furthermore, co-working opens up the possibilities for another kind of transition: transforming the prescribing practices across the medical team.

Considerations of co-working and interdependent learning here are, therefore, central to how transitions, first to effective practice and second for situated practice, can be advanced. The conceptual concern is how interdependence can effectively enact and support socio-genesis: the sourcing and learning of knowledge from the social world. Procedurally, interdependence is examined in the context of junior doctors and pharmacists working together to provide effective and safe pharmaceuticals to patients through prescribing practices. Throughout, data referring to the interactions among pharmacists, junior doctors and consultants are used to illustrate the salience of these interdependencies as processes of co-working. Finally, some suggestions are advanced about how such practices can secure the remaking of occupational practices as their requirements change.

The Case of Pharmacists and Junior Doctors Co-working and Learning

Prescribing is the process of making decisions about which medications to use, how to use them and how their usage is communicated, monitored and reviewed (Lum et al. 2013). It is acknowledged that effectively educating medical students about prescribing is difficult; therefore, it stands as a barrier to effective transition from medical school to practice (Rothwell et al. 2012). This transition is complicated by the dynamic nature of pharmaceutical work including the rapid increase in new products, more complex therapies and increasingly intense health care workloads (Aronson 2009) and the situational factors shaping effective and viable prescribing. Thus, the risk of junior doctors making prescribing errors that can cause patient harm is potentially high (Dornan et al. 2009). To date, these transition difficulties have been addressed through orthodox educational approaches and learner-initiated independent learning, such as simulated learning activities and prescribing education sessions (Dornan et al. 2009; Likic and Maxwell 2009; Rothwell et al. 2012). Yet, the evidence indicates that prescribing is learnt mostly through circumstances of practice, including the procedural and situational requirements such as preference and cost (McLellan et al. 2015).

The study whose findings are reported here investigated an alternative approach: How pharmacists contribute to the development of junior doctors' prescribing capacities and thereby support their transition to effective and safe clinical practice through co-working. Pharmacists and junior doctors interact when the pharmacists conduct regular ward visits; interaction also occurs by telephone. The study comprised interviews with junior doctors, pharmacists and consultants from the same Australian teaching hospital, all of whom worked in acute care wards. Thirty-four interviews were conducted with 11 junior doctors (three females and eight males), ten consultant clinical supervisors (three females and seven males) and 13 pharmacists (11 females and 2 males). The junior doctor participants, both interns and residents, were rotational doctors who worked in a range of clinical specialties including medicine, surgery and psychiatry. The consultants interviewed worked in the clinical specialty areas of medicine, surgery or psychiatry. The pharmacists' work practices varied, in that they tended to rotate through different clinical settings while seniors remained in a particular clinical specialty setting.

Each of these kinds of informants make important contributions to the practice and learning of prescribing in an acute health care setting. First, junior doctors are central to prescribing in this setting, usually under the direction of senior medical colleagues, but also with input from pharmacists and nursing staff (Dean et al. 2002; Tully et al. 2009). However, as junior doctors are often the least experienced members of the medical team, they have a high incidence of making prescribing errors (Lewis et al. 2014). In part, these errors arise because the medical hierarchy can make prescribing a difficult process for junior doctors, especially when they are uncertain of senior clinicians' prescribing intentions and decisions (Tully et al. 2009). Also, because of junior doctors' short tenures on these wards, ranging from five to ten weeks, they continually need to learn how to prescribe for new clinical contexts, often without sufficient opportunities to consolidate their learning from the previous ones.

Second, consultants tend to direct prescribing decisions and are accountable for those decisions. Despite this accountability, consultant supervisors often lack time to provide direct prescribing support to their trainees and dictate prescriptions without sufficient explanation for them to be comprehended and understood by junior doctors (Duncan et al. 2012; Hore et al. 2009; Kilminster et al. 2007).

Third, as previous studies have suggested, pharmacists make significant contributions to building junior doctors' prescribing capacities (Tamuz et al. 2011; Tully et al. 2009), thus they were selected as informants in this study. In particular, junior doctors report valuing interprofessional supervision by pharmacists and often rely on them when making prescribing decisions (Tamuz et al. 2011). Pharmacists also play pivotal roles in managing the risks associated with medication errors, thereby supporting and improving medication safety (Roughead et al. 2013). Increasingly, their contributions are becoming embedded in hospital practices (Weiss and Sutton 2009). These contributions include checking prescriptions and engaging with prescribing doctors if errors or inconsistencies are apparent. Hence, hospital pharmacists ordinarily and routinely interact with doctors as part of their clinical role. All this suggests that everyday work interactions with individuals who have particular expertise (e.g., pharmacists), albeit that these individuals sit outside of the immediate medical team, can make important contributions to learning within that work community. Yet, what remains unclear are the key elements of these contributions and how they can be enhanced to support junior doctors' work transitions.

The Relationship Between Transitioning and Co-working

How co-working can augment learning about prescribing by junior doctors is the key focus of this section, including their need to secure that transition expeditiously and effectively as active members of a medical team that is reliant on them for prescribing. From the data, the following factors associated with securing effective and safe prescribing were identified: (a) the prescribing readiness of junior doctors, (b) the need to engage with an authoritative source and (c) co-working as an outsider.

Prescribing Readiness of Transitioning Junior Doctors

In this study, as in others (Brennan et al. 2010; Hilmer et al. 2009; Kellett et al. 2015; McLellan et al. 2015), junior doctor participants indicated that in the transition from medical school to medical practice they felt inadequately prepared for prescribing in an acute health care setting. They reported not having the prescribing capacities, such as writing prescriptions and selecting medication regimens for patients. Factors contributing to this conclusion were their previous experiences as medical students, the workplace environment and the complex nature of prescribing in an acute care setting.

Most of the junior doctors described their experiences of learning to prescribe in medical school as being insufficient for developing the capacities required for prescribing. The types of educational experiences they were afforded (e.g. didactic teaching and assessments), while providing important conceptual knowledge about prescribing (e.g. selecting a drug for a particular condition), failed to provide opportunities to develop the procedural (e.g. writing a legal prescription) and dispositional (i.e. attitudes, values and interests) knowledge required to prescribe in clinical settings. The following excerpt illustrates the degree to which the junior doctors had experienced and engaged in these types of educational experiences:

> It [prescribing learning at university] was one of those things, for me, that wasn't practical at the time, cos I wasn't using it every day. So a list of 50 medications on a PowerPoint chart … is just mind-numbing. It doesn't make any sense until you're using it, until you're standing at the bedside with a patient with a chest infection, and then you need to go oh, what do I write? [Laughs]. (Junior Doctor 2)

The junior doctor participants acknowledged that they had developed some procedural knowledge of prescribing through assessment activities, when they simulated writing prescriptions and observing others during placement experiences. However, that development was constrained as they were not actually engaging in or responsible for the prescribing, nor was the experience wholly convincing. The following excerpt demonstrates this perception:

> it's never your real name signed on to a prescription. (Junior Doctor 5)

Despite the interprofessional nature of prescribing, most of the junior doctors did not mention interacting or working with pharmacists when developing their prescribing capacities on clinical placements from medical school. This suggested that the educational provision and the doctors' development proceeded without accessing those staff members who have much of the knowledge for successful prescribing. Therefore, when entering clinical workplaces, the junior doctors were unaware of pharmacists' roles in prescribing practices and of how to engage effectively with and learn from them. The junior doctors were entering the workplace without established ways of co-working with and securing guidance from pharmacists who have the capacity to assist their transition to effective prescribing practices. Thus among the many other challenges they faced was having to learn how to co-work with pharmacists. The following excerpt illustrates this experience:

> Yeah, I admit, I didn't quite understand what a pharmacist's role in the hospital was when I started. (Junior Doctor 9)

Some junior doctor participants also suggested that, as they had not developed the prescribing capacities required for their work, they were anxious about prescribing as they commenced clinical work, as illustrated in the following excerpt:

> So initially it [prescribing] was scary, because you don't want to write the wrong thing and then you'd be checking like three to four times, making sure you spelt everything right and you wrote it the right way. (Junior Doctor 1)

Yet, regardless of these junior doctors' estimations about their readiness to prescribe, once in the health care setting they were expected to adopt active roles in prescribing. This included writing up medication orders, rewriting medication charts and preparing discharge prescriptions for patients. So while these roles afforded junior doctors with opportunities to engage actively in prescribing, they demanded competence in a range of new tasks including prescribing decision-making based on a patient and condition within formulary requirements and in conjunction with the medical team and other health care professionals. These decision-making processes were further complicated by workplace factors such as busy workloads, fast-paced ward rounds and pressures to ensure patients are discharged in a timely fashion. As a result, junior doctors reported not being able to engage in prescribing practices as deliberately and effectively as they would have preferred. While there is probably no adequate way to prepare these new doctors for the realities of practice, it is worth attempting to do more to support that difficult transition.

For the most part, junior doctors reported lacking a coherent conception of prescribing practices as they were largely learning to prescribe through imitating their senior colleagues without always understanding what they were doing and why. This included lacking familiarity with the medications being prescribed and an inability to verify or consult clinical guidelines before actually prescribing. The following excerpt demonstrates the perceived risks of junior doctors lacking coherent conceptions of prescribing practices:

> because I know there are people [junior doctors] who just don't know basic stuff, the most simple [sic] process: Which anti-hypertensives to start first—for someone with—just really basic things that you see every day and they won't make a decision. Again, that flies completely under the radar because you call the med reg [registrar], call someone else or you just leave it and someone else will sort it. (Junior Doctor 9)

This perception was verified by some of the consultants in the study. They described instances and consequences of junior doctors' lack of understanding of prescribing practices, as the following excerpt illustrates:

> because the allergy list, what the patient says and the actual reality, it doesn't tally up … for example, we saw a patient … that said penicillin allergy. But, I knew and she was on Augmentin [penicillin antibiotic] and she has had Augmentin in the past. So, somehow the resident has just, like a parrot wrote what the patient says, doesn't think. That area probably needs to be tidied up. (Consultant 8)

In sum, these observations illustrate the ways in which transitions from medical school to engaging in prescribing practices were challenging for junior doctors. In part, this transitional issue can be attributed to the inadequacy of their educational experiences in preparing them to engage in prescribing. What was inadequate in the educational experience (i.e., access to authentic practice) became overwhelming in the clinical situation. These circumstances present an opportunity to improve prescribing readiness for transitioning junior doctors.

Need to Engage with an Accessible, Supportive and Authoritative Source

As noted in the preceding section, the transition into clinical settings afforded the opportunities to engage actively in prescribing that were absent in medical school. However, given the challenges experienced when engaged in prescribing, all the junior doctors indicated they needed guidance from accessible and authoritative sources to develop the capacities to prescribe safely and effectively in an acute care setting. This need is portrayed in the excerpt below:

> without the actual experience of going through and prescribing medication, you're not going to get any better at it and having a pharmacist or even somebody senior in your medical team, without there being further guidance sometimes you don't know necessarily as an intern what to do. (Junior Doctor 8)

To access this guidance, these doctors reported actively engaging with senior medical colleagues and pharmacists on prescribing matters. The findings suggest that how the junior doctors engaged with and were engaged by consultants and pharmacists differed.

Learning from Senior Doctors

The junior doctors reported the principal means of learning to prescribe was through being told what to prescribe by their consultant or registrars, and by observing others' (usually senior doctors) prescribing behaviors. From these experiences, junior doctors reported developing their prescribing capacities. The following excerpt illustrates this type of experience:

> a lot of it [prescribing] is driven from what your boss tells you, so your senior doctors. On the ward round, when most of these things are dealt with, it's, "okay put them on drug X"; "this much at this rate or this"… They [senior doctors] would tell you what to prescribe, but they would not really—there's no reason for it … so you pick it up eventually. (Junior Doctor 2)

The consultants reported augmenting this kind of interaction with regular appraisals of junior doctors' prescribing by reviewing medication charts while on ward rounds and delegating the supervision of prescribing to their registrars. However, most of the consultants admitted finding it difficult to provide comprehensive supervision of junior doctors' prescribing. They conceded that they rarely reviewed their patients' discharge prescriptions and that they did not always provide timely feedback to prescribers (e.g., the junior doctor may have been working on nights and had gone home). Some consultants justified this approach by noting that some prescribing processes are straightforward, and they often deferred the supervision responsibility to pharmacists, as the following demonstrates:

> I review the bedside [medication] chart every day, but I don't review the discharge prescriptions because it's essentially transcription from the inpatient pharmacy list to the outpatient thing, and that's reviewed by the pharmacist in any case. (Consultant 7)

Despite deferring some aspects of prescribing supervision to pharmacists, most consultants interviewed reported being unaware of interactions between pharmacists and junior doctors. Finally, they suggested that regardless of their limited availability to supervise prescribing, they assumed junior doctors would seek help from them, from registrars or from pharmacists should they need it.

> When in practice they [junior doctors] should ask questions if they don't know what to do, and to look things up or they should ask the ward pharmacist. (Consultant 6)

However, the junior doctors reported that they focused on learning about their consultants' prescribing preferences and how to prescribe for particular clinical conditions. Once the junior doctors understood and recognized the team's prescribing preferences, they began to exercise their capacities as prescribers within the medical team:

> If we're discharging them and the consultant's not there, I'll say to the reg [registrar], hey, do you want them to go home on this and this and I've kind of picked up what the consultants do. So it's kind of like I'm mimicking—you know, you kind of learn what they [consultants] want. (Junior Doctor 11)

Finally, although the consultants stated that junior doctors should seek prescribing guidance, junior doctors reported a reluctance to secure that advice or guidance from more senior medical staff out of concerns that they might be labeled as incompetent. Instead, the junior doctors indicated a tendency to trust unquestioningly their consultants' decision-making. The following excerpt illustrates this viewpoint:

> you don't always challenge them [senior doctors] … Because you trust that they [senior doctors] have more experience with certain drugs and certain reactions and … You, as a junior doctor not seeing a lot of reactions and drug—what certain drugs can do, so you just trust them basically. (Junior Doctor 3)

The junior doctors also reported wanting to appear to be making helpful contributions to the team, for example, by writing up prescriptions in a timely fashion and not slowing down the team's work. Moreover, they indicated that their ways of co-working and engaging with the consultants were shaped by the consultants' power over them, a perspective demonstrated by the following excerpt:

> your life is about trying to keep the boss [consultant] happy because he signs off your forms [assessment]. (Junior Doctor 2)

In these ways, junior doctors' engagement in prescribing was also being directed by their subjectivities (e.g., wanting approval from their bosses) and identity (e.g., being seen as a good doctor) (Billett 2006), which included not being seen by the consultants as someone who makes errors.

So, the guidance that they would seek out and engage with was set within a workplace context in which junior doctors, despite not being competent in prescribing, wanted to appear to be as competent as possible. Not needing to bother consultants with what might be perceived as unnecessary clarifications or advice was part of maintaining that appearance. Hence, in seeking support from the medical team, there were factors that made difficult the prospect of the benign and interdependent engagement required for effective co-working, let alone guided learning or participation.

In summary, junior doctors were learning to prescribe through their interactions and co-working with senior members of the medical team, yet team hierarchies meant that they avoided asking questions or seeking clarification to avoid being seen as incompetent. In these ways, the junior doctors' circumstances rendered them as independent learners through accepting and imitating senior clinicians' practices.

Learning from Pharmacists

The expertise needed for learning prescribing is not restricted to medical staff. All junior doctor and consultant participants agreed that junior doctors' engagement with pharmacists was vital for the development of their prescribing capacities. Similarly, the pharmacists acknowledged that their contributions were necessary for sustaining effective and safe prescribing practices. Yet, pharmacists' engagement with and contributions to developing these doctors' prescribing capacities were held as being quite different from those of consultants. These contributions were to be realized through: (a) direct guidance on prescribing matters, (b) identification of and feedback on prescribing errors and (c) providing explanations about prescribing practices. The contributions are outlined here to indicate how co-working between junior doctors and pharmacists might be enacted to improve the process of junior doctors' prescribing capacities. In particular, being positioned outside the medical team meant pharmacists were seen more as benign interlocutors than as critical supervisors.

The pharmacists all concurred that junior doctors were entering clinical work lacking familiarity with essential concepts and practices required to prescribe effectively. This included lacking awareness of legal requirements and economic constraints associated with prescribing and prescribing medications for discharge. All pharmacists described how they provided direct guidance to junior doctors. This variously comprised sitting with junior doctors and guiding them as they wrote their first prescriptions, conducting prescribing orientation sessions and providing feedback on junior doctors' prescriptions, as captured in the following excerpt:

> When the doctors are pretty new, so at the beginning of the year especially, most of the time you'll actually sit down with a doctor and you'll be there with them when they write their first script so I've experienced that a lot over the years. (Pharmacist 7)

The junior doctors confirmed their experiences of working with pharmacists as productive and effective, especially during the initial transition into a particular hospital ward. As noted, junior doctors' engagement with pharmacists was premised on their being outside the medical hierarchy; they were less concerned about the consequences of perceptions of incompetence through seeking advice and guidance. These interactions meant that the junior doctors' medical subjectivities were less likely to be challenged in this instance than when seeking advice from the medical team. Moreover, given their concerns about making prescribing errors, some junior doctors indicated they valued pharmacists' guidance as a "more informed partner" who also provided a safety net for their decision-making. The following excerpt illustrates these sentiments:

> You rely on them [pharmacists] fairly heavily … probably being one of the terms [rotation] where they have a lot more involvement than other [teams]. They either bring things to your attention; whether a patient's pre-existing medication history hasn't been adequately reflected or if something's been prescribed that doesn't quite fit—play well with other drugs or their current condition, then they'll—ward pharmacist will alert me to that. Similarly, on discharge as well. (Junior Doctor 10)

Second, as part of their role, pharmacists review medication charts and prescriptions before they dispense the medications. If they identify discrepancies or errors, their standard practice is to notify the prescribing doctor. These interactions were held to provide helpful and direct guidance to junior doctors who were able to evaluate their prescribing skills and advance their learning, as the following excerpt demonstrates:

> my role as a clinical pharmacist it's doing mainly clinical reviews [of] medication charts, so seeing transcriptions across from previous charts and then if there were any errors, which is often [when] junior doctors are writing up the charts, relaying that across [to the junior doctor] and just confirming any issues, and then the discharge process is probably another big thing where the junior doctors—there's often that liaising in terms of writing scripts; what's necessary, PBS [Pharmaceutical Benefits Scheme] kind of legislation and often some things are often missed when the initial script is presented. (Pharmacist 10)

Thus, a standard work process was reported as providing assurances and safeguards about prescribing while contributing to junior doctors' learning from mistakes in a supportive way. This type of co-working created moments for consideration and appraisal of their decision-making in and through their everyday work activities. All of this occurred in an area in which these doctors readily conceded they lacked readiness to practice confidently, as the following excerpt demonstrates:

> if you make a mistake … at least they'd [pharmacists] … give that sort of additional method of error prevention to make sure things are done properly but then also you then to learn that way as well. (Junior Doctor 8)

For the junior doctors, the frequency of interactions with pharmacists regarding prescribing errors became a measure of their progress and performance as a prescriber, as this excerpt illustrates:

> The number of phone calls we got from the pharmacy [laughs], because obviously if you've done something wrong you know straightaway because they [pharmacy] confirmed it over the phone. So I guess, yeah, that was really the only way, or if the pharmacist picked you up on it. (Junior Doctor 6)

Despite valuing these interactions, this co-working was challenging for some junior doctors. Some became concerned that their interactions were always focused on their deficiencies and created a perception that pharmacists were monitoring their prescribing performance, despite this being part of their role, as indicated in the following:

> it's their job to be the police and … have that attention to detail, which I accept and that's fine and just unfortunately I will never have that mindset which is always going to lead to a slight clash. (Junior Doctor 9)

Some of the more experienced junior doctor participants described how they were expressing their agency by making decisions about how they would engage with pharmacists' recommendations:

> pharmacy usually give us suggestions on what they think … ultimately, they always leave it with us. (Junior Doctor 5)

These junior doctors were imitating some of the consultant participants' perspectives, that doctors are ultimately responsible for prescribing decision-making:

> I think the final decision to prescribe rests with us. (Consultant 5)

Some pharmacists confirmed that they were cognizant of doctors' responsibilities for prescribing and were cautious about crossing professional boundaries and hampering junior doctors' responsibility for prescribing:

> if you're helping them [junior doctors] … you do take away a little bit of the autonomy from them as well. Like, you're helping them do what they need to do and learn, but at the same time if you're sitting there telling them this is what you need to do, this is the dose you need … and all those sorts of things, it … does take a little bit of their own kind of self away from them … but at the same time you're still helping guide and … for us it benefits from a medication safety standpoint. (Pharmacist 11)

The pharmacists also acknowledged that as their interactions with junior doctors usually did not involve consultants, they were not legitimated, nor seen as authoritative. Junior doctors reported not always accepting pharmacists' recommendations without reinforcement or agreement from consultants. Moreover, the consultants were seemingly often unaware of the amount of support being provided by pharmacists:

> At the moment we're just telling the person [junior doctor], nobody knows we're telling the person and nobody knows how often we're having to tell the person and seeing whether or not there's any change in habit. So formalizing the role would be giving them a forum where they can actually provide that feedback, perhaps in a less time-pressured situation. (Pharmacist 1)

As junior doctors were mainly learning to prescribe through instruction, most of them indicated that they frequently did not understand the rationale for the medications they were prescribing. However, pharmacists were often able to furnish explanations for prescribing decisions:

> because sometimes the consultant might know [about a drug interaction or contraindication], but I might not know that there's a—that some sort of interaction between the two or contraindication to a certain thing. At least [with a pharmacist's input] I'll learn that for the future. I might not know that, because the consultant had told me to [prescribe these] two basically. (Junior Doctor 3)

To sum up, co-working with pharmacists augmented junior doctors' learning about prescribing. Initially, that learning was often achieved through direct guidance, feedback on errors or provision of explanations. However, these interactions rarely involved both consultants and junior doctors together. The risk here is of a misalignment between pharmacists' and consultants' contributions to junior doctors' learning. This co-working offers an opportunity for pharmacists and consultants to align their contributions to prescribing learning that extends to securing changes in the entire medical team's knowledge. Also, as junior doctors gained more experience, they became less reliant on pharmacists and were able to exercise their discretion more confidently. This included being selective about which parts of pharmacists' advice were taken. So, the evidence here is of a developmental model that incrementally supports the junior doctors' learning through co-working with pharmacists in ways leading to their increasing competence and diminished reliance on direct guidance by pharmacists or consultants. This is not to suggest that learning processes become highly independent, but that there is a process of interdependence whereby it is incrementally more mediated by the junior doctors and others as they build their capacities.

Co-working as an Outsider

As noted previously, working with medical staff is a core part of pharmacists' routine work. In this section, pharmacists' experiences as outsiders are discussed as are the strategies they use to augment productive and engaged co-working relationships with junior doctors. Indeed, all pharmacist participants indicated that their motivation for co-working with junior doctors was to enable and sustain safe prescribing practices. This is a priority in acute health care settings where much prescribing is performed by junior doctors on short rotations. Indeed, part of the concern associated with such a situated practice is the challenges presented to pharmacists co-working with junior doctors. These challenges included time spent rectifying junior doctor prescribing errors at the expense of other important work activities and having to justify their interventions to the medical team as contributions to medication safety. The following excerpt demonstrates this concern:

> I spend so much time chasing up prescriptions and chasing up scripts and getting scripts edited and fixed in terms of doing a discharge for someone and organizing the medicines that that sometimes takes away from the fact that I could be actually reviewing a [patient's medication] chart. (Pharmacist 9)

The pharmacists' co-working is further complicated by differing perceptions of their contributions to prescribing practices and how of doctors understood them. For example, these pharmacists acknowledged that prescribing might be viewed by doctors as a clerical task; yet, their role is important for prescribing safety:

> I think prescribers do actually see prescribing as a clerical task in a lot of cases, which it is. A lot of the things we're getting them to do are clerical, but they're not putting the dots together always that it has clinical impact

on the patient. So while it's an administrative task, it still is a safety issue, as well as a funding issue. (Pharmacist 1)

In terms of prescribing safety, the pharmacists' roles were not always understood by junior doctor participants, a perspective further elaborated by a junior doctor who had previously trained as a pharmacist:

> Because you know pharmacists have a reputation of being hyper-vigilant about those sorts of rare, but serious things, whereas doctors are like, oh, I'll just give it a go. So it's like, where do we stand? (Junior Doctor 4)

So here, the view is that as pharmacists provide a safety net for prescribing errors, this encourages some junior doctors to relinquish being careful, informed and accurate when prescribing. This perspective highlights the importance of enhancing co-working, and thus learning, by heightening the levels of shared understanding (intersubjectivity) by informing junior doctors about pharmacists' motives (and vice versa).

As outsiders, the pharmacists described how they negotiated their engagement with junior doctors. Two ways in which pharmacists co-worked with junior doctors were identified in the data: negotiating a means of engagement and integrating into the medical team.

First, pharmacist informants reported the worth of getting to know new junior doctors as they commenced their rotation. They noted that interactions with junior doctors were less productive by phone and/or when they were unknown to junior doctors, with the most productive interactions occurring when engagements with the pharmacists were legitimized by their consultants. The following excerpt describes how pharmacists go about interacting with new junior doctors:

> just having a good relationship with them in the sense of introducing yourself, talking to them and building that rapport definitely helps. I've been on my current ward for about three months. When I first started there, talking to the doctors was—I don't feel like I necessarily did the best job I could do, because you were nervous, you were new to it, whereas I think over the time as I got to know the doctors better, as I got to know the cases and as I got better in my role as I progressed, I think that definitely helped. (Pharmacist 9)

These perceptions were shared by some junior doctor informants, in terms of establishing a means of engagement with a pharmacist:

> I think I decide relatively quickly which way it's going to go in terms of someone [pharmacist] who's just going to call me about every little thing instead of someone who's going to exercise their own clinical judgement first. I found, in general, I have a lot of time and trust for most of the pharmacists here. (Junior Doctor 9)

Second, all pharmacists indicated they were cognizant of their "outsider" position and understood that prescribing practices occur within a medical hierarchy. Thus, some of these pharmacists described how they attempted to engage with and integrate into the medical team, thereby facilitating effective interactions with junior doctors. One pharmacist explained this process in the following way:

> I have developed relationships with some consultants so… I can approach some consultants on certain things or I can have a discussion not even about patients but just general sort of hellos kind of thing. It almost automatically brings about a bit of a … like oh okay … so if the junior doctor sees me having a discussion with a consultant it kind of just brings instant respect. (Pharmacist 2)

More than building relationships with consultants, the pharmacists indicated that co-working could be augmented through integrating them more into the medical team's work practices. Strategies included attending the medical ward round, spending more time on wards (rather than in the dispensary) and orientating junior doctors when they commence new rotations.

> it would probably be more effective if you were integrated into that team and you spent most of your time with that team… Yeah I do think that if you were integrated with a team, if you followed that team and spent all your time with that team I think you could have a better impact than just being available on the ward to help when they needed it. (Pharmacist 7)

However, opportunities for pharmacists to participate in ward rounds and to be fully integrated into the medical team's work practices are not always available, or are subject to competing demands upon their work. Yet, the benefits of pharmacists being integrated into the medical team's work practices were supported by consultants who also suggested that such an integration would create opportunities for consultants and other medical team members to learn more about prescribing from pharmacists. Moreover, one consultant suggested that this integration provided opportunities for consultants and pharmacists to role-model interprofessional interactions to the junior doctors:

> There will be different opinions [between pharmacists and doctors] and for all practical purposes there's a respectful discussion there. So that way I think junior doctors are aware about how much we respect pharmacists' opinions and that's very important if we are discussing with the pharmacist in an open forum. (Consultant 2)

Finally, improving pharmacist integration and enhancing co-working might alleviate some of the anxiety when junior doctors have to challenge the medical hierarchy and risk their own nascent professional subjectivity and identity, in response to pharmacist-identified errors. The following demonstrates the risk likely experienced by junior doctors without pharmacist integration into the medical team:

> you don't want to be caught as the intern on the unit telling the consultant that the pharmacist recommended this because, again, the consultant's preference might just be their preference. Or it might be based on some amount of literature that they've recently been made abreast of that you don't ... that the pharmacist isn't aware about ... so sure, yeah, I think it has to be collaborative. (Junior Doctor 10)

Thus, an interdependence is apparent here with pharmacists recognizing the importance of engaging with the whole medical team so that junior doctors' subjectivities and identities are not threatened, while concurrently responding to the teams' need to incorporate safe prescribing practices. That is, co-working can potentially lead to the development of junior doctors' prescribing practices and patient safety realized through the continuity and further development of the medical team that provides patient care.

Enabling Productive Co-working to Support Effective Transitions

From the findings outlined above, this concluding section advances how co-working can be effectively enacted and supported as junior doctors make transitions to clinical work. In particular, the features, patterns and qualities of productive and effective interprofessional interactions are evident. The following four processes are advanced here: (a) reorganizing educational experiences to promote prescribing readiness, (b) working with the hierarchy, (c) augmenting co-working effectiveness through focusing on learning and (d) enhancing pharmacists' integration into the medical team.

First, junior doctors' lack of preparedness for prescribing as they make the transition to clinical work prompts consideration of how prescribing activities can be sequenced to promote co-working initially with pharmacists. This could include broadening experiences in medical school to alert medical students to the requirements for prescribing practices including implications of prescribing errors, strategies for preventing errors and legal and economic considerations related to prescribing. These experiences could also include sequencing prescribing learning through placement experiences during medical education, for example, initially writing up prescription charts under the direction of pharmacists, progressing to writing prescription charts in the context of a busy ward round or clinic and then having to respond to guidance and feedback from pharmacists and consultants. A key consideration should be encouraging medical students to co-work with pharmacists to ease the students' transition to practice.

Second, junior doctors' success in transitioning was dependent on guidance from both pharmacists and senior doctors. While pharmacists made significant contributions to supporting and enabling junior doctors' learning about prescribing, the medical hierarchy and junior doctors' positioning in it means that perceptions of advice and support are inevitably shaped by this hierarchy. However, these co-working experiences were independent of each other and meant that the junior doctors were left to reconcile the different types of guidance they were accessing. The junior doctors valued pharmacists' identifying and informing them of their errors and their learning about prescribing. However, the pharmacists' contributions seemed to be viewed as adjunctive and sometimes oppositional to medical guidance. As senior clinicians make judgments about junior doctors' performance, which influences their access to specialist training and continuity of employment, these junior doctors are subject to and tend to privilege the guidance of their senior counterparts. These may not be the best bases for fostering effective interdependent learning between pharmacists and junior doctors. Yet, this presents opportunities for pharmacists and consultants to strengthen their co-working through work practices such as collaboratively assessing junior doctors' readiness and selecting and planning appropriate learning experiences to augment prescribing readiness.

Third, while pharmacists can contribute to junior doctors' learning about prescribing through identifying errors, without the understanding that the purposes of those interactions are to ensure patient safety and support doctors' learning there is potential for misunderstandings about these interactions. The findings suggest that the prescribing practice norms are that consultants have responsibility for prescribing decisions whereas pharmacists are sanctioned and legitimized to provide guidance and information based on identified prescribing errors. This situation then influenced how junior doctors engage with the pharmacists, in that the doctors viewed themselves as ultimately being responsible for prescribing decisions although sometimes being challenged by an outsider (pharmacist). Strategies to address this potential tension could be to shift the pharmacists' role from error identification to explicit assistance in junior doctors' learning about prescribing. This approach has potential mutual benefits, in that junior doctors are more likely to engage with someone whose role is to guide and augment their learning, yet who sits outside decisions about their progress as a doctor. While for pharmacists, taking responsibility for prescribing learning (in conjunction with the medical team) is likely to facilitate the development of effective and safe junior doctor prescribing, ultimately this may mean that pharmacists can devote their time to other important medication safety matters. Certainly, in a teaching hospital of the kind where this study was conducted, and where the rotation of junior doctors is frequent, there is a need for pharmacists and others to have time and roles to assist junior doctors with their learning.

Fourth, the findings suggest that the pharmacists and medical participants in this study differed in how prescribing was valued and understood. Both groups of health care professionals had different procedural and dispositional capacities and ways of enacting effective prescribing practices. The risk is that misapprehensions may form between the two professions. Both parties need to establish a shared understanding of prescribing practices including the need to share procedures (i.e., how to do things) and dispositions (i.e., values, beliefs, interests). One way to address this could be to augment pharmacists' integration in the medical team by the restructuring of work practices to ensure pharmacists are able to engage in prescribing practices that involve the whole medical team, for example, by attending the ward rounds and so on. In these ways, pharmacists are likely to become more familiar with medical teams' practices, while junior doctors will come to understand shared prescribing procedures and dispositions through pharmacists and consultants role-modeling their interactions.

These findings present an opportunity for educators to consider alternative strategies to augment prescribing readiness with a focus on enabling an effective transition from educational to health care settings. The findings emphasize the contributions to readiness made through co-working with other professions and how these might be incorporated into the educational setting and workplace practices. These lessons are important because they contribute to the argument that rather than developing more conventional education programs to promote learner readiness, consideration might be given to developing procedural, conceptual and dispositional qualities associated with prescribing in practice settings. Co-working has been proposed here as an alternative to didactic processes, enabling an effective transition to work practice. It constitutes interdependence between two professions. This kind of interdependence is best supported and fostered within workplace practices. Such an approach prompts and supports readiness to engage in practice through developing procedural, conceptual and dispositional qualities associated with prescribing.

References

Aronson, J. K. (2009). Medication errors: EMERGing solutions. *British Journal of Clinical Pharmacology, 67*, 589–591.

Billett, S. (2001). Learning through work: Workplace affordances and individual engagement. *Journal of Workplace Learning, 13*, 209–214.

Billett, S. (2006). Relational interdependence between social and individual agency in work and working life. *Mind, Culture, & Activity, 13*, 53–69.

Billett, S. (2008). Learning throughout working life: A relational interdependence between personal and social agency. *British Journal of Educational Studies, 56*, 39–58.

Billett, S. (2014). Securing intersubjectivity through interprofessional workplace learning experiences. *Journal of Interprofessional Care, 28*, 206–211.

Billett, S. (2015). *Integrating practice-based experiences into higher education.* Dordrecht and New York: Springer.

Brennan, N., Corrigan, O., Allard, J., Archer, J., Barnes, R., Bleakley, A., et al. (2010). The transition from medical student to junior doctor: Today's experiences of tomorrow's doctors. *Medical Education, 44*, 449–458.

Brown, J. S., Collins, A., & Duguid, P. (1989). Situated cognition and the culture of learning. *Educational Researcher, 18*, 32–42.

Cleland, J., Leaman, J., & Billett, S. (2014). Developing medical capacities and dispositions through practice-based experiences. In C. Harteis, A. Rausch, & J. Seifried (Eds.), *Discourses on professional learning: On the boundary between learning & working* (pp. 211–230). Dordrecht: Springer Netherlands.

Dean, B., Schachter, M., Vincent, C., & Barber, N. (2002). Causes of prescribing errors in hospital inpatients: A prospective study. *The Lancet, 359*, 1373–1378.

Dornan, T., Ashcroft, D. M., Heathfield, H., Lewis, P. J., Miles, J., Taylor, D., et al. (2009). *An in depth investigation into the causes of prescribing errors by foundation trainees in relation to their medical education. EQUIP study.* Manchester, UK: University of Manchester.

Duncan, E., Francis, J., Johnston, M., Davey, P., Maxwell, S., Mckay, G., et al. (2012). Learning curves, taking instructions, and patient safety: Using a theoretical domains framework in an interview study to investigate prescribing errors among trainee doctors. *Implementation Science, 7*, 86.

Hilmer, S. N., Seale, J. P., Le Couteur, D. G., Crampton, R., & Liddle, C. (2009). Do medical courses adequately prepare interns for safe and effective prescribing in New South Wales public hospitals? *Internal Medicine Journal, 39*, 428–434.

Hore, C. T., Lancashire, W., & Fassett, R. G. (2009). Clinical supervision by consultants in teaching hospitals. *Medical Journal of Australia, 191*, 220–222.

Ingold, T. (2000). *The perception of the environment: Essays on livelihood, dwelling & skill.* London: Routledge.

Kellett, J., Papageorgiou, A., Cavenagh, P., Salter, C., Miles, S., & Leinster, S. J. (2015). The preparedness of newly qualified doctors—Views of foundation doctors and supervisors. *Medical Teacher, 37*, 949–954.

Kilminster, S., Cottrell, D., Grant, J., & Jolly, B. (2007). AMEE Guide No. 27: Effective educational and clinical supervision. *Medical Teacher, 29*, 2–19.

Lewis, P. J., Ashcroft, D. M., Dornan, T., Taylor, D., Wass, V., & Tully, M. P. (2014). Exploring the causes of junior doctors' prescribing mistakes: A qualitative study. *British Journal of Clinical Pharmacology, 78*, 310–319.

Likic, R., & Maxwell, S. R. J. (2009). Prevention of medication errors: Teaching and training. *British Journal of Clinical Pharmacology, 67*, 656–661.

Lum, E., Mitchell, C., & Coombes, I. (2013). The competent prescriber: 12 core competencies for safe prescribing. *Australian Prescriber, 36*, 13–16.

Mclellan, L., Yardley, S., Norris, B., De Bruin, A., Tully, M., & Dornan, T. (2015). Preparing to prescribe: How do clerkship students learn in the midst of complexity? *Advances in Health Sciences Education, 20*, 1339–1354.

Perrone, L., & Vickers, M. H. (2003). Life after graduation as a "very uncomfortable world": An Australian case study. *Education + Training, 45*, 69–78.

Rogoff, B. (1990). *Apprenticeship in thinking—Cognitive development in social context.* New York: Oxford University Press.

Rothwell, C., Burford, B., Morrison, J., Morrow, G., Allen, M., Davies, C., et al. (2012). Junior doctors prescribing: Enhancing their learning in practice. *British Journal of Clinical Pharmacology, 73*, 194–202.

Roughead, L., Semple, S., & Rosenfeld, E. (2013). *Literature review: Medication safety in Australia.* Sydney: Australian Commission on Safety and Quality in Health Care.

Tamuz, M., Giardina, T. D., Thomas, E. J., Menon, S., & Singh, H. (2011). Rethinking resident supervision to improve safety: From hierarchical to interprofessional models. *Journal of Hospital Medicine, 6*, 445–452.

Teunissen, P. W., & Westerman, M. (2011). Opportunity or threat: The ambiguity of the consequences of transitions in medical education. *Medical Education, 45*, 51–59.

Tully, M. P., Ashcroft, D. M., Dornan, T., Lewis, P. J., Taylor, D., & Wass, V. (2009). The causes of and factors associated with prescribing errors in hospital inpatients: A systematic review. *Drug Safety, 32*, 819–836.

Weiss, M. C., & Sutton, J. (2009). The changing nature of prescribing: Pharmacists as prescribers and challenges to medical dominance. *Sociology of Health & Illness, 31*, 406–421.

Index[1]

[1] Note: Page numbers followed by "n" denote notes.

S. Pekarek Doehler et al. (eds.), *Interactional Competences in Institutional Settings*, DOI 10.1007/978-3-319-46867-9

I

J

K

L

FSC
www.fsc.org
MIX
Papier | Fördert
gute Waldnutzung
FSC® C083411

Kolibri 360 GmbH
Ferdinand-Jühlke-Straße 7
99095 Erfurt, Deutschland
produktsicherheit@kolibri360.de